THE
EVERYTHING®
PRE-DIABETES COOKBOOK

Dear Reader,

The news that you have pre-diabetes is something you should take seriously. Whether you have just heard this news or you have known for a while, you probably realize that a lifestyle change is a necessary part of your future. *The Everything® Pre-Diabetes Cookbook* is designed to help you make the transition to a healthier way of preparing and eating food.

As a dietitian and diabetes educator in private practice, I have worked with many clients who have just learned they have pre-diabetes. Almost always, I am asked, "What can I eat?" Many people expect that favorite foods are going to be taken away, but after they learn how to make healthy eating and lifestyle choices, most are pleasantly surprised. They have learned that managing pre-diabetes is about common sense and moderation, not deprivation.

This cookbook has a wide array of recipes, some similar to your old favorites and some that will be completely new or different. I would like to encourage you to try new recipes or ideas to expand your food choices and variety. You may also want to take suggested ideas and apply them to your own favorite recipes.

For me, developing and testing the recipes found in this book has been a very enjoyable extension of my work as a Certified Diabetes Educator (CDE). When recipes result in great-tasting foods, cooking becomes a pleasure. It is my sincere hope that you enjoy using this cookbook and the recipes. I hope you will be pleasantly surprised!

Gretchen Scalpi, RD, CDN, CDE

Welcome to the EVERYTHING® Series!

These handy, accessible books give you all you need to tackle a difficult project, gain a new hobby, comprehend a fascinating topic, prepare for an exam, or even brush up on something you learned back in school but have since forgotten.

You can choose to read an Everything® book from cover to cover or just pick out the information you want from our four useful boxes: e-questions, e-facts, e-alerts, and e-ssentials.

We give you everything you need to know on the subject, but throw in a lot of fun stuff along the way, too.

We now have more than 400 Everything® books in print, spanning such wide-ranging categories as weddings, pregnancy, cooking, music instruction, foreign language, crafts, pets, New Age, and so much more. When you're done reading them all, you can finally say you know Everything®!

QUESTION

Answers to
common questions

FACT

Important snippets
of information

ALERT

Urgent
warnings

ESSENTIAL

Quick
handy tips

PUBLISHER Karen Cooper

MANAGING EDITOR, EVERYTHING® SERIES Lisa Laing

COPY CHIEF Casey Ebert

ASSISTANT PRODUCTION EDITOR Alex Guarco

ACQUISITIONS EDITOR Lisa Laing

SENIOR DEVELOPMENT EDITOR Brett Palana-Shanahan

EVERYTHING® SERIES COVER DESIGNER Erin Alexander

Visit the entire Everything® series at *www.everything.com*

THE
EVERYTHING®
PRE-DIABETES
COOKBOOK

Gretchen Scalpi, RD, CDN, CDE

Adams Media
New York London Toronto Sydney New Delhi

To all of my clients with pre-diabetes who have reaped the
rewards of a healthy lifestyle that includes eating well!

Adams Media
An Imprint of Simon & Schuster, Inc.
100 Technology Center Drive
Stoughton, MA 02072

An Everything® Series Book.
Everything® and everything.com® are registered trademarks of Simon & Schuster, Inc.

ADAMS MEDIA and colophon are trademarks of Simon and Schuster.

For information about special discounts for bulk purchases, please contact Simon & Schuster Special Sales at 1-866-506-1949 or business@simonandschuster.com.

The Simon & Schuster Speakers Bureau can bring authors to your live event. For more information or to book an event contact the Simon & Schuster Speakers Bureau at 1-866-248-3049 or visit our website at www.simon-speakers.com.

Manufactured in the United States of America

8 2021

Library of Congress Cataloging-in-Publication Data has been applied for.

ISBN 978-1-4405-7223-4
ISBN 978-1-4405-7224-1 (ebook)

Contains material adapted and abridged from *The Everything® Glycemic Index Cookbook, 2nd Edition* by LeeAnn Smith Weintraub, MPH, RD, copyright © 2010, 2006 by Simon & Schuster, Inc., ISBN: 978-1-4405-0584-3 and *The Everything® Diabetes Cookbook, 2nd Edition* by Gretchen Scalpi, RD, CDN, CDE, copyright © 2010, 2002 by Simon & Schuster, Inc., ISBN: 978-1-4405-0154-8.

Contents

Acknowledgments

I would like to thank Lisa Laing, Managing Editor, for all of her work in spearheading and guiding me through this project. A major thank you to Brett Palana-Shanahan, Senior Development Editor, for her help in finding the perfect words and clarifications for the recipes in this book.

Writing a cookbook and developing recipes is a challenging experience that takes time, testing, and patience. I would like to especially thank my family members and friends who sampled and critiqued the many new recipes that made their way to the table.

Introduction

IF YOU ARE READING THIS COOKBOOK, odds are that you have concerns about the fact that you or a loved one has pre-diabetes. Once diagnosed with pre-diabetes most people realize that they need to "do something" to take control of the situation.

Managing pre-diabetes means understanding what it is and what to do about it. The more you understand, the better you can take action to reverse it or minimize your risk of developing type 2 diabetes. Luckily, by reading and using this cookbook you can get ideas to put into practice right now. You will have taken the first steps toward learning about managing and reversing pre-diabetes.

In order to understand pre-diabetes, it's helpful to know more about diabetes. This quick overview will help you to see the connection to pre-diabetes and why action on your part should not be delayed.

Diabetes Mellitus

Every time you eat, your body converts the foods you consume into glucose (sugar). Insulin is a hormone the body makes that enables the glucose to get into cells, where the glucose is used for energy. People with diabetes either lack sufficient amounts of insulin or are unable to use the insulin they make. When insulin is absent or ineffective, the body is unable to get energy into cells and the level of glucose in the blood increases. To put it simply, your blood sugar level is too high. Genetics, obesity, and lack of exercise appear to be factors in most cases of diabetes. There are also several different types of diabetes.

Type 1 Diabetes

Approximately 5–10 percent of known cases of diabetes are classified as type 1 diabetes. Type 1 diabetes was formerly referred to as juvenile-onset diabetes because the onset typically occurs before the age of thirty. Type 1 diabetes is an autoimmune disorder that is thought to develop when stress factors (such as a viral infection) damage or destroy the beta cells of the pancreas. The person with type 1 diabetes is always dependent upon insulin because her pancreas no longer produces insulin. Type 1 diabetes is usually not associated with obesity or lack of exercise. Our discussion of pre-diabetes in this cookbook is mostly focused on type 2 diabetes rather than type 1 diabetes.

Type 2 Diabetes

The vast majority of individuals who have diabetes have type 2 diabetes. For most people with type 2 diabetes, the pancreas still produces insulin, but it is being produced in insufficient amounts, or the body simply is unable to use the insulin in an efficient way.

Most people with type 2 diabetes are diagnosed in mid- to late adulthood. Unfortunately, with the growing prevalence of obesity among children, we are now seeing children and young adults with type 2 diabetes as well.

Type 2 diabetes is often related to a sedentary lifestyle and an overweight or obese status. It is important to understand that diabetes is a disease that will progress, and while it can be controlled, it cannot be cured. Over time many people with type 2 diabetes may require oral medications and/or insulin injections to effectively treat and manage the disease. If untreated, a person with pre-diabetes may go on to develop type 2 diabetes.

Gestational Diabetes

Gestational diabetes is similar to type 2 diabetes because the body still makes insulin; however, a hormone secreted by the placenta interferes with the action of insulin. The result is elevated blood glucose levels usually starting between the twenty-fourth and twenty-eighth weeks of the pregnancy. In most cases, a pregnant woman's blood glucose returns to normal after the delivery of the baby and the diabetes is gone. A woman who has had gestational diabetes in the past has an increased risk of developing type 2 diabetes at a later time in her life, especially if she remains overweight or sedentary.

Seven Self-Care Behaviors

Managing diabetes and pre-diabetes is all about making lifestyle changes. The American Association of Diabetes Educators (AADE) believes that utilizing principles of the 7 Self-Care Behaviors is an effective way to make positive changes in lifestyle. The following self-care behaviors apply to those with pre-diabetes and diabetes:

THE 7 SELF-CARE BEHAVIORS

1. **Healthy Eating:** Make healthy food choices, understand portion sizes, and learn the best times to eat.
2. **Being Active:** Include regular activity for overall fitness, weight management, and blood glucose control.
3. **Monitoring:** Self-monitor blood glucose to assess how food, physical activity, and medications are working.
4. **Taking Medication:** Understand how prescribed medications work and when to take them.
5. **Problem-Solving:** Learn how to problem-solve. A high or low blood glucose episode requires the ability to make a quick decision about food, activity, or medication.
6. **Reducing Risks:** Develop behaviors that reduce risk. Smoking cessation and regular eye exams are examples of self-care that reduces risk of complications.
7. **Healthy Coping:** Develop good coping skills to deal with the challenges of diabetes and stay motivated to keep diabetes in control.

As you read this cookbook, you will find practical tools to empower you to learn about a healthier way of preparing and eating food. Taking control means having an action plan that you can live with! With practical tools and an effective plan, you have been given an opportunity to prevent or delay the onset of type 2 diabetes. Take it!

What Is Pre-Diabetes?

CHAPTER 1

Managing and Reversing Pre-Diabetes

Your doctor has just told you that you or your loved one has pre-diabetes. Your initial reactions might have been shock, anger, or a feeling of helplessness. Perhaps you knew something was not quite right all along, but you tried to put the whole thing out of your mind. Whatever the case, you are now faced with a medical diagnosis that has the potential to be serious. Many people in this situation do not know what pre-diabetes means or what to do about it. You can start by learning more about pre-diabetes and taking steps to stop pre-diabetes in its tracks.

What Is Pre-Diabetes?

The most recent data from the National Diabetes Fact Sheet, 2011, put out by the Centers for Disease Control and Prevention (CDC), estimates that there are 79 million Americans with pre-diabetes. Yes, you read that correctly: 79 million Americans! The numbers are growing annually; in large part because pre-diabetes is linked to America's other serious health problems: overweight and obesity. Being overweight and having elevated blood sugar tend to go hand in hand. Blood sugar that fluctuates too high or too low throughout the day has a direct influence on your hunger level and snacking habits. If your blood sugar is too low, you may eat too much food. If you eat too much food, over time you gain weight. Weight gain sets the stage for developing pre-diabetes, or worse yet, diabetes.

If you are obese, your risk for developing pre-diabetes is far greater than the risk for someone whose weight is normal. Recent data from the CDC indicates that 35.7 percent of adults in the United States are obese. One thing is very clear about this trend: It means that the number of people who will develop diabetes or pre-diabetes is going to continue to grow.

FACT

The term *pre-diabetes* was introduced by the American Diabetes Association in 2002 as a way to more clearly convey a state that is between normal blood sugar and type 2 diabetes. The old phrase "borderline diabetes" provides little meaning to the person hearing it, and it certainly does not convey the urgent need to do something about it.

When you have pre-diabetes your blood sugar level is higher than normal, but it's not yet high enough to be diagnosed as type 2 diabetes. Pre-diabetes means that you are on your way to developing diabetes if there are no interventions on your part. It is important to understand that progression from pre-diabetes to type 2 diabetes is not inevitable. There is a great deal that you can do to reverse pre-diabetes and bring your blood sugar level back to a normal range.

Pre-diabetes is a wake-up call that gives you an opportunity to improve your health and make healthy lifestyle changes. If you take action, you can prevent, or at the very least, halt, the progression to a serious, permanent disease.

Tests for Pre-Diabetes

To determine whether you have pre-diabetes, you will need to gather some information about your health. This information includes lab tests, blood pressure, and other measurements such as weight and waist circumference. Your prior health history helps to provide additional clues.

Fasting Blood Glucose Test

Fasting blood glucose is the first test that may indicate the possibility of pre-diabetes. This is a simple blood test where a sample of blood is drawn first thing in the morning after an overnight fast. A fasting blood glucose between 100 and 125 mg/dL on more than one occasion is an indicator for pre-diabetes. Some doctors prefer using a "glucose challenge" rather than a fasting test. In this case, you are given a glucose drink and blood is drawn two hours after taking the drink. With this test, a blood glucose result of 140–199 mg/dL two hours after taking the glucose drink indicates pre-diabetes. Two-hour readings that are above 200 mg/dL on more than one occasion indicate diabetes.

Hemoglobin A1c

When a fasting glucose test or two-hour glucose challenge is done, the reading provides a result for that moment in time. Because your glucose can vary throughout the day, these tests do not provide enough information about your blood sugar at other times of the day. That is why a test called the hemoglobin A1c is done when pre-diabetes or diabetes is suspected. Hemoglobin is the substance found in red blood cells that carries oxygen from the lungs to all cells in the body. When hemoglobin binds with glucose, an irreversible compound called glycated hemoglobin is formed. The A1c portion of glycated hemoglobin is the easiest portion of this compound to measure. A person with higher blood glucose has more glycated hemoglobin than a person with lower blood glucose. Hemoglobin found in red blood cells lasts for sixty to ninety days. As a result, a measurement of your Hemoglobin A1c indicates your average blood glucose level over the last sixty to ninety days. A hemoglobin A1c between 6% and 7% matches average glucose levels typically found in pre-diabetes. Monitoring your hemoglobin A1c routinely, and keeping it below 6%, should be part of your action plan.

QUESTION

Do you need a glucose meter even if you don't have diabetes? Periodically monitoring your blood sugar with a glucose meter can help you track your blood sugar. This information can show you how different foods affect your blood glucose, or what times of day you may be high or low. How often to check your blood glucose is up to you, but usually two to three times weekly is a good start.

Cholesterol and Triglycerides

People with pre-diabetes have more risk for heart disease; therefore monitoring your cholesterol level is important. You need to know the HDL (good cholesterol) and LDL (bad cholesterol) levels, in addition to total cholesterol. LDL and HDL levels are better predictors of heart-disease risk than the total cholesterol. Triglycerides, another type of fat found in the blood, are also associated with determining risk factors for heart disease. The following list indicates recommended cholesterol and triglyceride levels for adults.

- Total Cholesterol: Less than 200 mg/dL
- LDL Cholesterol: Less than 100 mg/dL
- HDL Cholesterol: Greater than 40 mg/dL for men; greater than 50 mg/dL for women
- Triglycerides: Less than 150 mg/dL

If you have pre-diabetes, your doctor may want to see readings even lower. If the results of your blood tests are abnormal, you and your doctor will discuss the results and appropriate treatment.

Blood Pressure

Just as the prevalence of pre-diabetes and diabetes is on the rise, high blood pressure is on the rise as well. Being overweight or having a sedentary lifestyle increases hypertension risk. The 2010 Dietary Guidelines for Americans recommends a reduction in daily sodium to less than 2,300 mg. daily. Although the recommendations for sodium have been reduced, many people consume much more sodium because they eat processed food. Processed food accounts for the largest percentage of the sodium Americans consume on a daily basis.

The American College of Endocrinology Task Force on the Prevention on Diabetes (2008) recommends a target blood pressure of 130/80 for persons with pre-diabetes.

Your Action Plan for Pre-Diabetes

Taking steps to stop the progression of pre-diabetes is necessary to restore good health. With pre-diabetes, there is still a chance for you to prevent the onset of type 2 diabetes. Even if you develop diabetes eventually at a later time, slowing down the progression will result in fewer complications.

There are three essential components to your action plan:

- Losing weight and keeping it off
- Eating healthier by changing poor eating habits
- Maintaining an exercise routine

It is important to develop an action plan to help you make lifestyle changes gradually. Have no more than two or three specific, tangible goals to work on at one time. This strategy prevents you from getting overwhelmed, and allows you to master a goal before moving on to something else. Have a small reward system for goals achieved; it's a way to keep you motivated and to celebrate success!

Losing Weight

Being overweight may be only one of several causes of pre-diabetes; however, it is one factor that you can control. Body Mass Index (BMI) is one way healthcare practitioners can determine whether you are at a healthy weight, overweight, or obese:

- A BMI of 18.5–24.9 = normal weight
- A BMI of 25–29.9 = overweight
- A BMI of 30 or greater = obese

Your doctor can tell you what your BMI is, or you can use the BMI calculator at *www.nhlbi.nih.gov/guidelines/obesity/BMI* to determine this yourself.

There are many rewards that come with weight loss. Weight loss of as little as 10–20 pounds can prevent or delay progression to diabetes. Modest weight loss also helps reduce insulin resistance, cholesterol, and blood pressure.

People who have advanced to type 2 diabetes gradually lose the ability to make adequate amounts of insulin. When this happens, weight loss and exercise alone are not enough to control blood glucose. Medications often are a necessary part of treatment. Knowing that you may be able to avoid medication is a good motivator for losing weight and keeping it off!

Eating Healthier

You probably can identify certain food choices that should be changed because of the ill effect they have on your health. Now is a good time to identify these problem foods and work on ways to reduce your exposure to them.

Make your food environment safe and keep it as free as possible from foods that cause problem eating and extra calories. Start by reviewing the foods you routinely buy at the grocery store. Are these foods helping you reach your goals or are they self-sabotaging? What kinds of foods are in your kitchen? Many people have a hard time cleaning up their food environment because of other people living in the household. Keeping less healthy foods in the house for others is not likely to help you stay on track. Remember that healthy eating should be for everyone, and having problem foods around the house makes it difficult to resist eating those foods. Discuss your food problems with your family and come to a compromise on how often these foods should be allowed in the household. Don't rely on willpower to stop you from eating irresistible foods. Make your food environment safer by keeping healthier food and snack alternatives available at all times. At the grocery store, be sure to purchase healthy snack items for everyone in the family. When healthy snacks are available, it becomes easier to avoid the impulsiveness of poor food decisions.

FACT

Having one or two snacks during the day is a good way to keep your blood glucose stable and take the edge off your hunger. Eat low-calorie snacks between meals to help you feel satisfied until your next meal. Keep snacks in the range of 100–200 calories. Here are a few examples:

- Carrot sticks with 2 tablespoons hummus
- Low-fat mozzarella cheese stick and a small apple
- 1 tablespoon peanut butter on 4 whole-grain crackers
- 6 ounces yogurt with ½ cup berries

Getting Started with Exercise

Exercise has to be part of your action plan for halting pre-diabetes. The role of exercise cannot be underestimated! Regular exercise will improve your blood glucose levels. Lower blood glucose levels are achieved when the glucose in blood is used for energy during and after exercise. Muscle cells become more sensitive to insulin, and insulin resistance improves. Gradually blood glucose levels go down.

First, talk to your doctor to make sure that exercise is appropriate for you. In most cases, your doctor will support your desire to start an exercise plan. If you have other health issues in addition to pre-diabetes, you and your doctor will want to discuss the best types of exercise for you. Once you have the okay to start, it's time to consider what type of exercise is right for you:

- Consider your physical ability and choose activities that you can do.
- Include activities you enjoy or those you already do on a regular basis. Walking, gardening, and house cleaning are all ways to get exercise.
- Think about how much time you have for exercise. An exercise plan that takes too much time will quickly be abandoned if you are short on time.
- Consider the resources available. If you do not have access to a gym, exercise equipment, or a pool, then walking may be your best bet.

Resist the temptation to purchase home exercise equipment until you have tried it out and are sure that you will use it! Many types of exercise equipment eventually just take up space after the owner tires of it. If you are considering buying exercise equipment, try it out first in the store, at a gym, or at a friend's house before purchasing it. Make sure you like the activity enough that you will want to do it often!

Making Time for Exercise

When planning your exercise routine, be honest about whether you will maintain the plan. Can you perform the activity outdoors year-round or will you need to find an alternate indoor activity for part of the year? Before you start, work through any barriers that could get in the way of your success. Short periods of time (ten to thirty minutes) will probably work much better than trying to carve out an hour for daily activity. Here are ways to slip in activity every day without making huge demands on your schedule:

- Park farther away from your destination, and then walk the rest of the way.
- During the workday, get up from your desk to walk or stretch every hour.
- Go for a ten-minute walk after lunch or dinner.
- Stand or walk in place while you are on the telephone or watching TV.

Try Walking

For most people, walking is a good place to begin because it is easy and requires no special equipment other than a pair of good walking shoes. Walking three times a week for ten to fifteen minutes at a time can help ease you into a regular routine. As you become stronger and gain more endurance, gradually increase your walking time by five minutes every week, until you are able to walk for a full thirty minutes at a time. Once you can walk for thirty minutes, increase your frequency to four or five times weekly. Brisk walking is an aerobic exercise and an effective strategy for weight loss.

QUESTION

What is the best time of day to exercise?
As long as you exercise, the time of day you actually do the exercise is the best time! Busy and demanding schedules often get in the way of good intentions. If your schedule is demanding, pencil in an appointment on your daily planner for exercise time. Remember that any time spent exercising is better than no time!

Slow and Steady Wins the Race

Consistent exercise benefits everyone and especially people with prediabetes. While diabetes prevention is at the top of the list, you will also enjoy lower blood pressure, lower lipid levels, reduced stress, and better sleep.

Once you have had success with maintaining exercise, find new ways to get active and keep it interesting. Varying the routine helps to keep you from getting bored, and it challenges your body in different ways. Your exercise program should be one that you can maintain for life. Think of your exercise program as a work in progress by finding new ways to improve it and keep it fun. Slow, steady progress will help you achieve your goals!

What Can You Eat?

You may think that having pre-diabetes means you will have to give up everything you like to eat. Nothing could be further from the truth! With the help and advice from a registered dietitian, you can develop healthy eating habits that fit into your lifestyle.

Think of changes in your eating habits as goals rather than inflexible rules. Start by making a list of the things you would like to change or improve. Decide exactly what you need to do in order to bring about change, and then select one or two changes to work on at a time. Here are a few ideas to help you start this process:

- **Eat meals at regular intervals.** Resolve not to skip meals or go for long periods of time without eating.
- **Include nutritious snacks in your daily eating plan.** Hint: fruits and vegetables are good choices!
- **Start reducing your portion sizes.** Cut back by 25–30 percent to get used to eating less.
- **Drink plenty of water every day.** Most adults need at least 48–64 ounces daily.

Balance and Moderation Are Key

Everyone should have a healthy diet regardless of whether or not they have pre-diabetes. You may be surprised to learn that your plan will have the same foods that everyone else should eat, and buying diet foods is usually unnecessary. You may wish to use an artificial sweetener or certain sugar-free foods to add variety; however, this is not essential. You will not have to prepare one meal for yourself and something different for the rest of your family. The recipes in this cookbook use ingredients suitable for everyone. To put it simply, a meal plan for managing pre-diabetes is a healthy plan that most people can follow.

Carbohydrates and Pre-Diabetes

Carbohydrates serve as the body's primary energy source. Simple carbohydrates include sugars, sweets, juices, and fruits. Complex carbohydrates include all types of grain products and starchy vegetables such as potatoes and corn. Recommendations for a healthy diet suggest that most carbohydrates come from the complex carbohydrates rather than simple sugars. Complex carbohydrates found in whole-grain foods provide better nutritional value and are a source of vitamins, minerals, and fiber. Fruit contains natural simple sugars, and they are also sources of essential nutrients. To get the most fiber from fruit, choose fresh or frozen, unsweetened fruit instead of fruit juice.

QUESTION

What are whole grains?
The Food and Drug Administration (FDA) has defined whole grains as "the intact, ground, cracked, or flaked fruit of the grains whose principal components—the starchy endosperm, germ, and bran—are present in the same relative proportions as they exist in the intact grain." In other words, no part of the grain has been removed during processing, so you are getting all parts of the grain.

Having pre-diabetes does not mean you must cut out all carbohydrates from your diet. Choose carbohydrates that have good nutritional value and maintain an appropriate portion size.

Proteins: Your Building Blocks to Good Health

Proteins are the building blocks of the body and are used for growth, building, and repair. Your plan can include lean sources of meat, fish, poultry, eggs, and milk products. Vegetable proteins are found in nuts, seeds, and legumes (beans and lentils). Most adults need three servings of foods from the protein group each day.

Fats: Monos, Polys, Saturated, and Trans

All fats, regardless of type, have a significant amount of calories. Therefore, moderation of any fat is recommended. Every gram of fat contains 9 calories.

Monounsaturated fat should make up most of the fat you consume. This type of fat is found in plant foods such as walnuts, canola oil, peanut oil, and olive oil. Monounsaturated fat does not raise blood cholesterol and may actually help reduce blood cholesterol levels if it replaces saturated fat in the diet.

Polyunsaturated fat should be consumed in moderation, and less often than monounsaturated fat. This fat comes mostly from vegetable sources such as corn oil, sunflower oil, and some types of margarine.

ALERT

Check food labels and ingredients and avoid trans fat as much as possible. This form of fat can raise LDL (bad) cholesterol and increase your risk for heart disease. Trans fat can be found in vegetable shortenings, solid margarines, certain crackers and cookies, and other foods made with partially hydrogenated oils.

Saturated fat should be used the least. This type of fat is found in animal-source foods such as meat, butter, and cheese. Baked goods may be high in saturated fat if lard or palm oil is used. Excessive intake of saturated fat can increase blood cholesterol levels.

Trans fat is the result of a food manufacturing process called hydrogenation. This process converts a liquid vegetable oil to a solid fat to make shortenings and solid (stick) types of margarine.

Cholesterol

Cholesterol is a waxy substance found in all body cells. The liver makes much of the cholesterol your body needs, but cholesterol is also obtained from the foods you eat. Cholesterol is found in animal foods such as meat, eggs, butter, and whole dairy products. Too much cholesterol in the blood can increase your risk for heart disease. Limit consumption of fatty meats, butter, and whole dairy foods.

Sodium

Sodium is a mineral that does not affect blood sugar, but it can alter your blood pressure. Keeping blood pressure under control is an important aspect of managing pre-diabetes and preventing heart disease. Here are some tips for reducing sodium:

- Leave out or reduce the amount of salt in standard recipes by 25–50 percent.
- Use commercial herb blends or make your own (see Chapter 15) to season food instead of using salt.
- Limit processed foods such as boxed mixes, TV dinners, and processed meats.
- Make more meals and side dishes from scratch.
- Watch your use of the salt shaker in cooking or at the table.

About Fiber and Whole Grains

There are two types of fiber found in foods: soluble and insoluble. It's important to include foods containing both types of fiber in your daily eating plan. Beans, fruit, barley, and oats are especially good sources of soluble fiber. Vegetables, whole-grain foods, and fruit are all sources of insoluble fiber.

FACT

The terms *multigrain*, *seven-grain*, and *stone-ground* do not necessarily mean a product is whole-grain. If a whole-grain ingredient is not listed as the first ingredient, the item may contain only a small portion of whole grains. One way to find a whole-grain product is to look for the Whole Grains Council stamp of approval, which labels foods containing whole grains. The logo that reads "100% Whole Grain" indicates that the food has only whole grains and at least 16g per serving.

Although all types of grains are sources of complex carbohydrates, those that have not been refined are better for you. Whole grains have not had the bran layer and germ removed during the milling process; therefore, the fiber as well as vitamins and minerals are preserved. Fiber helps to slow down the absorption of glucose into the bloodstream, which helps to keep blood glucose controlled. Refined grains such as white-flour products have the bran and germ removed, making them much lower in fiber. Whenever you can, choose whole grains over refined grains.

Great Ways to Get More Whole Grains

The best way to get more whole grains in your meals is to substitute whole-grain foods for refined products. Here are some tips:

- Instead of all-purpose flour, experiment by replacing some of the flour with a whole-grain variety.
- Use a whole grain as a side dish or combine it with vegetables or beans.
- Try a "new" grain that you have not used before. Quinoa, bulgur, or kasha may be unfamiliar, but they are as easy to prepare as white rice.
- Add whole grains to soups, salads, or casseroles instead of white rice or pasta.
- Gradually replace the refined grains in your pantry with whole-grain foods.

Learn How to Read Food Labels

The Nutrition Facts found on food labels contain information, but unless you understand how to read the labels, this information may not mean very much to you. Here are some of the items listed on the Nutrition Facts label:

- **Serving size:** Labels must identify the size of a serving. The nutritional information listed on a label is based on one serving of the food.
- **Amount per serving:** Each package identifies the quantities of nutrients and food constituents in one serving. This includes the caloric value of the food, as well as the amount of fat, cholesterol, sodium, carbohydrates, and protein per serving.
- **Percent daily value:** This indicates how much of a specific nutrient a serving of food contains based on an average 2,000-calorie diet.
- **Ingredient list:** This is a list of the ingredients in a food in descending order of predominance and weight.

Grams of Carbohydrate or Grams of Sugar?

There are several parts to the carbohydrate section of the nutrition label. Total Carbohydrate represents the full amount of carbohydrate grams found in a food. Beneath the Total Carbohydrate are other listings: Fiber, Sugars, and sometimes, Sugar Alcohols. It is important to know that all three are part of Total Carbohydrate. Grams of Sugars usually indicate *added* sugar.

By comparing the grams of Sugars to the grams of Total Carbohydrate you can decide whether a food contains too much sugar. For example, if a label says that a cup of cereal has 32g Total Carbohydrate and 16g of Sugars, it means that 50 percent of the carbohydrate in the cereal comes from sugar. Try to choose foods having no more than 25 percent of their grams from added sugars. Items such as milk, plain yogurt, and fresh fruit have *natural sugar,* not added sugar, therefore the 25 percent guideline does not apply.

Grocery Lists and Your Kitchen Makeover

Having the right foods on hand is the best way to keep you eating healthier. If you leave things up to chance, you could make poor food choices. Set aside time each week to plan meals. Keep a weekly shopping list visible and handy; when you think of food items you need, write them on your list. Consider what meals and snacks you will need for the coming week.

FIFTEEN FOODS TO ALWAYS HAVE ON HAND

1. Vegetables: Fresh, frozen, or reduced-sodium canned
2. Fruits: Fresh, frozen (unsweetened), or canned (juice- or water-packed)
3. Whole-grain bread or crackers
4. High-fiber (low-sugar) cereals with 4g or more fiber per serving
5. Canned beans, dried beans, or lentils
6. Boneless, skinless chicken or turkey breast
7. Eggs, egg substitutes, or egg whites
8. Tuna or salmon canned in water
9. Low-fat cheese or cheese sticks
10. Dried herbs and spices
11. Dry-roasted or raw nuts (unsalted)

12. Low-sodium chicken, vegetable, or beef broth
13. Leafy lettuce varieties or bagged mixes using leafy varieties
14. Low-sodium canned tomatoes
15. Nonfat yogurt: plain, vanilla, or low-sugar fruit-flavored

Let your shopping list be your guide at the grocery store and stick to your list as much as possible. The healthiest foods are found around the perimeter of the store, and everything else is found in the aisles. Spend most of your time shopping around the perimeter.

Make Over Your Food Supply

Making over your food supply is easy to do. You can gradually phase out foods of lesser nutritional quality and introduce newer ones that have more health benefits. As you run out of certain items, replace them with something new.

▼ SWITCH TO HEALTHIER OPTIONS

Instead of:	Replace with:
Garlic or onion salt	Fresh garlic or onion
Fruit juices	Fresh fruit
All-purpose flour	Whole-grain flour
Vegetable oil	Olive or canola oil
Sour cream	Plain, low-fat yogurt
Buttery snack crackers	Whole-grain crackers
Potato chips	Popcorn (make your own)

Recipe Adjustments for Your New Cooking Style

Your favorite recipes can be adjusted to lower fat, salt, or sugar content, yet still maintain good taste. Some of the recipes found in this cookbook may contain ingredients such as butter or salt in small amounts. These ingredients are usually part of a recipe because they improve the flavor or aid in the baking process. When baking bread, cookies, or cakes, salt is usually essential in the leavening process and should not be eliminated. If you must eliminate all butter from your diet, most recipes can use either olive or canola oil as a substitute.

The recipes for baked desserts found in this cookbook have different methods for addressing sugar. Some recipes will simply have a reduction in the amount of sugar used. There are others that use a different type of sugar such as honey or maple syrup. When these are used in the place of sugar, a lower quantity is used but the recipe is not sugar-free. Lastly, some recipes have a combination of an artificial sweetener with a very small amount of regular sugar. As you work with these or with your own recipes, you will learn how to adjust ingredients to get good results.

QUESTION

Can sugar be eliminated from my favorite baked dessert?
Completely eliminating sugar from baked desserts can be tricky. Although sugar is an empty-calorie food, it does serve as an important ingredient in baked foods. When sugar is reduced or replaced with an artificial sweetener, the result can be very different and not what you were hoping for. The baked item may lack a golden-brown color or have a flavor unlike the original recipe.

Tips for Replacing or Reducing Sugar and Fat

Try reducing a standard recipe's sugar content by starting with a 25-percent reduction and gradually decrease the amount of sugar each time you make it. Be sure to note whether the properties of the food change in any significant or undesirable ways, then adjust as needed. Use puréed, unsweetened fruit or fruit juice to replace some of the sugar in a recipe. Honey and maple syrup are sugars; however, either can add sweetness using a lesser amount. Many recipes can withstand up to a 50-percent reduction in fat. To replace fat, use plain yogurt, applesauce, mashed ripe banana, or other puréed fruit for half of the fat called for in a recipe. If the recipe requires sweetness, puréed fruit is a good option.

Using Sugar Substitutes

Sugar substitutes are never mandatory when you have pre-diabetes; however, they can offer options for those who wish to use them. Using a sugar substitute in a recipe can slash sugar content and calories. When using sugar substitutes in baking, keep in mind that sweetness is being added to the food but other traits unique to a baked product (volume, texture, color) may be altered. Check with the manufacturer on the best ways to use a sugar substitute for baking.

Cooking Styles

There are many ways to prepare foods that minimize the use of sugar, salt, and fat yet taste good! A little creativity with spices or herbs makes food more flavorful without the addition of extra fat, sodium, or calories. Stir-frying, broiling, and slow-cooking are examples of techniques that are time-saving and result in healthier food.

Stir-frying uses small amounts of oil to cook foods quickly at a high heat. Combine several foods together for a quick and healthy meal. Foods that work well using this method include vegetables, poultry, meats, fish, and cooked grains. Choose oil that allows for a high cooking temperature such as canola or peanut oil. Remember to use as little oil as possible; usually 1–2 teaspoons will do.

Broiling and grilling involve cooking food on a rack to allow fats to drip to a pan or flame below. Most meats, poultry, and fish can be grilled or broiled. Broiling instead of cooking in oil reduces fat and calories. When grilling outdoors, use aluminum foil to minimize the direct contact of food with the flame, and be sure to prevent foods from charring or overbrowning.

Slow cookers are often overlooked but can save time in the kitchen. Foods are placed in the slow cooker and allowed to cook at a low temperature for several hours or longer. Meals made in a slow cooker do not require the addition of fat, and the slow-cooking helps tenderize tougher cuts of meat. Soups, sauces, and stews are just a few examples of items you can cook in a slow cooker.

Breakfast and Brunch

Buckwheat Pancakes

PER SERVING: Calories: 220 | Protein: 11g | Carbohydrates: 44g | Fat: 1g | Saturated Fat: 0g | Cholesterol: 1mg
Sodium: 200mg | Fiber: 5g | PCF Ratio: 76-19-5 | Exchange Approx.: 2 Starches, ½ Skim Milk, ½ Fruit

INGREDIENTS | SERVES 2

1 cup whole-wheat flour
½ cup buckwheat flour
1½ teaspoons baking powder
2 egg whites
¼ cup apple juice concentrate
1¼–1½ cups skim milk

1. Sift flours and baking powder together into a large bowl.

2. In a medium bowl, combine egg whites, apple juice concentrate, and 1¼ cups milk.

3. Add the milk mixture to dry ingredients; mix well, but do not over-mix. Add remaining milk if necessary to reach desired consistency.

4. Cook pancakes for 1–2 minutes on each side in nonstick frying pan or on griddle treated with nonstick cooking spray over medium heat.

Egg White Pancakes

PER SERVING: Calories: 197 | Protein: 13g | Carbohydrates: 31g | Fat: 3g | Saturated Fat: 1g | Cholesterol: 0mg
Sodium: 120mg | Fiber: 4g | PCF Ratio: 27-61-12 | Exchange Approx.: 1 Free Sweet, 1 Lean Meat, 1½ Breads

INGREDIENTS | SERVES 2

4 egg whites
½ cup oatmeal
4 teaspoons reduced-calorie or low-sugar strawberry jam
1 teaspoon powdered sugar (optional)

1. Put all ingredients in blender; process until smooth.

2. Preheat nonstick pan treated with cooking spray over medium heat. Pour half of mixture into pan; cook for 4–5 minutes.

3. Flip pancake and cook until inside is cooked. Repeat using remaining batter for second pancake. Dust each pancake with powdered sugar, if using.

Creative Toppings

Experiment with toast and pancake toppings. Try a tablespoon of raisins, almonds, peanuts, walnuts, nut butters (limit these to 1 teaspoon per serving), apples, pears, bananas, berries, or wheat germ.

Buttermilk Pancakes

PER SERVING: Calories: 143 | Protein: 6g | Carbohydrates: 26g | Fat: 2g | Saturated Fat: 1g | Cholesterol: 49mg
Sodium: 111mg | Fiber: 1g | PCF Ratio: 16-74-10 | Exchange Approx.: 1½ Starches

INGREDIENTS | SERVES 2

1 cup all-purpose flour

2 tablespoons nonfat buttermilk powder

¼ teaspoon baking soda

½ teaspoon low-salt baking powder

1 cup water

Nut Butter Batter

For a change of pace, try adding 1 Exchange amount per serving of nut butter to pancake batter and use jelly or jam instead of syrup.

1. In a large bowl, blend together all the ingredients, adding more water if necessary to get desired batter consistency.

2. Pour ¼ of batter into nonstick skillet or skillet treated with nonstick cooking spray. Cook over medium heat until bubbles appear on top half of pancake. Flip and continue cooking until center of pancake is done. Repeat process with remaining batter.

Berry Puff Pancakes

PER SERVING: Calories: 110 | Protein: 5g | Carbohydrates: 37g | Fat: 2g | Saturated Fat: 1g | Cholesterol: 71mg
Sodium: 89mg | Fiber: 3g | PCF Ratio: 65-18-17 | Exchange Approx.: 1 Starch, ½ Fruit

INGREDIENTS | SERVES 6

2 whole eggs

1 egg white

½ cup skim milk

½ cup all-purpose flour

1 tablespoon granulated sugar

⅛ teaspoon sea salt

2 cups fresh berries such as raspberries, blackberries, boysenberries, blueberries, strawberries, or a combination

1 tablespoon powdered sugar

Syrup Substitutes

Spreading 2 teaspoons of your favorite Smucker's Low Sugar jam or jelly on a waffle or pancake not only gives you a sweet topping; it can be one of your Free Exchange List choices for the day.

1. Preheat oven to 450°F. Treat a 10" ovenproof skillet or deep pie pan with nonstick cooking spray. Once oven is heated, place pan in oven for a few minutes to get hot.

2. Add eggs and egg white to medium bowl; beat until mixed. Whisk in milk. Slowly whisk in flour, sugar, and salt.

3. Remove preheated pan from oven; pour batter into it. Bake for 15 minutes; then reduce heat to 350°F and bake for an additional 10 minutes, or until batter is puffed and brown.

4. Remove from oven and slide onto serving plate. Cover with fruit and sift powdered sugar over top. Cut into 6 equal wedges and serve.

Sweet Potato Pancakes

PER SERVING: Calories: 168 | Protein: 6g | Carbohydrates: 287g | Fat: 7g | Saturated Fat: 1g | Cholesterol: 0mg
Sodium: 139mg | Fiber: 3g | PCF Ratio: 13-49-37 | Exchange Approx.: 1 Starch, 1½ Fats

INGREDIENTS | SERVES 4

1½ cups cooked mashed sweet potatoes
¼ cup grated onions
1 egg
3 tablespoons whole-wheat pastry flour
½ teaspoon cinnamon
½ teaspoon baking powder
½ cup egg whites
2 tablespoons canola oil

1. In medium bowl, mix together the cooked sweet potatoes, grated onion, and egg. Add in flour, cinnamon, and baking powder.

2. In a separate small bowl, beat egg whites until rounded peaks are formed. Gently fold egg whites into potato mixture.

3. Heat canola oil in skillet (nonstick preferably) until hot. Spoon batter onto skillet to form pancakes approximately 4" in diameter. Brown on both sides.

4. Serve hot with unsweetened applesauce.

Cottage Cheese Pancakes

PER SERVING: Calories: 352 | Protein: 21g | Carbohydrates: 12g | Fat: 24g | Saturated Fat: 6g | Cholesterol: 376mg
Sodium: 557mg | Fiber: 0g | PCF Ratio: 24-14-62 | Exchange Approx.: 3 Medium-Fat Meats, 2½ Fats

INGREDIENTS | SERVES 4

½ cup whole-wheat flour
¼ teaspoon salt
¼ cup olive oil
1 cup low-fat milk
½ teaspoon vanilla extract
6 eggs
1 cup low-fat cottage cheese
Nonstick cooking spray, as needed

1. Blend all the ingredients except cooking spray in a blender until smooth.

2. Spray a pan with nonstick cooking spray and place over medium heat. Pour ¼-cup portions of batter onto hot pan to form pancakes. As the pan heats up, adjust the temperature to prevent the pancakes from becoming too dark.

3. Cook pancakes 2–3 minutes per side until golden brown. Make the pancakes in small batches and, when done, cover to keep warm before serving.

Blueberry Pancakes

Try adding a few handfuls of blueberries to your pancake batter. Blueberries are an excellent source of antioxidant phytonutrients, called anthocyanidins, which are responsible for the blue-red pigment seen in blueberries. Anthocyanidins help to protect the body from harm from free radicals.

Country-Style Omelet

PER SERVING: Calories: 253 | Protein: 17g | Carbohydrates: 7g | Fat: 17g | Saturated Fat: 5g | Cholesterol: 493mg
Sodium: 221mg | Fiber: 2g | PCF Ratio: 27-12-61 | Exchange Approx.: 1 Vegetable, 2 Medium-Fat Meats, 3 Fats

INGREDIENTS | SERVES 2

2 teaspoons olive oil
1 cup diced zucchini
¼ cup diced red pepper
1 cup skinned and cubed plum tomatoes
⅛ teaspoon pepper
4 eggs
1 tablespoon Parmesan cheese
1 teaspoon minced fresh basil

1. Heat oil in a nonstick skillet. Add zucchini and red pepper; sauté for 5 minutes.

2. Add tomatoes and pepper; cook uncovered for another 10 minutes, allowing fluid from tomatoes to cook down.

3. In a small bowl, whisk together eggs, Parmesan cheese, and fresh basil; pour over vegetables in skillet.

4. Cook over low heat until browned, approximately 10 minutes on each side.

Tomato and Feta Frittata

PER SERVING: Calories: 192 | Protein: 17g | Carbohydrates: 6g | Fat: 11g | Saturated Fat: 5g | Cholesterol: 227mg
Sodium: 421mg | Fiber: 1g | PCF Ratio: 35-11-54 | Exchange Approx.: 2 Medium-Fat Meats, 2 Fats, 1 Vegetable

INGREDIENTS | SERVES 1

2 egg whites
1 whole egg
2 tablespoons crumbled feta cheese
½ cup chopped tomatoes
Salt and pepper, to taste

Healthy Egg Dish

Quiches taste great, but they are loaded with fat, cholesterol, and calories. Plus, the crust often has a high glycemic value. Frittatas are a lighter option for a delicious and easy egg dish.

1. Place egg whites and whole egg in a medium bowl and whisk together.

2. Add the feta and tomatoes to the eggs and whisk together.

3. Place mixture into a small skillet coated with cooking spray over medium heat and cook for 4 minutes or until eggs are firm. Do not stir.

4. Flip and cook the other side for 2 more minutes. Season with salt and pepper to taste.

Herbed Omelet with Vegetables

PER SERVING: Calories: 178 | Protein: 18g | Carbohydrates: 5g | Fat: 9g | Saturated Fat: 4g | Cholesterol: 253mg
Sodium: 241mg | Fiber: 1g | PCF Ratio: 41-12-47 | Exchange Approx.: 2 Medium-Fat Meats, 1½ Fats, ½ Vegetable

INGREDIENTS | SERVES 2

Cooking spray, as needed
2 cups sliced white mushrooms
3 tablespoons low-fat milk, divided
2 tablespoons sour cream
Salt and pepper, to taste
2 tablespoons chopped green onions
1 tablespoon chopped chives
¼ teaspoon dried tarragon
4 egg whites
2 whole eggs

Low-Fat Alternative

Fresh herbs and mushrooms give this omelet tons of earthy flavor. In the summer, use fresh herbs from your own garden. To cut back on saturated fat, try using 6 egg whites and passing on the yolks.

1. Spray a large skillet with cooking spray and heat skillet over medium-high heat. Add mushrooms and cook for approximately 2 minutes or until mushrooms are soft and liquid evaporates.

2. In a medium bowl, mix together 1 tablespoon milk, sour cream, salt, and pepper. Whisk well and set aside.

3. In a separate bowl, mix remaining 2 tablespoons milk, green onion, chives, tarragon, egg whites, and whole eggs; whisk well.

4. Pour egg mixture into a greased pan over medium-high heat and spread evenly over pan. Once center is cooked, cover egg with mushrooms. Loosen omelet with spatula and fold in half.

5. Place omelet on a plate to serve and top with sour cream mixture.

Egg Clouds on Toast

PER SERVING: Calories: 57 | Protein: 4g | Carbohydrates: 9g | Fat: 1g | Saturated Fat: 0g | Cholesterol: 0mg Sodium: 101mg | Fiber: 0g | PCF Ratio: 30-63-7 | Exchange Approx.: ½ Very-Lean Meat, ½ Starch

INGREDIENTS | SERVES 1

2 egg whites

½ teaspoon sugar

1 cup water

1 tablespoon frozen apple juice concentrate

1 slice reduced-calorie oat-bran bread, lightly toasted

Tip

Additional serving suggestions: Spread 1 teaspoon of low-sugar or all-fruit spread on toast (½ Fruit Exchange) before ladling on the "clouds." For cinnamon French-style toast, sprinkle ¼ teaspoon cinnamon and ½ teaspoon powdered sugar (less than 10 calories) over top of the clouds.

1. In a copper bowl, beat egg whites until thickened. Add sugar; continue to beat until stiff peaks form.

2. In a small saucepan, heat water and apple juice over medium heat until it just begins to boil; reduce heat and allow mixture to simmer.

3. Drop egg whites by teaspoonful into simmering water. Simmer for 3 minutes; turn over and simmer for an additional 3 minutes.

4. Ladle "clouds" over bread and serve immediately.

Overnight Oatmeal

PER SERVING: Calories: 221 | Protein: 9g | Carbohydrates: 42g | Fat: 3g | Saturated Fat: 1g | Cholesterol: 1mg
Sodium: 25mg | Fiber: 6g | PCF Ratio: 15-73-11 | Exchange Approx.: 1 Fruit, 1 Starch, ½ Skim Milk

INGREDIENTS | SERVES 4

1 cup steel-cut oats

14 dried apricot halves

1 dried fig

2 tablespoons golden raisins

4 cups water

½ cup Mock Cream (see recipe in Chapter 12)

Add all ingredients to a slow cooker with a ceramic interior; set to low heat. Cover and cook overnight (8–9 hours).

Another Overnight Method

For another way to cook steel-cut oats, place 1 cup steel-cut oats, 4 cups water, and dried fruit in a medium saucepan; bring to a quick boil. Turn off the heat and cover the saucepan. When cooled, place in a covered container and refrigerate overnight. In the morning, the oatmeal will have absorbed all of the water. Scoop 1 portion of the oatmeal into a bowl; microwave on high for 1½–2 minutes. Add milk and serve. Heat up refrigerated leftover portions as needed; use within 3 days.

Quinoa Berry Breakfast

PER SERVING: Calories: 228 | Protein: 7g | Carbohydrates: 41g | Fat: 5g | Saturated Fat: 0g | Cholesterol: 0mg
Sodium: 2mg | Fiber: 5g | PCF Ratio: 12-69-19 | Exchange Approx.: 2 Starches, 1 Fruit, 1 Very-Lean Meat, 4 Fats

INGREDIENTS | SERVES 4

1 cup quinoa

2 cups water

¼ cup walnuts

1 teaspoon cinnamon

2 cups berries of your choice

Single Serving Quick Tip

Use this basic recipe to make 4 servings at once. Refrigerate any leftover portions; microwave 1–1½ minutes on high for single portions as needed. Use cooked quinoa within 3 days. Try other berries, nuts, or spices such as ginger or nutmeg to vary this nutritious breakfast cereal.

1. Rinse quinoa in fine mesh sieve before cooking.

2. Place quinoa, water, walnuts, and cinnamon in 1½-quart saucepan; bring to a boil. Reduce heat to low; cover and cook for 15 minutes or until all water has been absorbed.

3. Add berries and serve with milk, soy milk, or sweetener if desired.

Fruit Smoothie

PER SERVING: The Nutritional Analysis and Fruit Exchange for this recipe will depend on your choice of fruit. Otherwise, allow ½ Skim Milk Exchange and ½ Misc. Food Exchange. The wheat germ adds fiber, but at less than 20 calories a serving, it can count as 1 Free Exchange.

INGREDIENTS | SERVES 1

1 cup skim milk

2 Exchange servings of any diced fruit

1 tablespoon honey

4 teaspoons toasted wheat germ

6 large ice cubes

Put all the ingredients into blender or food processor and process until thick and smooth.

Batch 'Em

Make large batches of smoothies so you can keep single servings in the freezer. Get out a serving as you begin to get ready for your day. This should give the smoothie time to thaw enough for you to stir it when you're ready to have breakfast.

Yogurt Fruit Smoothie

PER SERVING: Calories: 149 | Protein: 10g | Carbohydrates: 26g | Fat: 1g | Saturated Fat: 0g | Cholesterol: 2mg Sodium: 96mg | Fiber: 2g | PCF Ratio: 25-67-8 | Exchange Approx.: 1 Milk, 1 Fruit

INGREDIENTS | SERVES 2

1 cup plain, low-fat yogurt
½ cup sliced strawberries
½ cup orange juice
½ cup peeled and sliced nectarines
2 tablespoons ground flaxseed

Variations and Combos

You can vary this smoothie by substituting other fruits of your choice. Good combinations are strawberry and banana, strawberry and kiwi, and banana and peach. Keep portions of each fruit to no more than ½ cup.

Put all the ingredients in blender and process until smooth.

Tofu Smoothie

PER SERVING: Calories: 289 | Protein: 20g | Carbohydrates: 35g | Fat: 11g | Saturated Fat: 2g | Cholesterol: 0mg Sodium: 19mg | Fiber: 8g | PCF Ratio: 25-44-31 | Exchange Approx.: 1 Meat Substitute, 2 Fruits

INGREDIENTS | SERVES 1

1⅓ cups frozen unsweetened strawberries
½ banana
½ cup (4 ounces) silken tofu

In a food processor or blender, process all ingredients until smooth. Add a little chilled water for a thinner smoothie if desired.

Banana-Kiwi Smoothie

**PER SERVING: Calories: 274 | Protein: 5g | Carbohydrates: 67g | Fat: 2g | Saturated Fat: 0g | Cholesterol: 0mg
Sodium: 12mg | Fiber: 9g | PCF Ratio: 7-87-6 | Exchange Approx.: 4 Fruits**

INGREDIENTS | SERVES 2

1 banana, peeled and cut in 2" segments

4 kiwi fruit, peeled and halved

Juice of 1 lime

1½ cups orange juice

2 tablespoons oat bran or Kashi

4 ice cubes

4 drops hot sauce (optional)

Place the banana, kiwi, lime juice, and orange juice in the blender and purée. Add the remaining ingredients and blend until smooth. Serve chilled.

Kick Up Your Breakfast with Kiwi

Kiwi fruit are delicious, inexpensive, and a bit exotic. They happen to be loaded with vitamins as well!

CHAPTER 3

Appetizers

Lemon Tahini Vegetable Dip

PER SERVING: Calories: 26 | Protein: 1g | Carbohydrates: 1g | Fat: 2g | Saturated Fat: 0g | Cholesterol: 0mg
Sodium: 61mg | Fiber: 1g | PCF Ratio: 16-11-73 | Exchange Approx.: ½ Fat

INGREDIENTS | MAKES ABOUT 5 CUPS; SERVING SIZE: 1 TABLESPOON

1 cup sesame seeds
¼ cup lemon juice
1 cup water
2 tablespoons ground flaxseed
1 teaspoon garlic powder
⅛ teaspoon cider vinegar
1 teaspoon sea salt

Put all the ingredients in food processor and blend until smooth.

Easy Onion Dip

PER SERVING: Calories: 50 | Protein: 2g | Carbohydrates: 4g | Fat: 3g | Saturated Fat: 2g | Cholesterol: 10mg
Sodium: 147mg | Fiber: 8g | PCF Ratio: 17-30-53 | Exchange Approx.: ½ Fat

INGREDIENTS | MAKES 2 CUPS; SERVING SIZE: 1½ TABLESPOONS

1 cup nonfat yogurt
1 cup reduced-fat sour cream
2 tablespoons dried onion flakes
½ teaspoon salt
¼ teaspoon lemon pepper
1 teaspoon dried dill

Mix all the ingredients together. Refrigerate for 2–3 hours in covered container before serving.

Horseradish Dip

PER SERVING: Calories: 12 | Protein: 1g | Carbohydrates: 1g | Fat: 1g | Saturated Fat: 0g | Cholesterol: 0mg
Sodium: 9mg | Fiber: 0g | PCF Ratio: 39-21-40 | Exchange Approx.: 1 Free Condiment

**INGREDIENTS | MAKES 1¾ CUPS;
SERVING SIZE: 1
TABLESPOON**

1 cup nonfat cottage cheese

1 tablespoon olive oil

½ cup plain, nonfat yogurt

3 tablespoons prepared horseradish

1 teaspoon lemon juice

Optional seasonings, to taste:

Onion powder

Ground cumin

Sea salt

Ground ginger

Combine all the ingredients in blender or food processor and process until smooth.

Garbanzo Dip

PER SERVING: Calories: 24 | Protein: 4g | Carbohydrates: 5g | Fat: 0g | Saturated Fat: 0g | Cholesterol: 0mg
Sodium: 1mg | Fiber: 1g | PCF Ratio: 25-73-2 | Exchange Approx.: ½ Very-Lean Meat

**INGREDIENTS | MAKES ABOUT 2 CUPS;
SERVING SIZE: 1
TABLESPOON**

3 cups cooked garbanzo or other white beans

½ teaspoon ground cumin

1 tablespoon lemon juice

1 tablespoon dried parsley

¼ teaspoon dried basil

1 teaspoon onion powder

¼ teaspoon garlic powder

1 tablespoon honey

Combine all the ingredients in food processor or blender and process until smooth. Add 1 teaspoon of water or bean broth if you need to thin the dip.

Artichoke Dip

PER SERVING: Calories: 47 | Protein: 1g | Carbohydrates: 4g | Fat: 3g | Saturated Fat: 1g | Cholesterol: 1mg | Sodium: 129mg | Fiber: 2g | PCF Ratio: 11-33-56 | Exchange Approx.: 1 Vegetable; ½ Fat

INGREDIENTS | MAKES ABOUT 1 CUP; SERVING SIZE: 1½ TABLESPOONS

1 cup artichoke hearts, drained

1 tablespoon chopped red onion

1 tablespoon chopped sun-dried tomatoes

1 tablespoon low-fat mayonnaise

1 tablespoon reduced-fat sour cream

2 teaspoons Parmesan cheese

1 teaspoon lemon juice

½ teaspoon minced garlic

1 tablespoon olive oil

Put all the ingredients in food processor and blend until smooth. Chill for at least 3 hours before serving.

Variation

For a variation on this recipe, you can use ¼ cup roasted red peppers instead of sun-dried tomatoes.

Garlic and Feta Cheese Dip

PER SERVING: Calories: 11 | Protein: 0g | Carbohydrates: 0g | Fat: 1g | Saturated Fat: 1g | Cholesterol: 0mg
Sodium: 22mg | Fiber: 0g | PCF Ratio: 9-10-80 | Exchange Approx.: 1 Free Condiment

**INGREDIENTS | MAKES 1½ CUPS;
SERVING SIZE:
1 TABLESPOON**

½ cup crumbled feta cheese

4 ounces cream cheese, softened

¼ cup real mayonnaise

1 clove dry-roasted garlic

¼ teaspoon dried basil

¼ teaspoon dried cilantro or oregano

⅛ teaspoon dried dill

⅛ teaspoon dried thyme

1. In food processor, combine all the ingredients and process until thoroughly mixed. Cover and chill until ready to serve with assorted vegetables.

2. This dip is somewhat high in fat if you use regular cream cheese, whereas nonfat cream cheese would lower the total fat in this recipe by 38 grams. People on a salt-restricted diet need to check with their dietitians about using nonfat cream cheese because it's much higher in sodium.

Dry-Roasted Garlic

To dry-roast garlic: Preheat oven to 350°F; lightly spray small, covered baking dish with nonstick cooking spray. Slice off ½" from top of each garlic head; rub off any loose skins, being careful not to separate cloves. Place in baking dish, cut-side up (if roasting more than 1 head, arrange in dish so they don't touch). Cover and bake until the garlic cloves are very tender when pierced, about 30–45 minutes. Roasted garlic heads will keep in refrigerator 2–3 days.

Fruit Skewers with Dip

PER SERVING: Calories: 166 | Protein: 5g | Carbohydrates: 36g | Fat: 2g | Saturated Fat: 1g | Cholesterol: 4mg
Sodium: 49mg | Fiber: 7g | PCF Ratio: 11-81-8 | Exchange Approx.: 2 Fruits, ½ Milk

INGREDIENTS | SERVES 4

4 kiwi fruit, peeled and sliced into ½"
pieces

8 large strawberries, sliced in half

2 medium pears, cut into ½" pieces

1 large orange, peeled and sliced into
½" pieces

1 cup plain, low-fat yogurt

Juice of 1 lime

2 teaspoons finely chopped fresh mint
leaves

1. Arrange cut fruit pieces on 8 wooden skewers, alternating fruit types.

2. In a small bowl, mix together yogurt, lime juice, and mint.

3. Serve fruit skewers with yogurt dip.

Fresh Herbed Yogurt

A forkless version of the fruit salad, this appetizer can be made with a variety of seasonal fruits. For a different flavor, try using fresh basil leaves and the juice of half a lemon in place of the mint and lime.

Black Bean Dip

PER SERVING: Calories: 20 | Protein: 1g | Carbohydrates: 2g | Fat: 1g | Saturated Fat: 0g | Cholesterol: 2mg
Sodium: 4mg | Fiber: 1g | PCF Ratio: 17-48-35 | Exchange Approx.: 1 Free Condiment

INGREDIENTS | MAKES 2 CUPS; SERVING SIZE: 2 TABLESPOONS

1½ cups canned black beans, drained and rinsed

½ cup finely minced Vidalia onion

4 cloves garlic, minced

2 teaspoons red hot pepper sauce, or to taste

Juice of 1 lime

½ cup sour cream

½ cup chopped cilantro or parsley

Salt and pepper, to taste

Pulse all the ingredients in the food processor or blender. Serve chilled or at room temperature.

Herbed Cheese Spread

PER SERVING: Calories: 20 | Protein: 1g | Carbohydrates: .5g | Fat: 2g | Saturated Fat: 1g | Cholesterol: 5mg
Sodium: 26mg | Fiber: 0g | PCF Ratio: 27-6-67 | Exchange Approx.: ¼ Skim Milk or 1 Free Condiment

INGREDIENTS | MAKES ABOUT 1 CUP; SERVING SIZE: 1 TABLESPOON

2 teaspoons chopped fresh parsley

2 teaspoons chopped fresh chives

1 teaspoon chopped fresh thyme

½ teaspoon freshly ground black pepper

½ cup nonfat cottage cheese

4 ounces Neufchâtel cheese, room temperature

1. Place herbs in a food processor and pulse till combined.

2. Add pepper and cheeses and process until smooth.

Easy Olive Spread

PER SERVING: Calories: 15 | Protein: 1g | Carbohydrates: 1g | Fat: 1g | Saturated Fat: .5g | Cholesterol: 1mg
Sodium: 56mg | Fiber: 0g | PCF Ratio: 17-19-64 | Exchange Approx.: 1 Free Condiment

**INGREDIENTS | MAKES ABOUT 3 CUPS;
SERVING SIZE: 1
TABLESPOON**

1 cup black olives

3 cloves garlic

1 tablespoon fresh Italian flat-leaf parsley

1 tablespoon fresh basil

2 teaspoons minced lemon zest

Freshly ground black pepper, to taste

½ cup nonfat cottage cheese

2 tablespoons cream cheese

1 tablespoon real mayonnaise

1. Combine olives, garlic, parsley, basil, lemon zest, and black pepper in a food processor and pulse until chopped. Transfer to a bowl and set aside.

2. Add cottage cheese, cream cheese, and mayonnaise to the food processor and process until smooth.

3. Fold cheese mixture into chopped olive mixture.

Delicious Substitutions

Substitute marinated mushrooms or artichoke hearts for olives in this recipe.

Herbed Yogurt Cheese Spread

PER SERVING: Calories: 36 | Protein: 4g | Carbohydrates: 5g | Fat: 0g | Saturated Fat: 0g | Cholesterol: 1mg Sodium: 146mg | Fiber: 0g | PCF Ratio: 41-56-3 | Exchange Approx.: ½ Milk

INGREDIENTS | MAKES ABOUT 2 CUPS; SERVING SIZE: 4 TABLESPOONS

1½ cups plain, nonfat yogurt
1 tablespoon minced scallion
1 tablespoon minced parsley
1 teaspoon minced garlic
2 tablespoons minced roasted red pepper
¼ teaspoon salt
Pinch cayenne pepper

1. Prepare yogurt cheese in advance: Line a fine mesh strainer with a coffee filter. Place plain yogurt in filter and set strainer over a bowl. Cover and refrigerate for 8 hours or overnight. When all fluid has drained, it should be the consistency of softened cream cheese.

2. Add scallion, parsley, garlic, red pepper, salt, and cayenne to the yogurt. Mix well, cover, and refrigerate for at least 3 hours before serving.

3. Serve with crackers or raw vegetables.

Get Your Calcium!

Yogurt is one of the top sources of calcium, a vital mineral for bone health. Yogurt cheese is very easy to make and can often be substituted in dip (or other) recipes that call for cream cheese. Cream cheese, unlike yogurt, contains mostly fat and is not a significant source of calcium or protein.

Mushroom Caviar

PER SERVING: Calories: 9 | Protein: 0g | Carbohydrates: 1g | Fat: 1g | Saturated Fat: 0g | Cholesterol: 0mg
Sodium: 1mg | Fiber: 0g | PCF Ratio: 11-32-57 | Exchange Approx.: 1 Free Condiment

INGREDIENTS | MAKES ABOUT 3 CUPS; SERVING SIZE: 1 TABLESPOON

1½ cups portobello mushrooms

1½ cups white mushrooms

¼ cup chopped scallions

4 cloves dry-roasted garlic (see recipe for Garlic and Feta Cheese Dip in this chapter)

1 teaspoon fresh lemon juice

½ teaspoon balsamic vinegar

1 tablespoon extra-virgin olive oil

½ teaspoon chopped fresh thyme (optional)

Sea salt and freshly ground black pepper, to taste (optional)

Pseudo-Sauté

When onions and scallions are sautéed in butter or oil, they go through a caramelization process that doesn't occur when they're steamed. To create this flavor without increasing fat in a recipe, transfer steamed vegetables to a nonstick wok or skillet (coated with nonstick cooking spray, or a small portion of oil called for in recipe) and sauté until extra moisture evaporates.

1. Cut portobello mushrooms into ¼" cubes. Cut white mushrooms into halves or quarters. (The mushroom pieces should be roughly uniform in size.) Place mushrooms and chopped scallions in microwave-safe bowl; cover and microwave on high 1 minute. Rotate bowl and microwave in 30-second intervals until tender.

2. Transfer scallions and mushrooms to a food processor. (Reserve any liquid to use for thinning, if necessary.) Pulse several times to chop mixture, scraping down sides of bowl as needed.

3. Add the remaining ingredients and pulse until mixed. Place in small crock or serving bowl; serve warm with toasted bread. Refrigerated leftovers will last a few days.

Fresh Baja Guacamole

PER SERVING: Calories: 59 | Protein: 2g | Carbohydrates: 11g | Fat: 13g | Saturated Fat: 2g | Cholesterol: 0mg
Sodium: 9mg | Fiber: 6g | PCF Ratio: 5-25-70 | Exchange Approx.: ½ Fruit, ½ Vegetable, 3 Fats

INGREDIENTS | SERVES 4

2 ripe avocados

½ red onion, minced (about ½ cup)

2 tablespoons finely chopped cilantro leaves

Juice of 1 lime

Salt and freshly ground black pepper, to taste

1 serrano chili, minced

½ tomato, chopped

1. Cut avocados in half. Remove the seeds. Scoop avocado away from the peel and place in a mixing bowl.

2. Use a fork to mash avocado. Add the chopped onion, cilantro, lime juice, salt, and pepper. Mix ingredients together.

3. Add the minced serrano chili to the guacamole to your desired degree of hotness.

4. Add chopped tomatoes just before serving.

Working with Hot Chilies

Put on rubber gloves when handling hot chili peppers. They can sting, burn, and irritate the skin. Avoid touching your eyes during or after working with chilies. Be sure to wash your hands with soap and warm water right after.

Homemade Hummus

PER SERVING: Calories: 158 | Protein: 4g | Carbohydrates: 13g | Fat: 10g | Saturated Fat: 1g | Cholesterol: 0mg
Sodium: 9mg | Fiber: 4g | PCF Ratio: 10-33-57 | Exchange Approx.: ½ Very-Lean Meat, 3 Fats

INGREDIENTS | MAKES 1½ CUPS, SERVES 12

1 (15-ounce) can chickpeas, drained

2 cloves garlic, chopped, or more to taste

½ small white onion, chopped

1 teaspoon Tabasco or other hot sauce

½ cup tightly packed fresh flat-leaf parsley or cilantro

Salt and black pepper, to taste

½ cup olive oil

Blend all the ingredients in a food processor or blender. Do not purée—you want a coarse consistency. Serve with bagel chips or warm pita bread.

Cucumber Slices with Smoked Salmon Cream

PER SERVING (1 TABLESPOON CREAM): Calories: 81 | Protein: 3g | Carbohydrates: 2g | Fat: 6g | Saturated Fat: 3g |
Cholesterol: 21mg | Sodium: 150mg | Fiber: .2g | PCF Ratio: 17-8-75 | Exchange Approx.: 1 Fat

INGREDIENTS | SERVES 8

2–3 cucumbers

1 ounce smoked salmon

8 ounces Neufchâtel cheese, room temperature

½ tablespoon lemon juice

½ teaspoon freshly ground pepper

Dried dill, to taste (optional)

1. Cut cucumbers into ¼" slices. Place on paper towels to drain while you prepare salmon cream.

2. Combine smoked salmon, Neufchâtel, lemon juice, and pepper in food processor; blend until smooth.

3. Fit a pastry bag with tip; spoon salmon cream into the bag. Pipe 1 teaspoon of salmon cream atop each cucumber slice. Garnish with dried dill, if desired.

Polenta Cubes with Salsa

PER SERVING: Calories: 85 | Protein: 2g | Carbohydrates: 6g | Fat: 6g | Saturated Fat: 1g | Cholesterol: 2mg
Sodium: 157mg | Fiber: 1g | PCF Ratio: 7-26-67 | Exchange Approx.: 1 Fat

INGREDIENTS | SERVES 20; SERVING SIZE: 4 CUBES

6 tomatillos, chopped, husks discarded

4 cloves garlic, minced

2 jalapeño peppers, cored and chopped, seeds included

½ cup sour cream

½ cup fresh cilantro, chopped

1½ teaspoons salt, divided

3 cups boiling water

1 cup yellow cornmeal

½ cup Parmesan cheese

½ cup finely minced chives

Nonstick cooking spray, as needed

½ cup canola oil

1. Place tomatillos, garlic, peppers, sour cream, cilantro, and ½ teaspoon salt in a blender and pulse until coarsely chopped. Rest in refrigerator for 2 hours.

2. Add 1 teaspoon salt to boiling water. Stir the cornmeal in a fine stream into boiling salted water. Cook, stirring for about 20 minutes or until the polenta comes away from the sides of the pan. Add Parmesan cheese and chives. Prepare a 9" × 9" glass baking pan with nonstick cooking spray and spread the polenta in the pan.

3. Chill the polenta. When polenta is firm, turn it out onto waxed paper and cut into 1" cubes.

4. Fry the cubes in canola oil at high heat, turning as the sides brown. Drain on paper towels and serve with salsa.

Deviled Eggs with Capers

PER SERVING: Calories: 54 | Protein: 3g | Carbohydrates: 0g | Fat: 3g | Saturated Fat: 1g | Cholesterol: 124mg
Sodium: 363mg | Fiber: 0g | PCF Ratio: 29-17-54 | Exchange Approx.: ½ Lean Meat, 1 Fat

INGREDIENTS | MAKES 12 HALF EGGS

6 hard-boiled eggs, shelled and cut in half lengthwise

½ cup low-fat mayonnaise

1 teaspoon Tabasco sauce

1 teaspoon celery salt

1 teaspoon onion powder

1 teaspoon garlic powder

1 chili pepper, finely minced, or to taste

2 tablespoons extra small capers

Garnish of paprika or chopped chives

1. Scoop out egg yolks and place in food processor along with mayonnaise, Tabasco, celery salt, onion powder, garlic powder, chili pepper, and capers. Blend until smooth and spoon into the hollows in the egg whites.

2. Add the garnish of paprika or chives. Cover with aluminum foil tented above the egg-yolk mixture and chill for at least 3 hours before serving.

Brine-Packed Capers

Capers are actually berries that have been pickled. You can get them packed in salt, but they are better when packed in brine. You can get larger ones or very, very small ones—the tiny ones are tastier.

Marinated Baby Artichoke Hearts

PER SERVING: Calories: 188 | Protein: 4g | Carbohydrates: 15g | Fat: 14g | Saturated Fat: 2g | Cholesterol: 0mg
Sodium: 91mg | Fiber: 7g | PCF Ratio: 9-29-62 | Exchange Approx.: 2½ Vegetables, 3 Fats

INGREDIENTS | SERVES 4

2 (9-ounce or 10-ounce) boxes frozen artichoke hearts

½ cup white wine vinegar

¼ cup olive oil

1 teaspoon Dijon mustard

½ teaspoon ground coriander

Salt and freshly ground black pepper, to taste

Easy Artichoke Hearts

Here's where frozen artichoke hearts work perfectly! They save you the time and energy of cutting out the choke and removing the leaves of fresh artichokes, and they taste delicious when marinated.

1. Thaw and cook the artichokes according to package directions. Drain and set aside.

2. Whisk the rest of the ingredients together in a bowl large enough to hold the artichokes. Add the warm artichokes and cover with the dressing. Cover and marinate for 2–4 hours. Serve as antipasto.

Baked Coconut Shrimp

PER SERVING: Calories: 173 | Protein: 20g | Carbohydrates: 4g | Fat: 9g | Saturated Fat: 3g | Cholesterol: 129mg
Sodium: 144mg | Fiber: 0g | PCF Ratio: 55-20-25 | Exchange Approx.: 2½ Lean Meats, ½ Fat

INGREDIENTS | SERVES 8

Nonstick cooking spray, as needed

⅓ cup almond flour

½ teaspoon ground red pepper

Salt, to taste

Juice of ½ lime

1 tablespoon agave nectar

⅓ cup egg whites

¾ cup shredded, unsweetened coconut

1½ pounds extra-large shrimp, shelled and cleaned with tails remaining

Agave Nectar

Agave nectar is used to sweeten the shrimp, keeping this appetizer low on the glycemic index. This substitute for sugar or honey is derived from the blue agave plant, which thrives in volcanic soils in southern Mexico.

1. Preheat oven to 425°F and lightly spray a baking sheet with nonstick cooking spray.

2. In a small bowl, combine almond flour, pepper, and salt.

3. In a separate bowl, mix lime juice and agave nectar and stir. Continuously stirring, add egg whites to lime-agave mixture.

4. Place coconut in a thin layer on a flat dish. Dip each shrimp first into the almond-flour mixture, then into the egg-white mixture, and then roll in coconut.

5. Place on baking sheet. Bake 10–15 minutes or until coconut appears lightly toasted.

Ceviche (Fresh Seafood in Citrus)

PER SERVING: Calories: 181 | Protein: 21g | Carbohydrates: 5g | Fat: 8g | Saturated Fat: 1g | Cholesterol: 105mg
Sodium: 238mg | Fiber: 0g | PCF Ratio: 48-10-42 | Exchange Approx.: 3 Very-Lean Meats, 1 Fat

INGREDIENTS | SERVES 4

½ pound raw tiny bay scallops

½ pound fresh raw shrimp, peeled and deveined

2 scallions, minced

1 green chili, seeded and minced

Juice of 1 fresh lime

2 tablespoons orange juice

1 tablespoon chili sauce

2 tablespoons fresh parsley or cilantro, chopped

Salt and pepper, to taste

2 tablespoons olive oil

1. Rinse scallops and pat dry in a paper towel.

2. Mix all ingredients except the olive oil in a nonreactive bowl. Cover and refrigerate for 8 hours or overnight.

3. Just before serving, sprinkle with olive oil. Serve in large cocktail glasses.

About Ceviche

Ceviche is made by using the acid from citrus juice instead of heat to cook fresh seafood. It has been enjoyed in South America for centuries. Ceviche is made differently all over the world, but it typically always contains fish and shellfish. Other common ingredients include thinly sliced onion, hot pepper, orange juice, lemon, garlic, corn, lettuce, and sweet potato.

Stuffed Mushrooms (Crabmeat or Shrimp)

PER SERVING: Calories: 90 | Protein: 8g | Carbohydrates: 11g | Fat: 2g | Saturated Fat: 0mg | Cholesterol: 58mg
Sodium: 382mg | Fiber: 1g | PCF Ratio: 16-50-34 | Exchange Approx.: ½ Starch, 1 Lean Meat

INGREDIENTS | SERVES 12

¼ pound cooked shrimp or crabmeat (canned or fresh)

1 cup soft white bread crumbs

½ cup light mayonnaise

Juice of ½ lemon

1 teaspoon fresh dill, or 1 teaspoon dried

Salt and pepper, to taste

12 white mushrooms, 1"–1½" across, stems removed

1. In a large bowl, mix together all the ingredients except the mushrooms.

2. Stuff the resulting mixture into the mushrooms. At this point, you can refrigerate or freeze the mushrooms, or you can continue the recipe.

3. Preheat oven to 400°F. Place stuffed mushrooms on a baking sheet and bake for 15–20 minutes. Serve hot.

Baked Stuffed Clams

PER SERVING: Calories: 150 | Protein: 7g | Carbohydrates: 8g | Fat: 11g | Saturated Fat: 5g | Cholesterol: 78mg
Sodium: 216mg | Fiber: 1g | PCF Ratio: 62-17-21 | Exchange Approx.: 1 Lean Meat, 2 Fats

INGREDIENTS | SERVES 4; (2 HALF CLAMS PER PERSON)

4 fresh cherrystone clams, well-scrubbed and opened, meat removed

1 tablespoon lemon juice

2 slices whole-grain wheat bread, toasted and crumbled

1 egg

1 tablespoon mayonnaise

½ teaspoon dried dill

2 tablespoons butter, melted

Salt and pepper, to taste

2 tablespoons Parmesan cheese

1. Preheat the oven to 350°F. Place the clam shells on a baking sheet.

2. Place the clam meat and the rest of the ingredients in a food processor or blender and pulse until mixed but not puréed.

3. Spoon the stuffing into the clam shells and bake for about 20 minutes. Serve immediately.

CHAPTER 4

Soups

Cold Roasted Red Pepper Soup

PER SERVING, WITHOUT SALT: Calories: 73 | **Protein:** 5g | **Carbohydrates:** 9g | **Fat:** 4g | **Saturated Fat:** 1g | **Cholesterol:** 3mg **Sodium:** 404mg | **Fiber:** 3g | **PCF Ratio:** 21-39-40 | **Exchange Approx.:** ½ Fat, ½ Starch

INGREDIENTS | SERVES 4

1 teaspoon olive oil

½ cup chopped onion

3 roasted red bell peppers, seeded and chopped (see recipe for Roasted Red Pepper and Plum Sauce in Chapter 12)

3¼ cups low-fat, reduced-sodium chicken broth

½ cup plain, nonfat yogurt

½ teaspoon sea salt (optional)

4 sprigs fresh basil (optional)

1. Heat a saucepan over medium-high heat. Add olive oil and sauté onion until transparent.

2. Add peppers and broth. Bring to a boil; reduce heat and simmer for 15 minutes. Remove from heat; purée in blender or food processor until smooth.

3. Allow to cool. Stir in yogurt and salt, if using; chill well for at least 4 hours in refrigerator. Garnish the soup with fresh basil sprigs, if desired.

Lentil-Vegetable Soup

PER SERVING, WITH WATER: Calories: 273 | **Protein:** 16g | **Carbohydrates:** 53g | **Fat:** 1g | **Saturated Fat:** 0g | **Cholesterol:** 0mg **Sodium:** 34mg | **Fiber:** 19g | **PCF Ratio:** 23-74-3 | **Exchange Approx.:** 1 Very-Lean Meat, 3 Starches, 1 Vegetable

INGREDIENTS | SERVES 4

5 cups water or your choice of broth

1 medium sweet potato, peeled and chopped

1 cup uncooked lentils

2 medium onions, chopped

¼ cup barley

2 tablespoons dried parsley

2 carrots, sliced

1 stalk celery, chopped

2 teaspoons ground cumin

Combine all the ingredients in soup pot. Simmer covered until lentils are soft, about 1 hour.

Lentil Soup with Herbs and Lemon

PER SERVING: Calories: 214 | Protein: 15g | Carbohydrates: 34g | Fat: 3g | Saturated Fat: 1g | Cholesterol: 0mg
Sodium: 353mg | Fiber: 16g | PCF Ratio: 27-61-12 | Exchange Approx.: 1 Lean Meat, 2 Starches, 1 Vegetable

INGREDIENTS | SERVES 4

1 cup lentils, soaked overnight in 1 cup water

6 cups low-fat, reduced-sodium chicken broth

1 carrot, sliced

1 stalk celery, sliced

1 yellow onion, thinly sliced

2 teaspoons olive oil

1 tablespoon dried tarragon

½ teaspoon dried oregano

Sea salt and black pepper, to taste (optional)

1 tablespoon lemon juice

4 thin slices lemon

1. Drain and rinse lentils. Add lentils and broth to soup pot over medium heat; bring to a boil. Reduce heat and simmer until lentils are tender, approximately 15 minutes. (If you did not presoak the lentils, increase cooking time by about 15 more minutes.)

2. While lentils are cooking, sauté carrot, celery, and onion in oil in a nonstick pan for 8 minutes, or until onion is golden brown. Remove from heat and set aside.

3. When lentils are tender, add vegetables, tarragon, oregano, and salt and pepper, if using, and cook for 2 minutes. Stir in lemon juice. Ladle into 4 serving bowls; garnish with lemon slices.

Fresh Tomato Basil Soup

PER SERVING: Calories: 87 | Protein: 3g | Carbohydrates: 12g | Fat: 4g | Saturated Fat: 2g | Cholesterol: 10mg
Sodium: 449mg | Fiber: 3g | PCF Ratio: 13-50-37 | Exchange Approx.: 2 Vegetables, 1 Fat

INGREDIENTS | SERVES 6

1 tablespoon butter

¼ cup chopped onion

4 cups (2 pounds) crushed tomatoes

¼ cup loosely chopped fresh basil leaves

1 cup low-sodium chicken broth

2 ounces reduced-fat cream cheese or Neufchâtel

Freshly ground pepper, to taste

1. Melt butter in soup pot. Add onion and sauté until soft. Add crushed tomatoes, basil, and chicken broth.

2. Bring mixture to a boil. Reduce heat; cook for another 15 minutes. Remove from heat; stir in cream cheese until melted.

3. Transfer to food processor or blender; purée until smooth. Depending on size of processor or blender, you may need to purée a portion at a time. Transfer to serving bowls and sprinkle with pepper, if using.

Tomato-Vegetable Soup

**PER SERVING: Calories: 158 | Protein: 5g | Carbohydrates: 31g | Fat: 3g | Saturated Fat: 1g | Cholesterol: 0mg
Sodium: 349mg | Fiber: 5g | PCF Ratio: 12-72-16 | Exchange Approx.: 1½ Starches, 1 Vegetable**

INGREDIENTS | SERVES 6

1 tablespoon olive oil

2 teaspoons minced garlic

⅔ teaspoon ground cumin

2 carrots, chopped

2 stalks celery, diced

1 medium onion, chopped

⅔ cup unsalted tomato paste

½ teaspoon red pepper flakes

2 cups canned, unsalted, peeled tomatoes, with juice

⅔ teaspoon chopped fresh oregano

3 cups low-fat, reduced-sodium chicken broth

3 cups fat-free beef broth

2 cups diced potatoes

2 cups shredded cabbage

½ cup green beans

½ cup fresh or frozen corn kernels

½ teaspoon freshly ground black pepper

¼ cup lime juice or balsamic vinegar

1. Heat olive oil in large stockpot. Add the garlic, cumin, carrot, and celery and sauté for 1 minute. Add onion and cook until onion is transparent.

2. Stir in tomato paste and sauté until it begins to brown.

3. Add remaining ingredients except for lime juice or balsamic vinegar. Bring to a boil; reduce heat and simmer for 20–30 minutes, adding additional broth or water if needed. Just before serving, add lime juice or balsamic vinegar.

Easy Measures

Consider freezing broth in an ice cube tray. Most ice cube tray sections hold ⅛ cup (2 tablespoons) of liquid. Once the broth is frozen, you can transfer the cubes to a freezer bag or container. This makes it easy to measure out the amount you need for recipes.

Minestrone Soup Genoese-Style

PER SERVING: Calories: 201 | Protein: 9g | Carbohydrates: 29g | Fat: 6g | Saturated Fat: 2g | Cholesterol: 5mg
Sodium: 271mg | Fiber: 6g | PCF Ratio: 17-56-27 | Exchange Approx.: 1½ Starches, 1 Vegetable, 1 Fat

INGREDIENTS | SERVES 6

4 cloves garlic, minced

2 tablespoons chopped fresh basil

¼ teaspoon salt

2 tablespoons olive oil

1 ounce Romano cheese

2 cups shredded cabbage

1 cup diced zucchini

1 cup chopped (1" pieces) green beans

1 cup peeled and chopped potatoes

2 cups cooked navy beans

½ cup chopped celery

¼ cup fresh or frozen peas

1 tablespoon tomato paste

3 cups water

Salt and pepper, to taste

1. In a small bowl, combine garlic, basil, and salt. Add olive oil and Romano cheese; mix well into a paste and set aside. (Using a mortar and pestle works very well.)

2. In a 4- or 6-quart soup pot, combine cabbage, zucchini, green beans, potatoes, cooked navy beans, celery, peas, tomato paste, and water.

3. Bring to a boil; reduce heat and simmer for 45–60 minutes, or until tender.

4. Mix garlic paste into soup; simmer an additional 5 minutes. Serve with salt and pepper to taste.

Tip

Make extra garlic paste (using first 5 ingredients and step 1) and keep refrigerated. You'll have instant garlic-cheese flavor on hand for soups, sauces, garlic bread, and pasta dishes. Garlic paste keeps in the refrigerator for up to 2 weeks.

Broccoli and Whole-Grain Pasta Soup

PER SERVING: Calories: 86 | Protein: 6g | Carbohydrates: 10g | Fat: 3g | Saturated Fat: 1g | Cholesterol: 9mg
Sodium: 185mg | Fiber: 2g | PCF Ratio: 25-43-32 | Exchange Approx.: ½ Starch, 1 Vegetable, 1 Fat

INGREDIENTS | SERVES 6

1–3 slices bacon, cut into 1" pieces

1 tablespoon chopped onion

2 cloves garlic, minced

1 tablespoon tomato paste

3 cups water

1 cup peeled and cubed eggplant

¾ teaspoon salt

¼ teaspoon pepper

½ teaspoon oregano

8 ounces broccoli florets

1 cup whole-grain pasta shells, cooked al dente

1 ounce Romano cheese, grated

1. Place bacon, onion, and garlic in a 4-quart soup pot and brown over medium heat.

2. Add tomato paste, water, eggplant, salt, pepper, and oregano. Bring to a boil; reduce heat and simmer for 20 minutes, or until eggplant is soft-cooked.

3. Add broccoli florets; simmer for 5 minutes or until broccoli is tender but still slightly crisp. Add cooked pasta.

4. Serve soup immediately with a sprinkling of grated cheese.

Broccoli Soup with Cheese

PER SERVING: Calories: 311 | Protein: 11g | Carbohydrates: 25g | Fat: 17g | Saturated Fat: 4g | Cholesterol: 7mg
Sodium: 722mg | Fiber: 5g | PCF Ratio: 15-34-51 | Exchange Approx.: 1 Starch, 2 Vegetables, 1 Lean Meat, 3½ Fats

INGREDIENTS | SERVES 4

¼ cup olive oil

1 medium sweet onion, chopped

2 cloves garlic, chopped

1 large baking potato, peeled and chopped

1 large bunch broccoli, coarsely chopped

½ cup dry white wine

3 cups chicken broth

Salt and pepper, to taste

Pinch ground nutmeg

4 heaping tablespoons grated extra sharp Cheddar cheese (for garnish)

1. Heat the olive oil in a large soup pot. Sauté the onion, garlic, and potato over medium heat until softened slightly. Add the broccoli, wine, broth, and seasonings.

2. Cover and simmer over low heat for 45 minutes.

3. Cool slightly. Purée in a blender. Reheat and place in bowls.

4. Spoon the cheese over the hot soup to serve.

Save the Stalks

When you prepare broccoli, save the stems. They can be grated and mixed with carrots in a slaw, cut into coins and served hot, or cooked and puréed as a side. Broccoli marries well with potatoes and carrots and is good served raw with a dipping sauce.

White Bean and Escarole Soup

PER SERVING: Calories: 163 | Protein: 11g | Carbohydrates: 27g | Fat: 2g | Saturated Fat: 0g | Cholesterol: 7mg
Sodium: 349mg | Fiber: 9g | PCF Ratio: 26-64-10 | Exchange Approx.: 1½ Starches, ½ Vegetable, 1½ Very-Lean Meats, 2 Fats

INGREDIENTS | SERVES 6

1 cup dried navy beans

3 cups water

1 cup chopped onion

½ cup peeled and chopped potato

1 clove garlic, minced

3 ounces Canadian bacon, cut in ½"
cubes

2½ cups water

½ teaspoon salt

¼ teaspoon pepper

1 teaspoon vegetable oil

8 ounces escarole, coarsely chopped

1. Place dry beans and 3 cups of water in medium saucepan. Bring to a boil; remove from heat. Allow beans to soak several hours or overnight.

2. Drain beans; place in a pressure cooker with onion, potatoes, garlic, Canadian bacon, 2½ cups water, salt, pepper, and vegetable oil. Close cover securely, place pressure regulator on vent pipe, and cook for 30 minutes with pressure regulator rocking slowly. (If using an electric pressure cooker, follow manufacturer instructions.) Let pressure drop on its own.

3. Add chopped escarole; simmer for 5–10 minutes, until escarole is wilted and tender.

Slow-Cooker Method

This soup can also be prepared using a slow cooker. Soak beans as described in step 1; drain. Add beans, onion, potatoes, garlic, Canadian bacon, and 2½ cups water to slow cooker. Cook for 8–10 hours. At end of cooking, add escarole; simmer for 5–10 minutes, until escarole is wilted and tender. Add salt and pepper to taste.

Winter Squash and Red Pepper Soup

PER SERVING: Calories: 137 | Protein: 3g | Carbohydrates: 24g | Fat: 3g | Saturated Fat: 1g | Cholesterol: 0mg
Sodium: 445mg | Fiber: 6g | PCF Ratio: 10-70-20 | Exchange Approx.: 1 Starch, 1 Vegetable, ½ Fat

INGREDIENTS | SERVES 6

3½ cups winter squash

1 tablespoon olive oil

1 cup chopped onions

1 tablespoon chopped garlic

4 ounces roasted red pepper

3 cups low-sodium chicken broth

½ cup dry white wine

2 teaspoons sugar

1 teaspoon cinnamon

½ teaspoon ground ginger

1 tablespoon reduced-fat sour cream (optional)

1. Preheat oven to 400°F and oil a 9" × 13" glass baking dish.

2. Wash and cut squash in half and remove seeds. Place halves face down on prepared baking dish and bake for 50–60 minutes, or until squash is tender. When cool enough to handle, scoop squash out of shells and set aside.

3. In large nonstick frying pan, heat olive oil. Add onions and garlic; sauté until tender and continue to cook until the onions are soft and have turned brown (caramelized).

4. Add roasted pepper and chicken broth; simmer for another 15 minutes.

5. Add cooked winter squash, white wine, sugar, cinnamon, and ginger; simmer for another 5 minutes.

6. Transfer to food processor or blender; purée until smooth. Depending on size of processor or blender, you may need to purée a portion at a time. If desired, stir in reduced-fat sour cream and serve.

Vegetable and Bean Chili

**PER SERVING: Calories: 205 | Protein: 12g | Carbohydrates: 35g | Fat: 3g | Saturated Fat: 1g | Cholesterol: 0mg
Sodium: 156mg | Fiber: 13g | PCF Ratio: 22-65-13 | Exchange Approx.: 1 Lean Meat, 2 Starches, 1 Vegetable**

INGREDIENTS | SERVES 8

4 teaspoons olive oil

2 cups chopped onions

½ cup chopped green bell pepper

3 cloves garlic, chopped

1 small jalapeño pepper, finely chopped (include the seeds if you like the chili extra hot)

1 tablespoon chili powder

1 teaspoon ground cumin

1 (28-ounce) can unsalted, chopped tomatoes, undrained

2 zucchinis, peeled and chopped

2 (15-ounce) cans unsalted kidney beans, drained and rinsed

1 tablespoon chopped semisweet chocolate

3 tablespoons chopped fresh cilantro

1. Heat heavy pot over medium-high heat. Add olive oil, onions, bell pepper, garlic, and jalapeño; sauté until vegetables are softened, about 5 minutes. Add chili powder and cumin; sauté for 1 minute, stirring frequently to mix well.

2. Add tomatoes with juice and zucchini; bring to a boil. Lower heat and simmer, partially covered, for 15 minutes, stirring occasionally.

3. Stir in beans and chocolate; simmer, stirring occasionally, for additional 5 minutes, or until beans are heated through and chocolate is melted. Stir in cilantro and serve.

Black Bean Soup with Chilies

PER SERVING: Calories: 308 | Protein: 10g | Carbohydrates: 11g | Fat: 26g | Saturated Fat: 7g | Cholesterol: 26mg
Sodium: 698mg | Fiber: 2g | PCF Ratio: 13-14-73 | Exchange Approx.: 1½ Vegetable, 1½ Meat, 2 Fats

INGREDIENTS | SERVES 4

4 strips bacon

4 cloves garlic, chopped

1 medium sweet onion, chopped

2 hot chilies, seeded and minced

2 cans (or 1 pound) black beans

8 ounces beef broth

½ cup tomato juice

2 ounces dark rum

Salt and black pepper, to taste

Garnish of fresh lime wedges, sour cream, chopped cilantro, and pepper jack cheese

1. In a large pot, fry the bacon until crisp. Remove bacon to a paper towel–lined plate and leave the bacon fat in the pot. Crumble bacon and reserve for garnish.

2. Add garlic, onion, and chilies to the pot. Sauté until softened, about 5 minutes.

3. Stir in the black beans, beef broth, tomato juice, rum, salt, and pepper. Cover and simmer for 1 hour.

4. You may either purée the soup or serve it as is. Garnish with any or all of the suggestions.

Heart-Healthy Substitution

Beans make for a very nutritious meal. You have a few options to make this recipe more heart-healthy. Instead of bacon, flavor the soup with a ham bone (which you must remove before puréeing or serving) or use vegetarian "bacon."

Egg Drop Soup with Lemon

PER SERVING: Calories: 230 | Protein: 13g | Carbohydrates: 7g | Fat: 16g | Saturated Fat: 4g | Cholesterol: 246mg
Sodium: 666mg | Fiber: 1g | PCF Ratio: 23-12-65 | Exchange Approx.: 2 Meats, 1½ Fat

INGREDIENTS | SERVES 2

1 tablespoon peanut oil

1 clove garlic, minced

2 cups low-sodium chicken broth

Juice of ½ lemon

1 tablespoon hoisin sauce

1 teaspoon soy sauce

1 teaspoon Asian fish sauce

½ teaspoon chili oil, or to taste

1" fresh gingerroot, peeled and minced

2 eggs

1. Heat the peanut oil in a large saucepan. Sauté the garlic over medium heat until softened, about 5 minutes.

2. Add chicken broth, lemon juice, hoisin sauce, soy sauce, fish sauce, chili oil, and gingerroot. Stir and cover. Cook over low heat for 20 minutes.

3. Just before serving, whisk the eggs in a bowl with a fork. Add to the boiling soup and continue to whisk until the eggs form thin strands.

Flavorful Asian Sauces

This is a lovely, spicy version of the Chinese staple, made with a variety of Asian sauces. Asian fish sauce is a liquid made from salted fish that is used in place of salt in many Asian recipes. Hoisin sauce is made from crushed soybeans and garlic, has a sweet and spicy flavor, and is a rich brown color.

Pumpkin Soup

PER SERVING: Calories: 130 (with heavy cream, add 50 calories) | Protein: 5g | Carbohydrates: 26g | Fat: 1g | Saturated Fat: 0g Cholesterol: 0mg | Sodium: 390mg | Fiber: 4g | PCF Ratio: 14-77-9 | Exchange Approx.: ½ Starch, 1 Fruit, 1 Vegetable

INGREDIENTS | SERVES 4

1 cup finely chopped Vidalia or other sweet onion

½" fresh gingerroot, peeled and minced

2 cups orange juice

2 cups chicken broth

1 (13-ounce) can pumpkin (unflavored)

1 teaspoon brown sugar

½ teaspoon ground cinnamon

¼ teaspoon ground nutmeg

¼ teaspoon ground cloves

½ cup heavy cream (optional)

Add all the ingredients except the heavy cream to a soup pot, one by one, whisking after each addition. Cover and simmer for 10 minutes. If you decide to use the cream, add at the last minute.

Beef, Barley, and Vegetable Soup

PER SERVING: Calories: 368 | Protein: 38g | Carbohydrates: 40g | Fat: 6g | Saturated Fat: 2g | Cholesterol: 51mg Sodium: 670mg | Fiber: 10g | PCF Ratio: 41-44-15 | Exchange Approx.: 2 Starches, 3 Lean Meats, 1 Vegetable, 1 Fat

INGREDIENTS | SERVES 8

1 tablespoon olive oil

1 pound top round beef, cubed

8 cups low-sodium beef broth

1 (8-ounce) can tomato sauce

1½ cups chopped carrots

1½ cups peas

1½ cups trimmed green beans, cut into 1" pieces

1½ cups barley

4 cloves garlic, minced

1 tablespoon onion powder

Salt and pepper, to taste

1. Heat olive oil in a large pot over medium heat. Add beef cubes to pot and brown on all sides.

2. Add broth and tomato sauce and simmer for 1 hour.

3. Add carrots, peas, green beans, barley, garlic, and onion powder to the pot. Stir to combine.

4. Simmer for 45 minutes, until barley is cooked. Add salt and pepper as desired.

Creamy Cauliflower Soup

PER SERVING: Calories: 314 | Protein: 22g | Carbohydrates: 9g | Fat: 21g | Saturated Fat: 9g | Cholesterol: 40mg
Sodium: 321mg | Fiber: 1g | PCF Ratio: 28-12-60 | Exchange Approx.: 2 Vegetables, 1 Meat, 4 Fats

INGREDIENTS | SERVES 4

2 tablespoons olive oil
½ cup finely chopped onion
½ cup chopped celery
1 cup cauliflower florets
4 cups low-sodium chicken stock
1 cup shredded Cheddar cheese
Salt and pepper, to taste
1 cup low-fat milk

1. Heat oil in a large pot, add onion and celery, and sauté until translucent. Add cauliflower and chicken stock and bring to a boil. Reduce heat, cover, and simmer for 25 minutes, stirring occasionally.

2. Purée soup in food processor or blender until smooth.

3. Return soup to pot over medium-low heat. Add cheese, salt, and pepper, continue to cook, and stir until cheese is melted and well integrated.

4. Add milk and stir into the soup. Add more chicken stock if the consistency of the soup is too thick.

Chicken Corn Chowder

PER SERVING: Calories: 193 | Protein: 17g | Carbohydrates: 21g | Fat: 5g | Saturated Fat: 3g | Cholesterol: 39mg
Sodium: 155mg | Fiber: 2g | PCF Ratio: 22-36-42 | Exchange Approx.: 1½ Very-Lean Meats, ½ Starch,
1 Vegetable, ½ Skim Milk, ½ High-Fat Meat

INGREDIENTS | SERVES 10

1 pound boneless, skinless chicken breast, cut into chunks

1 medium onion, chopped

1 red bell pepper, diced

1 large potato, peeled and diced

2 (16-ounce) cans low-fat, reduced-sodium chicken broth

1 (8¼-ounce) can unsalted, cream-style corn

½ cup all-purpose flour

2 cups skim milk

4 ounces Cheddar cheese, diced

½ teaspoon sea salt

Freshly ground pepper, to taste

½ cup processed bacon bits

Tip

To trim down the fat in this recipe, use a reduced-fat cheese, such as Cabot 50% Reduced Fat Cheddar.

1. Spray large soup pot with nonstick cooking spray; heat on medium setting until hot. Add chicken, onion, and bell pepper and sauté over medium heat until chicken is browned and vegetables are tender.

2. Stir in potatoes and broth; bring to a boil. Reduce heat to low and simmer, covered, for 20 minutes. Stir in corn.

3. In a medium bowl, blend flour and milk. Gradually stir milk mixture into pot. Increase heat to medium; cook until mixture comes to a boil, then reduce heat and simmer until soup is thickened, stirring constantly.

4. Add cheese; stir until melted and blended in. Add salt and pepper to taste and sprinkle with bacon bits before serving.

Nutty Greek Snapper Soup

PER SERVING: Calories: 309 | Protein: 39g | Carbohydrates: 25g | Fat: 6g | Saturated Fat: 1g | Cholesterol: 46mg
Sodium: 240mg | Fiber: 2g | PCF Ratio: 50-33-17 | Exchange Approx.: 4 Lean Meats, 1 Skim Milk, 1 Vegetable

INGREDIENTS | SERVES 4

1 pound red snapper fillets

2 large cucumbers

4 green onions, chopped

4 cups plain, nonfat yogurt

1 cup packed fresh parsley, basil, cilantro, arugula, and chives, mixed

3 tablespoons lime juice

Salt and pepper, to taste (optional)

¼ cup chopped walnuts

Herb sprigs for garnish (optional)

Tip

You can make this soup using leftover fish or substitute halibut, cod, or sea bass for the snapper.

1. Rinse red snapper fillets and pat dry with paper towels. Broil fillets until opaque through the thickest part, about 4 minutes on each side depending on the thickness of fillets. Let cool. (Alternatives would be to steam or poach the fillets.)

2. Peel and halve cucumbers and scoop out and discard seeds; cut into 1" pieces. Put half of cucumber with green onions in bowl of food processor; pulse to coarsely chop. Transfer to a large bowl.

3. Add remaining cucumber, yogurt, and herb leaves to food processor; process until smooth and frothy. (Alternatively, you can grate cucumbers, finely mince green onion and herbs, and stir together with yogurt in large bowl.) Stir in lime juice and season with salt and pepper to taste, if using. Cover and refrigerate for at least 1 hour, or up to 8 hours; the longer the soup cools, the more the flavors will mellow.

4. While soup cools, break cooled red snapper fillet into large chunks, discarding skin and any bones. Ladle chilled soup into shallow bowls and add red snapper chunks. Sprinkle chopped walnuts over soup, garnish with herb sprigs, and serve.

Rich and Creamy Sausage-Potato Soup

PER SERVING: Calories: 326 | Protein: 17g | Carbohydrates: 53g | Fat: 6g | Saturated Fat: 2g | Cholesterol: 19mg | Sodium: 259mg | Fiber: 3g | PCF Ratio: 20-64-16 | Exchange Approx.: 1 Fat, ½ Medium-Fat Meat, 1 Starch, 1½ Skim Milks, 1 Vegetable

INGREDIENTS | SERVES 2

1 teaspoon olive oil

½ teaspoon butter

½ cup chopped onion, steamed

1 clove dry-roasted garlic (see recipe for Garlic and Feta Cheese Dip in Chapter 3)

1 ounce crumbled, cooked Mock Chorizo (see recipe in Chapter 5)

¼ teaspoon celery seed

2 Yukon gold potatoes, peeled and diced into 1" pieces

½ cup fat-free chicken broth

1½ cups Mock Cream (see recipe in Chapter 12)

1 teaspoon white wine vinegar

1 teaspoon vanilla extract

Optional seasonings to taste:

    Fresh parsley

    Sea salt and freshly ground black pepper

1. In a large saucepan, heat olive oil and butter over medium heat. Add onion, roasted garlic, Mock Chorizo, celery seed, and potatoes and sauté until heated.

2. Add chicken broth and bring to a boil. Cover saucepan, reduce heat, and maintain simmer for 10 minutes, or until potatoes are tender. Add Mock Cream and heat.

3. Remove saucepan from burner and stir in vinegar and vanilla. Serve with parsley, salt, and pepper to taste, if using.

Skim the Fat

You can remove fat from soups and stews by dropping ice cubes into the pot. The fat will cling to the cubes as you stir. Be sure to take out the cubes before they melt. Fat also clings to lettuce leaves; simply sweep them over the top of the soup. Discard ice cubes or leaves when done.

Salmon Chowder

PER SERVING: Calories: 364 | Protein: 20g | Carbohydrates: 61g | Fat: 6g | Saturated Fat: 2g | Cholesterol: 28mg | Sodium: 199mg | Fiber: 7g | PCF Ratio: 22-65-14 | Exchange Approx.: ½ Fat, 2 Starches, 2 Lean Meats, 2 Vegetables, ½ Skim Milk

INGREDIENTS | SERVES 4

1 (7.5-ounce) can unsalted salmon

2 teaspoons butter

1 medium onion, chopped

2 stalks celery, chopped

1 sweet green bell pepper, seeded and chopped

1 clove garlic, minced

4 carrots, peeled and diced

4 small potatoes, peeled and diced

1 cup fat-free chicken broth

1 cup water

¾ teaspoon freshly ground black pepper, divided

½ teaspoon dill seed

1 cup diced zucchini

1 cup Mock Cream (see recipe in Chapter 12)

1 (8¼-ounce) can unsalted cream-style corn

½ cup chopped fresh parsley (optional)

1. Drain and flake salmon; discard liquid.

2. In large nonstick saucepan, melt butter over medium heat; sauté onion, celery, green pepper, garlic, and carrots, stirring often, until tender, about 5 minutes.

3. Add potatoes, broth, water, ½ teaspoon pepper, and dill seed; bring to a boil. Reduce heat, cover, and simmer for 20 minutes, or until potatoes are tender.

4. Add zucchini; simmer, covered, for another 5 minutes.

5. Add salmon, Mock Cream, corn, and remaining pepper; cook over low heat just until heated through. Just before serving, add parsley, if desired.

CHAPTER 5
Beef, Pork, and Lamb

Beef Broth: Easy Slow-Cooker Method

PER SERVING: Calories: 58 | Protein: 9g | Carbohydrates: 0g | Fat: 2g | Saturated Fat: 1g | Cholesterol: 27mg
Sodium: 14mg | Fiber: 0g | PCF Ratio: 65-0-35 | Exchange Approx.: 1 Lean Meat

INGREDIENTS | MAKES ABOUT 3 CUPS BROTH; SERVING SIZE: ½ CUP

1 pound lean round steak
1 onion, chopped
2 carrots, peeled and chopped
2 stalks celery with leaves, chopped
1 bay leaf
4 sprigs parsley
6 black peppercorns
¼ cup dry white wine
4½ cups water

Trade Secrets

Some chefs swear that a hearty beef broth requires oven-roasted bones. Place bones on a roasting tray and bake in 425°F oven for 30–60 minutes. Blot fat from bones before adding to rest of broth ingredients. You may need to reduce the amount of water in your slow cooker, which will produce a more concentrated broth.

1. Cut beef into several pieces; add to slow cooker with all other ingredients. Use high setting until mixture reaches a boil, then reduce heat to low. Allow to simmer, covered, overnight, or up to 16 hours.

2. Remove beef and drain on paper towels to absorb any fat. Strain broth, discarding meat and vegetables. (You don't want to eat vegetables cooked directly with the beef because they will have absorbed too much of the residue fat.) Put broth in a covered container and refrigerate for several hours or overnight; this allows time for fat to congeal on top of broth. Remove hardened fat and discard. (When you remove fat from broth, the Exchange Approximation for it will be a Free Exchange.) Broth will keep in refrigerator for a few days. Freeze any you won't use within that time.

Stovetop Grilled Beef Loin

PER SERVING: Calories: 105 | Protein: 15g | Carbohydrates: 1g | Fat: 4g | Saturated Fat: 1g | Cholesterol: 2mg
Sodium: 27mg | Fiber: 0g | PCF Ratio: 58-5-37 | Exchange Approx.: 2½ Lean Meats

INGREDIENTS | MAKES 1 (5-OUNCE) LOIN; SERVING SIZE: 2½ OUNCES

1 lean beef tenderloin fillet, no more than 1" thick

½ teaspoon paprika

1½ teaspoons garlic powder

⅛ teaspoon freshly ground black pepper

¼ teaspoon onion powder

Pinch to ⅛ teaspoon cayenne pepper (according to taste)

⅛ teaspoon dried oregano

⅛ teaspoon dried thyme

½ teaspoon brown sugar

½ teaspoon olive oil

Weights and Measures: Before and After

Exchanges are based on cooking weight of meats; however, in the case of lean meats trimmed of all fat, very little weight is lost during the cooking process. Therefore, amounts given for raw lean meat in recipes equal cooked weights. If you find your cooking method causes more variation in weight, adjust accordingly.

1. Remove loin from refrigerator 30 minutes before preparing it to allow it to come to room temperature. Pat meat dry with paper towels.

2. Mix together all the dry ingredients in a bowl. Rub ¼ teaspoon of olive oil on each side of the fillet. (The olive oil is used in this recipe to help the "rub" adhere to the meat and to aid in the caramelization process.) Divide seasoning mixture; rub into each oiled side.

3. Heat a grill pan on high for 1–2 minutes, until the pan is sizzling hot. Place beef fillet in pan, reduce heat to medium-high, and cook 3 minutes. Use tongs to turn fillet, being careful not to pierce meat. Cook for another 2 minutes for medium or 3 minutes for well-done.

4. Remove from heat and let the meat rest in pan for at least 5 minutes, allowing juices to redistribute throughout meat and complete cooking process, which makes for a juicier fillet.

The Ultimate Grilled Cheeseburger Sandwich

PER SERVING: Calories: 262 | Protein: 17g | Carbohydrates: 15g | Fat: 15g | Saturated Fat: 5g | Cholesterol: 60mg
Sodium: 252mg | Fiber: 1.22g | PCF Ratio: 26-24-50 | Exchange Approx.: 2 Lean Meats, 1 Fat, 1 Starch

INGREDIENTS | SERVES 1

1 tablespoon olive oil

1 teaspoon butter, softened

2 slices of 7-Grain Bread (see recipe in Chapter 13)

1 ounce Cheddar cheese

¼ pound ground round

1 teaspoon Worcestershire sauce, or to taste

Fresh minced garlic, to taste

Balsamic vinegar, to taste

Toppings of your choice, such as stone-ground mustard, mayonnaise, etc.

The Olive Oil Factor

Once you've used an olive oil and butter mixture to butter the bread for a toasted or grilled sandwich, you'll never want to use just plain butter again! Olive oil helps make the bread crunchier and imparts a subtle taste difference to the sandwiches.

1. Preheat indoor grill. In a small bowl, combine olive oil and butter; use ½ to butter 1 side of each slice of bread. Place Cheddar cheese on unbuttered side of 1 slice of bread; top with other slice, buttered-side up.

2. In a large bowl, combine ground round with Worcestershire sauce, garlic, and balsamic vinegar, if using. Shape ground round into large, rectangular patty, a little larger than slice of bread. Grill patty and then cheese sandwich. (If you are using a large indoor grill, position hamburger at lower end, near area where fat drains; grill cheese sandwich at higher end.)

3. Once cheese sandwich is done, separate slices of bread, being careful not to burn yourself on cheese. Top 1 slice with hamburger and add your choice of condiments. Cover with remaining slice of bread.

Southwest Black Bean Burgers

PER SERVING: Calories: 230 | Protein: 20g | Carbohydrates: 10g | Fat: 12g | Saturated Fat: 4g | Cholesterol: 55mg
Sodium: 102mg | Fiber: 4g | PCF Ratio: 36-18-46 | Exchange Approx.: 2½ Lean Meats, ½ Starch, 1 Fat

INGREDIENTS | SERVES 5

1 cup black beans, cooked

¼ cup chopped onion

1 teaspoon chili powder

1 teaspoon ground cumin

1 tablespoon minced fresh parsley

1 tablespoon minced fresh cilantro

½ teaspoon salt (optional)

¾ pound lean ground beef

Swapping Fresh Herbs for Dried

If you do not have fresh herbs such as parsley or cilantro available, 1 teaspoon dried can be used in place of 1 tablespoon fresh.

1. Place beans, onion, chili powder, cumin, parsley, cilantro, and salt in food processor. Combine ingredients using pulse setting until beans are partially puréed and all ingredients are mixed. (If using canned beans, drain and rinse first.)

2. In a separate bowl, combine ground beef and bean mixture. Shape into 5 patties.

3. Meat mixture is quite soft after mixing and should be chilled or partially frozen prior to cooking. Grill or broil on oiled surface for approximately 6 minutes on each side, until internal temperature is 160°F when checked with a meat thermometer.

Slow-Cooker Beef Braciola

PER SERVING: Calories: 367 | Protein: 29g | Carbohydrates: 293g | Fat: 16g | Saturated Fat: 5g | Cholesterol: 69mg
Sodium: 162mg | Fiber: 5g | PCF Ratio: 32-29-39 | Exchange Approx.: 3½ Very-Lean Meats, 2½ Fats, 3 Vegetables, 1 Starch

INGREDIENTS | SERVES 4

4 cups tomato sauce

1 tablespoon olive oil

¼ cup finely chopped onion

1 teaspoon finely chopped garlic

¼ cup finely chopped carrots

¼ cup finely chopped celery

2 slices whole-wheat bread, cubed

1 egg, lightly beaten

1 pound thinly sliced round beef, cut into 4 pieces

1. Heat tomato sauce in a slow cooker and maintain at medium heat.

2. Heat olive oil in large nonstick skillet. Add the onions, garlic, carrots, and celery and sauté until softened. Remove from heat.

3. Add cubed bread and egg to sautéed vegetables; mix well.

4. Pound each piece of beef on both sides to flatten and tenderize. Each slice of meat should be about ¼" thick. Place approximately ½ cup of bread and vegetable stuffing down center of each meat slice and press in place. Starting at one end, roll meat up like a jelly roll; secure with 6" wooden skewer.

5. Place meat rolls in tomato sauce. Set slow cooker on low to medium setting; cook for at least 4 hours. (On low setting, the meat rolls can be left in slow cooker for 6–8 hours.) Remove wooden skewers before serving.

Soy and Ginger Flank Steak

PER SERVING: Calories: 304 | Protein: 29g | Carbohydrates: 1g | Fat: 19g | Saturated Fat: 7g | Cholesterol: 95mg
Sodium: 213mg | Fiber: 0g | PCF Ratio: 40-2-58 | Exchange Approx.: 4 Lean Meats, 1½ Fats

INGREDIENTS | SERVES 4

1 pound lean London broil
1 tablespoon minced fresh ginger
2 teaspoons minced fresh garlic
1 tablespoon reduced-sodium soy sauce
3 tablespoons dry red wine
¼ teaspoon pepper
½ tablespoon olive oil

Slicing Meats Against the Grain

Certain cuts of meat such as flank steak, brisket, and London broil have a distinct grain (or line) of fibers running through them. If you slice with the grain, meat will seem tough and difficult to chew. These cuts of meat should always be thinly sliced across (or against) the grain so fibers are cut through and meats remain tender and easy to chew.

1. Marinate meat at least 3–4 hours in advance: Place meat, ginger, garlic, soy sauce, red wine, pepper, and olive oil in a shallow baking dish. Coat meat with marinade on both sides. Cover and refrigerate meat in marinade, turning meat once or twice during marinating so all marinade soaks into both sides of meat.

2. Lightly oil barbecue grill and preheat. Place flank steak on grill and discard marinade. Grill steak, turning once, until done to your preference. Medium-rare will take approximately 12–15 minutes. Slice meat diagonally and against grain into thin slices.

London Broil with Grilled Vegetables

PER SERVING: Calories: 375 | Protein: 29g | Carbohydrates: 24g | Fat: 19g | Saturated Fat: 4g | Cholesterol: 62mg
Sodium: 151mg | Fiber: 3g | PCF Ratio: 30-26-44 | Exchange Approx.: 3½ Vegetables, 4 Lean Meats, 2 Fats

INGREDIENTS | SERVES 2

2 tablespoons olive oil

1 teaspoon red wine vinegar

1 tablespoon steak sauce

1 teaspoon red pepper flakes, or to taste

1 zucchini, cut into 1" chunks

1 orange or yellow pepper, seeded and cored, cut into quarters

2 sweet onions, cut into thick chunks

4 cherry tomatoes

½ pound London broil, cut into chunks

4 wooden skewers, presoaked for 30 minutes

1. In a small bowl, mix the olive oil, vinegar, steak sauce, and red pepper flakes.

2. Brush the vegetables with the dressing.

3. Toss the London broil in the rest of the dressing to coat.

4. Skewer the vegetables and London broil, alternating between meat and different vegetables.

5. Heat grill to 350°F and roast the vegetables and meat to the desired level of doneness.

Keep Your Eye on the Beef

Beef is high-quality protein, but beware—when you eat too much of it or have it with rich sauces, the caloric count skyrockets.

Beef Brisket with Onions and Mushrooms

**PER SERVING: Calories: 537 | Protein: 24g | Carbohydrates: 20g | Fat: 32g | Saturated Fat: 11g | Cholesterol: 92mg
Sodium: 553mg | Fiber: 4g | PCF Ratio: 21-17-62 | Exchange Approx.: 3 Medium-Fat Meats, 3½ Vegetables, 3 Fats**

INGREDIENTS | SERVES 4

4 cloves garlic

½ teaspoon salt

2 tablespoons olive oil, divided

½ bunch rosemary, chopped

1 pound beef brisket

Freshly ground pepper, to taste

3 large onions, quartered

3 cups white mushrooms, sliced

3 stalks celery, cut into large chunks

2 cups dry red cooking wine

1 (16-ounce) can whole tomatoes

2 bay leaves

1. Preheat oven to 325°F.

2. Using a mortar and pestle or the back of a spoon and bowl, mash together the garlic, ½ teaspoon salt, 1 tablespoon oil, and chopped rosemary leaves to make a paste. Set aside.

3. Season the brisket with pepper. Heat remaining olive oil in large pan, place the brisket in the pan, and sear over medium-high heat to make a dark crust on both sides.

4. Place brisket in a large roasting pan and spread the rosemary paste on the brisket. Place the onion, mushrooms, and celery around the brisket in the pan. Pour wine and tomatoes over top and toss in the bay leaves.

5. Tightly cover the pan with foil and place in the oven. Bake for about 4 hours, basting with pan juices every 30 minutes, until the beef is very tender.

6. Let the brisket rest for 15 minutes before slicing it across the grain at a slight diagonal. Remove bay leaves before serving.

Beef and Broccoli Stir-Fry

PER SERVING: Calories: 360 | Protein: 28g | Carbohydrates: 9g | Fat: 23g | Saturated Fat: 7g | Cholesterol: 58mg
Sodium: 655mg | Fiber: 2g | PCF Ratio: 32-10-58 | Exchange Approx.: 3 Lean Meats, 1 Vegetable, 2 Fats

INGREDIENTS | SERVES 4

¾ pound sirloin steak sliced into ½"-thick pieces

Salt and pepper, to taste

1½ tablespoons cornstarch

3 tablespoons peanut oil, divided

1 teaspoon minced fresh ginger

½ pound broccoli florets

3 cloves garlic

2 tablespoons soy sauce

Juice of 1 large orange

¼ cup water

½ teaspoon red pepper flakes

1. Season beef with salt and pepper. Coat beef with cornstarch.

2. Heat 2 tablespoons of oil in a wok over medium-high heat, then stir-fry beef and ginger for 1–2 minutes. Transfer beef to a bowl, cover, and set aside.

3. Add remaining oil to the hot wok. Add broccoli and garlic and stir-fry for 3–4 minutes, until broccoli is tender. Take care not to burn garlic.

4. Pour soy sauce, orange juice, water, and red pepper flakes into the wok with the broccoli and bring to a boil. Return the cooked beef to the wok. Stir until sauce thickens, about 2–3 minutes.

Steak and Mushroom Kabobs

PER SERVING: Calories: 380 | Protein: 36g | Carbohydrates: 4g | Fat: 24g | Saturated Fat: 7g | Cholesterol: 77mg
Sodium: 416mg | Fiber: 1g | PCF Ratio: 38-4-58 | Exchange Approx.: ½ Vegetable, 4 Meats, 2 Fats

INGREDIENTS | SERVES 4

1 pound sirloin steak

3 tablespoons olive oil

¼ cup balsamic vinegar

1 tablespoon Worcestershire sauce

½ teaspoon salt

2 cloves garlic, minced

Freshly ground pepper, to taste

½ pound large white mushrooms

1. Cut steak into 1½" cubes.

2. In a small bowl, combine oil, vinegar, Worcestershire sauce, salt, garlic, and pepper to make a marinade.

3. Wash mushrooms and cut in half. Place steak and mushrooms in a shallow bowl with marinade and place in refrigerator for 1–2 hours.

4. Place mushrooms and steak cubes on separate wooden or metal skewers. Grill 4 minutes per side for medium-rare steak. You may need additional cooking time for mushrooms.

Outdoors or In

These meaty, juicy kabobs are a hit at summer barbecues. They can also be cooked indoors on a well-seasoned grill pan.

Pork Roast with Caramelized Onions and Apples

PER SERVING: Calories: 373 | Protein: 31g | Carbohydrates: 8g | Fat: 23g | Saturated Fat: 9g | Cholesterol: 96mg
Sodium: 156mg | Fiber: 1g | PCF Ratio: 34-9-57 | Exchange Approx.: 1 Vegetable, 4 Lean Meats, 2 Fats

INGREDIENTS | SERVES 6

2 pounds lean pork loin roast
Freshly ground pepper, to taste
½ tablespoon olive oil
½ tablespoon butter
2 cups chopped onion
1 tablespoon Marsala wine
⅓ cup low-sodium chicken broth
1 apple, peeled and chopped

1. Preheat oven to 375°F. Season pork loin with pepper.

2. Heat olive oil in a large frying pan over medium heat. Add pork and sear to brown all sides.

3. Transfer pork to 9" × 13" glass baking dish; place in oven for approximately 1 hour and 15 minutes.

4. While pork is roasting, prepare onions: In large nonstick frying pan over medium heat, melt butter and add onions. Sauté onions until soft. Add wine, chicken broth, and apple. Continue cooking on low heat until onions are soft, brown in color, and caramelized.

5. When pork has reached an internal temperature of 130°F, spoon onions over top; place a loose foil tent over pork.

6. Remove pork from oven when an internal temperature of 145°F has been reached. (Temperature will continue to rise as meat rests.) Keep roast loosely covered with foil and allow to stand for 10–15 minutes before slicing.

Fruited Pork Loin Roast Casserole

PER SERVING: Calories: 170 | Protein: 7g | Carbohydrates: 27g | Fat: 4g | Saturated Fat: 1g | Cholesterol: 19mg
Sodium: 32mg | Fiber: 3g | PCF Ratio: 17-63-20 | Exchange Approx.: 1 Lean Meat, 1 Fruit, 1 Starch

INGREDIENTS | SERVES 4

4 small Yukon Gold potatoes, peeled and sliced

2 (2-ounce) pieces trimmed boneless pork loin, pounded flat

1 apple, peeled, cored, and sliced

4 apricot halves

1 tablespoon chopped red onion or shallot

⅛ cup apple cider or apple juice

Optional seasonings, to taste:

> Olive oil
>
> Parmesan cheese
>
> Salt and freshly ground pepper

Tip

To enhance the flavor of this dish, top with the optional ingredients when it's served. Just be sure to make the appropriate Exchange Approximations adjustments if you do.

1. Preheat oven to 350°F (325°F if using a glass casserole dish); treat casserole dish with nonstick cooking spray.

2. Layer ½ of potato slices across bottom of dish; top with 1 piece of flattened pork loin. Arrange apple slices over top of loin; place apricot halves on top of apple. Sprinkle red onion over apricot and apples. Add second flattened pork loin; layer remaining potatoes atop loin. Drizzle apple cider or apple juice over top of casserole.

3. Cover and bake for 45 minutes to 1 hour, or until potatoes are tender. Keep casserole covered and let sit for 10 minutes after removing from oven.

White Wine and Lemon Pork Roast

PER SERVING: Calories: 172 | Protein: 18g | Carbohydrates: 2g | Fat: 7g | Saturated Fat: 2g | Cholesterol: 50mg
Sodium: 47mg | Fiber: 0g | PCF Ratio: 53-5-42 | Exchange Approx.: 3 Lean Meats

INGREDIENTS | SERVES 4

1 clove garlic, crushed

½ cup dry white wine

1 tablespoon lemon juice

1 teaspoon olive oil

1 tablespoon minced red onion or shallot

¼ teaspoon dried thyme

⅛ teaspoon ground black pepper

12 ounces pork loin roast

Marmalade Marinade

For a variation on this recipe, combine 1 teaspoon Dijon or stone-ground mustard, 1 tablespoon Smucker's Low-Sugar Orange Marmalade, 1 clove crushed garlic, and ¼ teaspoon dried thyme leaves. Marinate and prepare a ½-pound pork loin as you would the White Wine and Lemon Pork Roast, substituting this marinade. The Nutritional Analysis for a 2-ounce serving is: Calories: 89.52; Protein: 126g; Carbohydrate: 1.90g; Fat: 26g; Saturated Fat: 1.11g; Cholesterol: 345mg; Sodium: 466mg; Fiber: 0.09g; PCF Ratio: 57-9-34; Exchange Approximations: 2 Lean Meats.

1. In heavy, freezer-style plastic bag, make the marinade by combining garlic, white wine, lemon juice, olive oil, red onion or shallot, thyme, and black pepper. Add roast and marinate in refrigerator 1 hour or overnight, according to taste. (Note: Pork loin is already tender, so you're marinating the meat to impart the flavors only.)

2. Preheat oven to 350°F. Remove meat from marinade; put on nonstick cooking spray–treated rack in roasting pan. Roast for 20–30 minutes, or until meat thermometer reads 150°F to 170°F, depending on how well done you prefer it.

Pork Lo Mein

PER SERVING: Calories: 266 | Protein: 23g | Carbohydrates: 25g | Fat: 8g | Saturated Fat: 2g | Cholesterol: 50mg
Sodium: 386mg | Fiber: 5g | PCF Ratio: 35-38-27 | Exchange Approx.: 2½ Lean Meats, 1 Starch, 1 Vegetable

INGREDIENTS | SERVES 4

1½ tablespoons reduced-sodium soy sauce

1 teaspoon grated fresh ginger

1 tablespoon rice vinegar

¼ teaspoon turmeric

¾ pound lean pork loin, cut into 1" cubes

½ tablespoon canola oil

½ cup sliced green onion

2 teaspoons minced garlic

2 cups shredded cabbage

1 cup chopped (1" pieces) snap peas

¼ teaspoon red pepper flakes

2 cups cooked whole-grain spaghetti

1 teaspoon sesame oil

1 teaspoon sesame seeds

1. In a medium bowl, combine soy sauce, ginger, rice vinegar, and turmeric. Mix in cubed pork and set aside.

2. In large skillet or wok, heat oil and sauté green onion and garlic. Add meat; cook quickly until meat and onions are slightly browned.

3. Add in cabbage and snap peas; continue to stir-fry for another 3–4 minutes. Sprinkle in red pepper flakes.

4. When vegetables are crisp-tender, add cooked pasta, sesame oil, and sesame seeds. Toss lightly and serve.

Sweet and Sour Pork Skillet

PER SERVING: Calories: 198 | Protein: 26g | Carbohydrates: 12g | Fat: 5g | Saturated Fat: 2g | Cholesterol: 67mg
Sodium: 164mg | Fiber: 3g | PCF Ratio: 47-30-25 | Exchange Approx.: 3½ Very-Lean Meats, 1½ Vegetables, ½ Other
Carbohydrate, ½ Fat

INGREDIENTS | SERVES 4

12 ounces lean pork tenderloin

1 tablespoon honey

2 tablespoons rice vinegar or white vinegar

2 teaspoons soy sauce

½ teaspoon grated fresh ginger

½ cup chopped onions

½ cup julienned carrots

2 cups cauliflower florets

¼ teaspoon Chinese five-spice powder

Aromatic Five-Spice Powder

Chinese five-spice powder is a blend of cinnamon, anise, fennel (or star anise), ginger, and clove. Five-spice powder is an essential base seasoning for many Chinese dishes. A little of this aromatic mix goes a long way, giving dishes a hint of sweet, savory, and sour.

1. Cut pork into 1" strips. In medium bowl, combine pork, honey, vinegar, soy sauce, and ginger. Coat pork strips with mixture and allow to marinate for at least 15 minutes.

2. Heat large nonstick skillet or wok over medium-high heat. Add pork strips and onion; quickly stir-fry over high heat for 2–3 minutes. Reserve any leftover marinade to add with vegetables.

3. Add carrots, cauliflower, and marinade. Toss all ingredients and continue to stir-fry, allowing marinade to coat all vegetables. Cook over high heat for an additional 3–4 minutes, or until vegetables are crisp-tender.

4. Add five-spice powder and combine just before serving.

Country-Style Pork Ribs

PER SERVING: Calories: 434 | Protein: 28g | Carbohydrates: 31g | Fat: 22g | Saturated Fat: 8g | Cholesterol: 181mg
Sodium: 830mg | Fiber: 0g | PCF Ratio: 25-28-47 | Exchange Approx.: 3 Meats, 1½ Other Carbs, 4 Fats

INGREDIENTS | SERVES 4

2½ pounds country-style pork ribs

Salt and pepper, to taste

Garlic powder, to taste

Cayenne pepper, to taste

1 cup water

1 teaspoon liquid smoke

2 tablespoons Worcestershire sauce

1 cup barbecue sauce of your choice

Liquid Smoke

Liquid smoke is used to give food a smoky, barbecued flavor without the wood chips. It is most often made out of hickory wood, which producers burn to capture and condense the smoke. They filter out impurities in the liquid and bottle the rest.

1. Sprinkle the ribs with salt and pepper, garlic powder, and cayenne pepper. Rub the spices into the meat and bone on both sides. Place them in a roasting pan with the water and liquid smoke on the bottom. Sprinkle with Worcestershire sauce.

2. Set the oven at 225°F. Cover the ribs tightly with aluminum foil. Roast them for 4–5 hours. The meat should be "falling-off-the-bone" tender.

3. Remove foil and brush the ribs with barbecue sauce. Bake for another 15–20 minutes or until dark brown.

Italian Sausage

PER SERVING, WITHOUT SALT: Calories: 135 | Protein: 15g | Carbohydrates: 0g | Fat: 8g | Saturated Fat: 3g | Cholesterol: 45mg Sodium: 27mg | Fiber: 0g | PCF Ratio: 47-0-53 | Exchange Approx.: 1 Medium-Fat Meat

INGREDIENTS | MAKES ABOUT 2 POUNDS; SERVING SIZE: 2 OUNCES

2 pounds pork shoulder

1 teaspoon ground black pepper

1 teaspoon dried parsley

1 teaspoon Italian-style seasoning

1 teaspoon garlic powder

¾ teaspoon crushed anise seeds

⅛ teaspoon red pepper flakes

½ teaspoon paprika

½ teaspoon instant minced onion flakes

1 teaspoon kosher or sea salt (optional)

1. Remove all fat from meat; cut the meat into cubes. Put in food processor; grind to desired consistency.

2. Add remaining ingredients to the meat in the food processor; mix until well blended. You can put sausage mixture in casings, but it works equally well broiled or grilled as patties.

Simple (and Smart!) Substitutions

Game meats—buffalo, venison, elk, moose—are low in fat, as are ground chicken or turkey. Substitute one of these for pork in any of the sausage recipes in this chapter.

Italian Sweet Fennel Sausage

PER SERVING, WITHOUT SALT: Calories: 139 | Protein: 15g | Carbohydrates: 1g | Fat: 8g | Saturated Fat: 3g | Cholesterol: 45mg Sodium: 27mg | Fiber: 0g | PCF Ratio: 46-3-51 | Exchange Approx.: 1 Medium-Fat Meat

INGREDIENTS | MAKES ABOUT 2 POUNDS; SERVING SIZE: 2 OUNCES

1 tablespoon fennel seeds

¼ teaspoon cayenne pepper

2 pounds pork butt

½ teaspoon black pepper

2½ teaspoons crushed fresh garlic

1 tablespoon sugar

1 teaspoon kosher or sea salt (optional)

Better the Second Day

Ideally, sausage is made the night before and refrigerated to allow the flavors to merge. Leftover sausage can be frozen for up to 3 months.

1. Toast fennel seeds and cayenne pepper in nonstick skillet over medium heat, stirring constantly, until seeds just begin to darken, about 2 minutes. Set aside.

2. Remove all fat from meat; cut the meat into cubes. Put in food processor; grind to desired consistency.

3. Add remaining ingredients, including the toasted fennel seeds, to the meat in the food processor; mix until well blended. You can put sausage mixture in casings, but it works equally well broiled or grilled as patties.

Grilled Lamb Chops with Garlic, Rosemary, and Thyme

PER SERVING: Calories: 269 | Protein: 21g | Carbohydrates: 1g | Fat: 20g | Saturated Fat: 7g | Cholesterol: 79mg Sodium: 357mg | Fiber: 0g | PCF Ratio: 32-1-67 | Exchange Approx.: 3 Meats, 2 Fats

INGREDIENTS | SERVES 2

2 cloves garlic

½ teaspoon salt

1 teaspoon chopped fresh rosemary

1 teaspoon chopped fresh thyme

1 tablespoon olive oil

1 teaspoon lemon zest

Pepper, to taste

4 (1¼"-thick) lamb chops

1. In a medium bowl, mash garlic cloves into a paste. Add salt.

2. Add rosemary, thyme, oil, and lemon zest to the garlic paste and stir well to combine. Add pepper to taste. Rub the herb-garlic paste onto the lamb chops and set them aside to marinate for 15 minutes.

3. Grill lamb chops for 4–5 minutes on each side for medium-rare doneness.

Mock Chorizo

PER SERVING, WITHOUT SALT: Calories: 137 | **Protein:** 15g | **Carbohydrates:** 1g | **Fat:** 8g | **Saturated Fat:** 3g | **Cholesterol:** 45mg
Sodium: 27mg | **Fiber:** 0g | **PCF Ratio:** 47-1-52 | **Exchange Approx.:** 1 Medium-Fat Meat

INGREDIENTS | MAKES ABOUT 2 POUNDS; SERVING SIZE: 2 OUNCES

2 pounds lean pork

4 tablespoons chili powder

¼ teaspoon ground cloves

2 tablespoons paprika

2½ teaspoons crushed fresh garlic

1 teaspoon dried oregano

3½ tablespoons cider vinegar

1 teaspoon kosher or sea salt (optional)

Break from Tradition

Traditionally, chorizo is very high in fat. This mock chorizo recipe is a lower-fat alternative. It makes an excellent flavor replacement in recipes that call for bacon. In fact, 1 or 2 ounces of chorizo can replace an entire pound of bacon in cabbage, bean, or potato soup.

1. Remove all fat from meat; cut the meat into cubes. Put in food processor; grind to desired consistency.

2. Add remaining ingredients to the meat in the food processor; mix until well blended.

3. Tradition calls for aging this sausage in an airtight container in the refrigerator for 4 days before cooking. Leftover sausage can be stored in the freezer for up to 3 months.

Kousa (Squash Stuffed with Lamb and Rice)

PER SERVING: Calories: 430 | Protein: 27g | Carbohydrates: 36g | Fat: 20g | Saturated Fat: 7g | Cholesterol: 82mg
Sodium: 692mg | Fiber: 5g | PCF Ratio: 25-33-42 | Exchange Approx.: 3 Lean Meats, 1 Starch, 3 Vegetables, 3 Fats

INGREDIENTS | SERVES 4

3 cups chopped tomatoes

1 cup chopped onion

2 cups water

½ teaspoon salt

⅛ teaspoon freshly ground pepper

2 tablespoons minced fresh mint

4 small zucchini (7"–8" long)

¾ pound very lean ground lamb

½ cup uncooked white rice

2 tablespoons pine nuts

½ teaspoon salt

⅛ teaspoon ground allspice

⅛ teaspoon freshly ground pepper

Summer Harvest

Kousa (stuffed squash) is a traditional Lebanese dish that uses a pale green summer squash very similar to zucchini. This squash is not always easy to find, but zucchini is very abundant and works quite well. If you have a large garden crop of zucchini: Pick them small, hollow out the squash, blanch in boiling water for 2 minutes, then freeze. You'll have squash ready to stuff all year long.

1. Prepare tomato sauce first: Combine tomatoes, onion, water, salt, pepper, and fresh mint in a large pot over high heat. Bring to a boil; reduce heat and simmer 30 minutes.

2. Scrub squash and dry with paper towels. Remove stem ends of each squash and carefully core center, leaving about ¼" of shell.

3. Make stuffing: In a large bowl, thoroughly mix ground lamb, rice, pine nuts, salt, allspice, and pepper.

4. Spoon stuffing into each squash, tapping bottom end of squash to get stuffing down. Fill each squash to top; stuffing should be loosely packed to allow rice to expand while cooking.

5. Place squash in tomato sauce, laying them on their sides. Bring sauce to a slow boil; cover and cook over low heat for 45–60 minutes, or until squash is tender and rice has cooked. Serve squash with tomato sauce spooned over top.

Baked Stuffed Kibbeh

PER SERVING: Calories: 226 | Protein: 18g | Carbohydrates: 13g | Fat: 12g | Saturated Fat: 4g | Cholesterol: 62mg
Sodium: 343mg | Fiber: 3g | PCF Ratio: 32-22-46 | Exchange Approx.: 1 Starch, 2 Lean Meats, 2 Fats

INGREDIENTS | SERVES 8

Nonstick cooking spray
¾ cup fine-grind bulgur wheat
2 cups boiling water
1 pound lean ground lamb
1 cup grated onion, divided
1 teaspoon salt
¼ teaspoon pepper
Small bowl ice water
3 tablespoons butter, divided
¼ cup pine nuts
¼ teaspoon cinnamon
¼ teaspoon ground allspice

Making Lean Ground Lamb

Unless you have a butcher, very lean ground lamb is difficult to find. Make it yourself using chunks of meat trimmed from a leg of lamb. Be sure to remove all visible fat from the lamb and grind twice using a medium or fine grinder blade. Removing all visible fat prevents lamb from having a strong "mutton" taste.

1. Spray 9" × 9" baking dish with nonstick cooking spray.

2. Put bulgur wheat in small bowl. Cover with boiling water and allow wheat to absorb liquid, approximately 15–20 minutes.

3. Line colander with small piece of cheesecloth. Drop bulgur wheat into cloth; drain and squeeze as much liquid out of wheat as possible.

4. On large cutting board, combine lamb, ½ cup grated onions, wheat, salt, and pepper; mix with hands, kneading together all ingredients.

5. Place ½ meat mixture in bottom of baking dish by dipping hands into ice water to spread meat mixture smoothly over bottom of dish. Cover bottom of dish completely.

6. In a small pan, melt 1½ tablespoons of butter; sauté remaining onions, pine nuts, cinnamon, and allspice until onions are soft.

7. Spread onion and pine nut mixture evenly over first layer of meat in baking dish. Take remaining ½ of meat mixture and spread smoothly on top, using procedure in Step 5.

8. Score top in diamond shapes with a knife dipped in cold water. Melt remaining 1½ tablespoons of butter; drizzle over top of meat. Bake at 350°F for approximately 40–45 minutes, or until golden brown.

Balsamic Venison Pot Roast

PER SERVING: Calories: 188 | Protein: 28g | Carbohydrates: 6g | Fat: 6g | Saturated Fat: 2g | Cholesterol: 96mg
Sodium: 75mg | Fiber: 1g | PCF Ratio: 60-13-28 | Exchange Approx.: 4 Very-Lean Meats, ½ Fat

INGREDIENTS | SERVES 8

2½ tablespoons all-purpose flour

2 teaspoons paprika

1 (2-pound) venison roast

1½ tablespoons olive oil

1 (14-ounce) can low-sodium beef broth

½ cup chopped onion

2 tablespoons dried onion flakes

⅓ cup balsamic vinegar

⅛ teaspoon Worcestershire sauce

1 teaspoon sugar

1. In a shallow bowl, mix flour and paprika together. Dredge venison in flour mixture and coat completely.

2. Heat oil in Dutch oven or deep skillet. Add the venison and brown on all sides.

3. Add beef broth, onion, onion flakes, balsamic vinegar, Worcestershire sauce, and sugar. Bring to a quick boil; reduce heat to low.

4. Cover and cook over low heat for 2–3 hours, or until venison is tender and cuts easily. Serve with whole-grain noodles.

Recipe Adaptation

This recipe also works well cooked in a slow cooker for 6–8 hours, until tender. Slow cookers with a ceramic interior maintain low temperatures better than those with a metal cooking surface.

Venison Pepper Steak

PER SERVING: Calories: 237 | Protein: 26g | Carbohydrates: 12g | Fat: 9g | Saturated Fat: 3g | Cholesterol: 39mg
Sodium: 344mg | Fiber: 2g | PCF Ratio: 44-20-36 | Exchange Approx.: 3½ Very-Lean Meats, 2 Vegetables, 1½ Fats

INGREDIENTS | SERVES 4

1 pound venison loin

2 tablespoons reduced-sodium soy sauce

1 clove garlic, minced

1½ teaspoons grated fresh ginger

1 tablespoon canola oil

1 cup thinly sliced onion

1 cup thinly sliced green or red peppers

½ cup thinly sliced celery

1 tablespoon cornstarch

1 cup water

1½ cups chopped tomatoes

Whole-Grain Additions

Instead of serving white rice, substitute brown rice or quinoa mixed with sautéed vegetables with this dish.

1. Cut meat across grain into ¼" strips.

2. In a large bowl, combine soy sauce, garlic, and ginger. Add sliced meat; mix well and marinate for at least 1 hour.

3. Heat canola oil in large wok or skillet. Add meat and cook for 2–3 minutes over high heat. Cover, reduce heat, and simmer for 15 minutes.

4. Add onions, peppers, and celery to meat; cover and cook on low heat for another 15 minutes, or until sliced meat is tender.

5. In a small bowl, mix cornstarch with water, and then add to meat. Cook for 5 minutes, or until sauce thickens slightly. Add tomatoes and heat through.

Slow-Cooker Venison and Vegetable Pot Roast

PER SERVING: Calories: 309 | Protein: 27g | Carbohydrates: 28g | Fat: 10g | Saturated Fat: 3g | Cholesterol: 39mg
Sodium: 237mg | Fiber: 4g | PCF Ratio: 35-36-28 | Exchange Approx.: 3½ Very-Lean Meats, 1 Starch, 3 Vegetables, 1½ Fats

INGREDIENTS | SERVES 4

1 (1-pound) venison roast
1 tablespoon all-purpose flour
1 tablespoon olive oil
1 tablespoon instant brown gravy mix
1 teaspoon Worcestershire sauce
1 cup chopped onions
½ pound potatoes, cut into 1" pieces
1 cup chopped carrots
1 cup chopped celery
½ cup crushed tomatoes
½ teaspoon dried thyme leaves

1. Dredge roast in flour. Heat olive oil in large skillet; sear roast until browned on all sides. Put roast in slow cooker.

2. Sprinkle instant gravy mix and Worcestershire sauce over top of roast. Place onions, potatoes, carrots, and celery around roast; spoon crushed tomatoes evenly around vegetables. Sprinkle thyme over meat and vegetables.

3. Cook in slow cooker on low setting for 6–8 hours.

Variation

You can also use ⅓ cup water and 2 tablespoons red wine for the liquid instead of crushed tomatoes.

CHAPTER 6
Chicken and Turkey

Chicken Broth: Easy Slow-Cooker Method

PER SERVING: Calories: 67 | Protein: 9g | Carbohydrates: 0g | Fat: 3g | Saturated Fat: 1g | Cholesterol: 24mg
Sodium: 22mg | Fiber: 0g | PCF Ratio: 53-0-47 | Exchange Approx.: ½ Very-Lean Meat, ½ Lean Meat

INGREDIENTS | **MAKES ABOUT 4 CUPS;**
SERVING SIZE: ½ CUP

1 small onion, chopped
2 carrots, peeled and chopped
2 stalks celery with leaves, chopped
1 bay leaf
4 sprigs parsley
6 black peppercorns
¼ cup dry white wine
2 pounds chicken pieces, skin removed
4½ cups water

Reduced Broth

Reducing broth is the act of boiling it to decrease the amount of water so you're left with a richer broth. Nonfat, canned chicken broth won't reduce as a homemade broth would. The broth from this recipe will be richer than what most recipes call for, so unless you need reduced broth, thin it with water as needed. Assuming you remove the fat from the broth, it will be a Free Exchange.

1. Add all ingredients except water to slow cooker. The chicken pieces and vegetables should be loosely layered and fill no more than ¾ of slow cooker. Add enough water to just cover ingredients; cover slow cooker.

2. Set slow cooker to high setting until mixture almost reaches a boil, then reduce heat to low. Allow to simmer overnight or up to 16 hours, checking occasionally and adding more water, if necessary.

3. Remove chicken pieces and drain on paper towels to absorb any fat. Allow to cool; remove meat from bones. Strain vegetables from broth and discard. (You don't want to eat vegetables cooked directly with chicken because they will have absorbed too much of the residue fat.) Put broth in a covered container; refrigerate for several hours or overnight, allowing fat to congeal on top. Remove hardened fat and discard.

4. To separate broth into small amounts for use when you steam vegetables or potatoes, fill up an ice cube tray with broth. Let freeze, then remove cubes from tray and store in labeled freezer bag. Common ice cube trays allow for ⅛ cup or 2 tablespoons of liquid per section.

Pineapple-Orange Grilled Chicken Breasts

PER SERVING: Calories: 165 | Protein: 27g | Carbohydrates: 10g | Fat: 2g | Saturated Fat: 0g | Cholesterol: 58.40mg
Sodium: 75mg | Fiber: 0g | PCF Ratio: 67-25-9 | Exchange Approx.: 3½ Lean Meats, ½ Fruit

INGREDIENTS | SERVES 4

6 ounces pineapple juice

4 ounces orange juice

¼ cup cider vinegar

1 tablespoon chopped fresh tarragon

½ tablespoon fresh rosemary

1 pound boneless, skinless chicken breast, cut into 4 pieces

1. In a large, shallow dish make the marinade by combining pineapple juice, orange juice, vinegar, tarragon, and rosemary.

2. Add pieces of raw chicken breast to marinade; cover and refrigerate for 3–4 hours. Turn pieces of chicken to cover with marinade.

3. Heat grill to medium-high; place chicken on grill. Grill approximately 7–10 minutes on each side, until chicken is cooked through.

Herbed Chicken and Brown Rice Dinner

PER SERVING: Calories: 300 | Protein: 33g | Carbohydrates: 26g | Fat: 6g | Saturated Fat: 1g | Cholesterol: 75mg
Sodium: 112mg | Fiber: 0g | PCF Ratio: 45-36-19 | Exchange Approx.: 1½ Starches, 2 Very-Lean Meats, 2 Lean Meats

INGREDIENTS | SERVES 4

1 tablespoon canola oil

4 (4-ounce) boneless, skinless chicken breast pieces

¾ teaspoon garlic powder, divided

¾ teaspoon dried rosemary, divided

1 (10.5-ounce) can low-fat, reduced-sodium chicken broth

⅓ cup water

2 cups uncooked instant brown rice

1. Heat oil in large nonstick skillet on medium-high. Add chicken; sprinkle with ½ of garlic powder and ½ of dried rosemary. Cover, and cook 4 minutes on each side, or until cooked through. Remove chicken from skillet and set aside.

2. Add broth and water to skillet; stir to deglaze pan and bring to a boil. Stir in rice and remaining garlic powder and rosemary. Top with chicken and cover; cook on low heat 5 minutes. Remove from heat and let stand, covered, 5 minutes.

Chicken Breasts in Balsamic Vinegar Sauce

PER SERVING: Calories: 200 | Protein: 28g | Carbohydrates: 2g | Fat: 8g | Saturated Fat: 3g | Cholesterol: 73mg | Sodium: 381mg | Fiber: 0g | PCF Ratio: 58-4-38 | Exchange Approx.: 4 Lean Meats, 1½ Fats

INGREDIENTS | SERVES 4

1 pound boneless, skinless chicken breasts, cut into 4 (4-ounce) pieces

Pinch salt

¼ teaspoon pepper

1 tablespoon butter

1 tablespoon olive oil

¼ cup chopped red onion

2 teaspoons finely chopped garlic

3 tablespoons balsamic vinegar

1½ cups low-sodium chicken broth

1 teaspoon dried oregano

1. Sprinkle chicken with salt and pepper.

2. Heat butter and olive oil in large skillet over medium heat. Add chicken; cook until browned, about 5 minutes each side. Reduce heat and cook 12 minutes. Transfer to platter; cover and keep warm.

3. Add red onions and garlic to skillet; sauté over medium heat 3 minutes, scraping up browned bits. Add balsamic vinegar; bring to a boil. Boil 3 minutes, or until reduced to a glaze, stirring constantly.

4. Add chicken broth; boil until reduced to about ¾ cup liquid. Remove sauce from heat; add dried oregano. Spoon sauce over chicken and serve immediately.

Oven-Fried Chicken Thighs

PER SERVING, NO OIL: Calories: 74 | Protein: 9g | Carbohydrates: 5g | Fat: 2g | Saturated Fat: 1g | Cholesterol: 34mg Sodium: 331mg | Fiber: 0g | PCF Ratio: 53-26-21 | Exchange Approx.: 2 Very-Lean Meats

INGREDIENTS | SERVES 4

4 chicken thighs, skin removed

1 tablespoon unbleached, white all-purpose flour

1 egg white

½ teaspoon sea salt

½ teaspoon olive oil (optional; see Comparison Analysis for using olive oil)

1 tablespoon rice flour

1 tablespoon cornmeal

If You Use Oil . . .

Comparison Analysis (with olive oil): Calories: 78.53; Protein: 9.46g; Carbohydrate: 65g; Fat: 27g; Saturated Fat: 0.50g; Cholesterol: 303mg; Sodium: 331.03mg; Fiber: 0.06g; PCF Ratio: 49-24-27; Exchange Approx.: 2 Lean Meats.

1. Preheat oven to 350°F. Place rack on baking sheet; spray both with nonstick cooking spray. Rinse and dry chicken thighs. Put white flour on plate.

2. In small, shallow bowl, whip egg white with the sea salt. Add olive oil, if using; mix well.

3. Put rice flour and cornmeal on another plate; mix together.

4. Roll each chicken thigh in white flour, dip it into egg-white mixture, and roll in rice-flour mixture. Place thighs on rack so they aren't touching. Bake 35–45 minutes, until meat juices run clear.

Easy Chicken Paprikash

PER SERVING, USING EQUAL AMOUNTS OF LIGHT- AND DARK-MEAT CHICKEN: Calories: 376 | Protein: 22g | Carbohydrates: 58g | Fat: 6g | Saturated Fat: 2g | Cholesterol: 78mg | Sodium: 135mg | Fiber: 4g | PCF Ratio: 23-62-15
Exchange Approx.: ½ Very-Lean Meat, ½ Lean Meat, 2½ Starches, 1 Vegetable, 1 Skim Milk

INGREDIENTS | SERVES 4

1 recipe Condensed Cream of Chicken Soup (see recipe in Chapter 8)

½ cup skim milk

2 teaspoons paprika

⅛ teaspoon ground red pepper (optional)

¼ pound (4 ounces) boneless, skinless chicken, cooked and chopped

1½ cups sliced steamed mushrooms

½ cup diced steamed onion

½ cup plain, nonfat yogurt

4 cups medium egg noodles, cooked

1. In large saucepan, combine soup, skim milk, paprika, and pepper (if using); whisk until well mixed. Bring to a boil over medium heat, stirring occasionally.

2. Reduce heat to low and stir in chicken, mushrooms, and onion; cook until chicken and vegetables are heated through, about 10 minutes. Stir in yogurt.

3. To serve, put 1 cup of warm, cooked noodles on each of 4 plates. Top each portion with an equal amount of chicken mixture. Garnish by sprinkling with additional paprika, if desired.

For Best Results . . .

Mock condensed-soup recipes are used in the dishes in this book so that you know the accurate information. In all cases, you can substitute commercial canned condensed soups; however, be sure to use the lower-fat and lower-sodium varieties.

Chicken and Broccoli Casserole

PER SERVING: Calories: 328 | Protein: 26g | Carbohydrates: 20g | Fat: 17g | Saturated Fat: 6g | Cholesterol: 67mg
Sodium: 254mg | Fiber: 3g | PCF Ratio: 31-24-45 | Exchange Approx.: 1 Very-Lean Meat, 1 Lean Meat, ½ High-Fat Meat,
1 Fat, 1 Vegetable, 1 Skim Milk, ½ Starch

INGREDIENTS | SERVES 4

2 cups broccoli

½ pound chicken, cooked and chopped

½ cup skim milk

2 tablespoons real mayonnaise

¼ teaspoon curry powder

1 recipe Condensed Cream of Chicken Soup (see recipe in Chapter 8)

1 tablespoon lemon juice

½ cup (2 ounces) grated Cheddar cheese

½ cup bread crumbs

1 teaspoon melted butter

1 teaspoon olive oil

1. Preheat oven to 350°F. Treat 11" × 7" casserole dish with nonstick cooking spray.

2. Steam broccoli until tender; drain.

3. Spread out chicken on bottom of dish; cover with steamed broccoli.

4. In medium bowl, combine milk, mayonnaise, curry powder, soup, and lemon juice; pour over broccoli.

5. In small bowl, mix together cheese, bread crumbs, butter, and oil; sprinkle over top of casserole. Bake 30 minutes.

Chicken Kalamata

PER SERVING: Calories: 311 | Protein: 31g | Carbohydrates: 25g | Fat: 11g | Saturated Fat: 2g | Cholesterol: 66mg
Sodium: 787mg | Fiber: 6g | PCF Ratio: 38-31-31 | Exchange Approx.: 4 Lean Meats, 2 Vegetables, 1 Starch, 2 Fats

INGREDIENTS | SERVES 4

2 tablespoons olive oil

1 cup chopped onion

1 teaspoon minced garlic

1½ cups chopped green peppers

1 pound boneless, skinless chicken breasts, cut into 4 (4-ounce) pieces

2 cups diced tomatoes

1 teaspoon oregano

½ cup pitted, chopped kalamata olives

1. Heat olive oil over medium heat in large skillet. Add onions, garlic, and peppers and sauté for about 5 minutes until onions are translucent.

2. Add chicken pieces. Cook for about 5 minutes each side until lightly brown.

3. Add tomatoes and oregano. Reduce heat and simmer 20 minutes.

4. Add olives. Simmer an additional 10 minutes before serving.

Chicken and Green Bean Stovetop Casserole

PER SERVING: Calories: 305 | Protein: 23g | Carbohydrates: 36g | Fat: 8g | Saturated Fat: 2g | Cholesterol: 48mg
Sodium: 101mg | Fiber: 6g | PCF Ratio: 30-46-24 | Exchange Approx.: 1 Very-Lean Meat, 1 Lean Meat, 1 Vegetable,
1 Starch, 1 Skim Milk

INGREDIENTS | SERVES 4

1 recipe Condensed Cream of Chicken Soup (see recipe in Chapter 8)

¼ cup skim milk

2 teaspoons Worcestershire sauce (recipe for homemade in Chapter 12)

1 teaspoon real mayonnaise

½ teaspoon onion powder

¼ teaspoon garlic powder

¼ teaspoon ground black pepper

1 (4-ounce) can sliced water chestnuts, drained

2½ cups frozen green beans, thawed

1 cup sliced mushrooms, steamed

½ pound chicken, cooked and chopped

1⅓ cups cooked brown long-grain rice

1. In a large saucepan, combine soup, milk, Worcestershire, mayonnaise, onion powder, garlic powder, and pepper; bring to a boil.

2. Reduce heat; add water chestnuts, green beans, mushrooms, and chicken. Simmer until vegetables and chicken are heated through, about 10 minutes. Serve over rice.

Veggie Filler

Steamed mushrooms are a low-calorie way to add flavor to a dish and "stretch" the meat. If you don't like mushrooms, you can substitute an equal amount of other low-calorie steamed vegetables like red and green peppers and not significantly affect the total calories in a recipe.

Chicken Pasta with Herb Sauce

PER SERVING: Calories: 393 | Protein: 26g | Carbohydrates: 52g | Fat: 8g | Saturated Fat: 2g | Cholesterol: 48mg
Sodium: 71mg | Fiber: 4g | PCF Ratio: 27-53-20 | Exchange Approx.: 2 Lean Meats, 3 Starches, ½ Skim Milk

INGREDIENTS | SERVES 4

1 recipe Condensed Cream of Chicken Soup (see recipe in Chapter 8)

¼ cup skim milk

½ teaspoon Worcestershire sauce (recipe for homemade in Chapter 12)

1 teaspoon real mayonnaise

¼ cup grated Parmesan cheese

¼ teaspoon chili powder

½ teaspoon garlic powder

¼ teaspoon dried rosemary

¼ teaspoon dried thyme

¼ teaspoon dried marjoram

1 cup sliced mushrooms, steamed

½ pound chicken, cooked and chopped

4 cups cooked pasta

Freshly ground black pepper, to taste (optional)

1. In a large saucepan, combine soup, milk, Worcestershire, mayonnaise, and cheese and bring to a boil.

2. Reduce heat and add chili powder, garlic powder, rosemary, thyme, and marjoram; stir well. Add mushrooms and chicken; simmer for 10 minutes until heated through.

3. Serve over pasta and top with freshly ground pepper, if desired.

Chicken and Asparagus in White Wine Sauce

PER SERVING: Calories: 186 | Protein: 21g | Carbohydrates: 7g | Fat: 8g | Saturated Fat: 2g | Cholesterol: 51mg
Sodium: 57mg | Fiber: 2g | PCF Ratio: 46-16-38 | Exchange Approx.: 2½ Very-Lean Meats, 1½ Vegetables, 1 Fat

INGREDIENTS | SERVES 4

4 boneless, skinless chicken breast halves

½ tablespoon butter

1 tablespoon olive oil

1 teaspoon finely chopped garlic

½ cup finely chopped onion

10 ounces asparagus spears, cut diagonally in 2" pieces

½ pound mushrooms

¼ cup dry white wine

¼ cup water

1 tablespoon chopped parsley

Salt and pepper, to taste

1. Pound chicken pieces to ¼" thickness.

2. In a large skillet over medium heat, melt butter and olive oil. Add chopped garlic and onions and sauté 1–2 minutes.

3. Add chicken; cook 5 minutes, or until the chicken is brown on both sides. Remove chicken and set aside.

4. Add asparagus and mushrooms to skillet and cook 2–3 minutes.

5. Return chicken to skillet; add white wine and water. Bring to a quick boil; boil 2 minutes to reduce the liquid.

6. Reduce heat; cover and simmer 3 minutes, or until chicken and vegetables are tender. Add chopped parsley, salt and pepper to taste, and serve.

Grilled San Francisco–Style Chicken

PER SERVING: Calories: 298 | Protein: 21g | Carbohydrates: 1g | Fat: 23g | Saturated Fat: 6g | Cholesterol: 112mg
Sodium: 44mg | Fiber: 0g | PCF Ratio: 29-1-70 | Exchange Approx.: 3 Meats, 1 Fat

INGREDIENTS | SERVES 4

1 tablespoon olive oil

1 tablespoon Dijon mustard

2 tablespoons raspberry white wine vinegar

1 small chicken (about 2½–3 pounds), cut in quarters

Celery salt and pepper, to taste

Olive oil, as needed

1. Heat grill to 400°F.

2. In a small bowl, mix the olive oil, mustard, and vinegar. Sprinkle the chicken with celery salt and pepper.

3. Paint the skin side of the chicken with the mustard mixture. Spray a few drops of olive oil on the bone side.

4. Grill the chicken, bone side to flame, for 15 minutes. Reduce heat to 325°F; cover and cook for 15 minutes.

Fried Chicken with Cornmeal Crust

PER SERVING: Calories: 408 | Protein: 40g | Carbohydrates: 16g | Fat: 20g | Saturated Fat: 3g | Cholesterol: 104mg
Sodium: 539mg | Fiber: 1g | PCF Ratio: 40-16-44 | Exchange Approx.: 1 Starch, 4 Lean Meats, 3 Fats

INGREDIENTS | SERVES 4

4 (4-ounce) boneless, skinless chicken breast halves

½ cup buttermilk

½ cup coarse cornmeal

1 teaspoon baking powder

½ teaspoon salt

Freshly ground pepper, to taste

¼ cup canola or other vegetable oil

1. Soak the chicken in buttermilk for 15 minutes.

2. On a piece of waxed paper, mix the cornmeal, baking powder, salt, and pepper. Remove the chicken from the buttermilk and coat the chicken with the cornmeal mixture.

3. In a large nonstick frying pan, heat the oil to 350°F. Fry chicken for 8–10 minutes per side. Drain on paper towels.

Indian Tandoori-Style Chicken

PER SERVING: Calories: 253 | Protein: 41g | Carbohydrates: 5g | Fat: 6g | Saturated Fat: 2g | Cholesterol: 107mg
Sodium: 133mg | Fiber: 0g | PCF Ratio: 68-9-23 | Exchange Approx.: ½ Milk, 4 Lean Meats, 1 Fat

INGREDIENTS | SERVES 4

4 boneless, skinless chicken breast
halves, pounded thin

1 tablespoon garam masala

2 cloves garlic, mashed

1 cup low-fat yogurt

1. In a large glass pan, marinate the chicken breasts overnight in a mixture of garam masala, garlic, and yogurt.

2. Preheat the oven or grill to 400°F. Broil or grill the chicken for 4 minutes per side. The hot oven recreates the clay oven, or tandoori, used in India to bake meats.

Garam Masala

Garam masala is a combination of spices used in most Indian cooking. A basic recipe contains coriander, cinnamon, cloves, cardamom, and cumin. Try ½ teaspoon of each as a base, and then make changes to suit your taste.

Chicken Thighs Cacciatore

PER SERVING: Calories: 370 | Protein: 19g | Carbohydrates: 48g | Fat: 9g | Saturated Fat: 2g | Cholesterol: 39mg
Sodium: 166mg | Fiber: 4g | PCF Ratio: 21-55-24 | Exchange Approx.: 1½ Lean Meats, 2½ Starches, 1 Fat, 1 Vegetable

INGREDIENTS | SERVES 4

2 teaspoons olive oil

½ cup chopped onion

2 cloves garlic, minced

4 chicken thighs, skin removed

½ cup dry red wine

1 (14½-ounce) can unsalted diced tomatoes, undrained

1 teaspoon dried parsley

½ teaspoon dried oregano

¼ teaspoon pepper

⅛ teaspoon sugar

¼ cup grated Parmesan cheese

4 cups cooked spaghetti

2 teaspoons extra-virgin olive oil

For Cheese Lovers!

Indulge your love of extra cheese and still have a main dish that's under 400 calories. Prepare Chicken Thighs Cacciatore according to recipe instructions. Top each portion with 1 tablespoon freshly grated Parmesan cheese. With cheese, analysis is: Calories: 398.22; Protein: 21.39g; Carbohydrates: 48.43g; Fat: 11.15g; Saturated Fat: 62g; Cholesterol: 487mg; Sodium: 2,814mg; Fiber: 81g; PCF Ratio: 23-51-26; Exchange Approx.: 2 Lean Meats, 2½ Starches, 1 Fat, 1 Vegetable.

1. Heat deep, nonstick skillet over medium-high heat; add 2 teaspoons olive oil. Add onion and sauté until transparent.

2. Add garlic and chicken thighs and sauté 3 minutes on each side, or until lightly browned.

3. Remove thighs from pan; add wine, tomatoes and juices, parsley, oregano, pepper, and sugar. Stir well, bring to a boil. Add chicken back to pan; sprinkle Parmesan cheese over top. Cover, reduce heat, and simmer 10 minutes. Uncover and simmer 10 more minutes.

4. To serve, put 1 cup of cooked pasta on each of 4 plates. Top each serving with a chicken thigh; divide sauce between dishes. Drizzle ½ teaspoon extra-virgin olive oil over top of each dish and serve.

Chicken with Portobello Mushrooms and Roasted Garlic

PER SERVING: Calories: 335 | Protein: 26g | Carbohydrates: 39g | Fat: 10g | Saturated Fat: 4g | Cholesterol: 56mg
Sodium: 261mg | Fiber: 3g | PCF Ratio: 30-45-25 | Exchange Approx.: 2½ Lean Meats, ½ Fat, 8 Vegetables

INGREDIENTS | SERVES 4

1 tablespoon olive oil

4 boneless, skinless chicken breasts

1 cup reduced-sodium chicken broth

1 bulb dry-roasted garlic (see recipe for Garlic and Feta Cheese Dip in Chapter 3), mashed into paste

2 cups chopped portobello mushrooms

½ teaspoon thyme

1 tablespoon butter

2 tablespoons crumbled feta cheese

1. Heat olive oil in large nonstick skillet; brown chicken breasts on both sides over medium heat, about 5 minutes per side.

2. Add chicken broth and roasted-garlic paste to pan; cover and simmer on low 10 minutes.

3. Meanwhile, in a separate, smaller pan, sauté mushrooms and thyme in butter. Simmer 2 minutes.

4. Add the mushrooms to the chicken and simmer for an additional 2 minutes.

5. When serving, top each chicken breast with 1½ teaspoons feta cheese and pour sauce over the top.

Chipotle Chicken Wrap

PER SERVING: Calories: 284 | Protein: 24g | Carbohydrates: 28g | Fat: 8g | Saturated Fat: 2g | Cholesterol: 40mg
Sodium: 415mg | Fiber: 2g | PCF Ratio: 35-41-25 | Exchange Approx.: 2 Starches, ½ Vegetable, 3 Lean Meats

INGREDIENTS | SERVES 4

12 ounces boneless, skinless chicken breast

1 tablespoon lime juice

1 tablespoon olive oil

1 teaspoon chipotle seasoning

⅛ teaspoon freshly ground pepper

4 whole-wheat tortillas

½ cup jarred salsa

1 cup chopped lettuce

1. Cut chicken into ½" strips. Place chicken, lime juice, olive oil, chipotle seasoning, and pepper in a dish; mix well. Cover and allow chicken to marinate for 1 hour.

2. Heat outdoor grill. Wrap tortillas in aluminum foil and place on top rack. Cook chicken strips 7–9 minutes until done, turning strips once during cooking.

3. When ready to make wraps, place chicken strips in center of each heated tortilla, add 2 tablespoons salsa to each, top with chopped lettuce, and wrap.

Spicy Grilled Turkey Burgers

PER SERVING: Calories: 176 | Protein: 26g | Carbohydrates: 5g | Fat: 5g | Saturated Fat: 2g | Cholesterol: 125mg
Sodium: 155mg | Fiber: 0g | PCF Ratio: 63-12-25 | Exchange Approx.: 3½ Very-Lean Meats, 1 Fat

INGREDIENTS | SERVES 4

1 pound ground turkey

¼ cup bread crumbs

1 tablespoon Cajun Blend seasoning (see recipe in Chapter 15) or commercial salt-free blend

1 egg

1 tablespoon finely chopped fresh cilantro

2 teaspoons minced jalapeño pepper

Nonstick cooking spray

1. In a large bowl, combine all ingredients, except the cooking spray, well. Shape mixture into 4 patties.

2. Spray grill with nonstick cooking spray. Grill burgers approximately 6 minutes on each side, or until cooked through.

Buttermilk Ranch Chicken Salad

PER SERVING: Calories: 147 | Protein: 18g | Carbohydrates: 11g | Fat: 4g | Saturated Fat: 1g | Cholesterol: 33mg
Sodium: 184mg | Fiber: 2g | PCF Ratio: 49-29-22 | Exchange Approx.: 2 Very-Lean Meats, ½ Vegetable, 1 Free Vegetable, ½ Skim Milk

INGREDIENTS | SERVES 4

1 tablespoon real mayonnaise

3 tablespoons plain, nonfat yogurt

½ cup nonfat cottage cheese

½ teaspoon cider vinegar

1 teaspoon brown sugar

1 teaspoon Dijon mustard

½ cup buttermilk

2 tablespoons dried parsley

1 clove garlic, minced

2 tablespoons grated Parmesan cheese

¼ teaspoon sea salt (optional)

¼ teaspoon freshly ground pepper (optional)

1 cup chopped, cooked chicken breast

½ cup sliced cucumber

½ cup chopped celery

½ cup sliced carrots

4 cups salad greens

½ cup red onion slices

Fresh parsley for garnish (optional)

1. In blender or food processor, combine mayonnaise, yogurt, cottage cheese, vinegar, brown sugar, mustard, buttermilk, parsley, garlic, cheese, salt, and pepper and process until smooth.

2. In a large bowl place the chicken, cucumber, celery, and carrots. Pour the yogurt mixture over top and mix. Chill at least 2 hours.

3. To serve, arrange 1 cup of salad greens on each of 4 serving plates. Top each salad with an equal amount of chicken salad. Garnish with red onion slices and fresh parsley, if desired.

Get More Mileage from Your Meals

Leftover chicken salad makes great sandwiches. Put it between two slices of bread with lots of lettuce for a quick lunch. The lettuce helps keep the bread from getting soggy if the sandwich is to-go.

Stovetop Grilled Turkey Breast

PER SERVING: Calories: 207 | Protein: 31g | Carbohydrates: 2g | Fat: 8g | Saturated Fat: 2g | Cholesterol: 85mg
Sodium: 68mg | Fiber: 0g | PCF Ratio: 62-3-35 | Exchange Approx.: 4 Very-Lean Meats, ½ Fat

INGREDIENTS | SERVES 4

1 teaspoon cider vinegar

1 teaspoon garlic powder

1 teaspoon Dijon mustard

1 teaspoon brown sugar

¼ teaspoon black pepper

2 teaspoons olive oil

4 (4-ounce) turkey breast cutlets

Tip

Cutlets prepared this way tend to cook faster than on an outdoor grill. If using an indoor grill that cooks both sides at once, allow 4–5 minutes total cooking time. You can also use a well-seasoned cast-iron frying pan instead of a grill pan; however, you may need to introduce more oil to the pan to prevent the cutlets from sticking. Cooking time will be the same as with a grill pan. Be sure to adjust the Fat Exchange, if necessary.

1. In a medium bowl, combine vinegar, garlic powder, mustard, brown sugar, and black pepper; slowly whisk in olive oil to thoroughly combine and make a thin paste.

2. Rinse turkey cutlets and dry thoroughly on paper towels. If necessary, to ensure a uniform thickness, put between sheets of plastic wrap and pound to flatten.

3. Pour paste into heavy-duty freezer-style resealable plastic bag. Add cutlets, moving around in mixture to coat all sides. Seal bag, carefully squeezing out as much air as possible. Refrigerate to allow turkey to marinate at least 1 hour, or as long as overnight.

4. Place nonstick, hard-anodized stovetop grill pan over high heat. When pan is heated thoroughly, add cutlets. Lower heat to medium-high; cook cutlets 3 minutes on 1 side. Use tongs to turn; cook another 3 minutes, or until juices run clear.

Turkey Kielbasa with Red Beans and Rice

PER SERVING: Calories: 297 | Protein: 15g | Carbohydrates: 41g | Fat: 9g | Saturated Fat: 3g | Cholesterol: 32mg Sodium: 679mg | Fiber: 7g | PCF Ratio: 19-54-26 | Exchange Approx.: 2 Starches, 1½ Vegetables, 1 Lean Meat, 1 Very-Lean Meat, 3 Fats

INGREDIENTS | SERVES 5

2 cups canned pinto beans, drained and rinsed

2 cups canned diced tomatoes

2 cups water, divided

1 cup diced onion

2 teaspoons Cajun Blend seasoning (see recipe in Chapter 15)

8 ounces turkey kielbasa, cut into 1" pieces

½ cup brown rice

1. In a slow cooker, combine pinto beans, canned tomatoes, ½ cup water, onion, Cajun seasoning, and kielbasa. Set slow cooker on low and cook for 4–6 hours.

2. In a medium saucepan, bring brown rice and remaining 1½ cups water to a boil; reduce heat, cover, and simmer on low heat 35–40 minutes.

3. Serve beans and sausage over rice.

Turkey Chili

PER SERVING: Calories: 281 | Protein: 26g | Carbohydrates: 38g | Fat: 4g | Saturated Fat: 1g | Cholesterol: 49mg Sodium: 347mg | Fiber: 11g | PCF Ratio: 35-52-13 | Exchange Approx.: 2 Starches, 2 Vegetables, 3 Very-Lean Meats, 1½ Fats

INGREDIENTS | SERVES 6

1 pound ground turkey

1 cup chopped onion

½ cup chopped green pepper

2 teaspoons finely chopped garlic

2 (28-ounce) cans crushed tomatoes

1 cup canned black beans, drained

1 cup canned red kidney beans, drained

3 tablespoons chili powder

1 tablespoon ground cumin

1 teaspoon red pepper flakes

Dash Tabasco Sauce

1. Brown ground turkey in large nonstick pot over medium-high heat.

2. Drain off any fat; add chopped onion, green pepper, and garlic. Continue cooking until onion is translucent, about 5 minutes. Add remaining ingredients; bring to a slow boil.

3. Reduce heat, cover, and let simmer at least 2–3 hours before serving.

Turkey Mushroom Burgers

PER SERVING: Calories: 100 | Protein: 15g | Carbohydrates: 3g | Fat: 3g | Saturated Fat: 1g | Cholesterol: 34mg
Sodium: 36mg | Fiber: 1g | PCF Ratio: 60-10-30 | Exchange Approx.: 1 Lean Meat, 1 Vegetable, ½ Fat

INGREDIENTS | MAKES 8 LARGE BURGERS

1 pound turkey breast
1 pound fresh white mushrooms
1 tablespoon olive oil
1 teaspoon butter
1 clove garlic, minced
1 tablespoon chopped green onion
¼ teaspoon dried thyme
¼ teaspoon dried oregano
¼ teaspoon freshly ground black pepper
Cayenne pepper or red pepper flakes, to taste (optional)

1. Cut turkey into even pieces about 1" square. Place cubes in freezer 10 minutes, or long enough to allow turkey to become somewhat firm.

2. In a covered microwave-safe container, microwave mushrooms on high 3–4 minutes, or until they begin to soften and sweat. Set aside to cool slightly.

3. Process turkey in food processor until ground, scraping down sides of bowl as necessary. Add oil, butter, garlic, onion, and mushrooms (and any liquid resulting from microwaving the mushrooms); process until mushrooms are ground, scraping down sides of bowl as necessary.

4. Add remaining ingredients; pulse until mixed. Shape into 8 equal-size patties. Cooking times will vary according to method used and how thick burgers are.

Turkey Marsala with Fresh Peas

PER SERVING: Calories: 278 | Protein: 30g | Carbohydrates: 14g | Fat: 7g | Saturated Fat: 3g | Cholesterol: 78mg
Sodium: 208mg | Fiber: 2g | PCF Ratio: 50-24-27 | Exchange Approx.: 4 Very-Lean Meats, ½ Starch, ½ Vegetable, 1 Fat

INGREDIENTS | SERVES 4

¼ cup all-purpose flour

¼ teaspoon salt

¼ teaspoon pepper

½ teaspoon paprika

1 pound turkey breast cutlets, sliced ¼" thick

1 tablespoon olive oil

1 tablespoon butter

½ cup thinly sliced onion

½ cup Marsala wine

½ cup fresh or frozen peas

Quick Tip

It's easy to prepare quick and healthy meals if you keep boneless, skinless chicken or turkey in the freezer. If you use an indoor grill, you don't even need to thaw them first. You can prepare a quick sauce or glaze in the time it takes for the chicken or turkey to cook.

1. In a plastic zip-top bag, mix together flour, salt, pepper, and paprika. Place turkey cutlets in plastic bag; shake to coat cutlets with flour mixture.

2. Heat olive oil and butter in large skillet. Add the onions and sauté for about 5 minutes, until browned.

3. Add coated turkey cutlets and brown on both sides, approximately 7–8 minutes on each side.

4. Add Marsala to pan; stir well to combine. Bring to a boil; reduce heat. Turn cutlets to coat both sides.

5. Add peas; continue to cook, stirring, another 2–3 minutes. Serve.

CHAPTER 7

Fish and Seafood

Salmon Patties

PER SERVING: Calories: 168 | Protein: 17g | Carbohydrates: 3g | Fat: 9g | Saturated Fat: 2g | Cholesterol: 70mg
Sodium: 92mg | Fiber: 0g | PCF Ratio: 42-8-50 | Exchange Approx.: 2 Lean Meats, ½ Fat, ½ Starch

INGREDIENTS | SERVES 5

2 cups flaked cooked salmon (no salt added)

6 soda crackers, crushed

1 egg

½ cup skim milk

1 small onion, chopped

1 tablespoon chopped fresh parsley

1 tablespoon unbleached all-purpose flour

1 tablespoon olive oil

Ener-G rice flour (optional)

1. Place salmon in a large bowl. Add crushed crackers, egg, milk, onion, parsley, and flour; mix well. Gently form 5 patties.

2. Heat oil in nonstick skillet over medium heat. (Optional: Lightly dust patties with some Ener-G rice flour for crispier patties.) Fry on both sides until browned, about 5 minutes per side.

Salmon and Broccoli Stir-Fry

PER SERVING: Calories: 327 | Protein: 26g | Carbohydrates: 7g | Fat: 22g | Saturated Fat: 3g | Cholesterol: 67mg
Sodium: 138mg | Fiber: 4g | PCF Ratio: 31-9-60 | Exchange Approx.: 1 Vegetable, 3 Lean Meats, 2½ Fats

INGREDIENTS | SERVES 2

½ pound broccoli florets

2 (¼-pound) salmon fillets, skin removed

1 tablespoon canola oil

1 teaspoon Asian sesame oil

1 teaspoon minced fresh ginger

2 slices pickled ginger, chopped

1 clove garlic, minced

1 teaspoon hoisin sauce

1 cup brown rice (optional)

Garnish of 5 scallions, chopped

1. Steam the broccoli for 3–4 minutes.

2. In a large skillet, over medium-high heat, toss the broccoli and salmon with the canola oil and sesame oil. Cook, stirring for 3–4 minutes.

3. Add the fresh ginger, pickled ginger, garlic, and hoisin sauce and cook for another minute until heated through. Serve over rice, garnished with scallions.

Grilled Salmon with Roasted Peppers

PER SERVING: Calories: 269 | Protein: 24g | Carbohydrates: 8g | Fat: 16g | Saturated Fat: 3g | Cholesterol: 67mg
Sodium: 321mg | Fiber: 1g | PCF Ratio: 36-11-53 | Exchange Approx.: 3½ Lean Meats, 1 Vegetable, 1 Fat

INGREDIENTS | SERVES 4

4 (4-ounce) salmon steaks
1 tablespoon reduced-sodium soy sauce
1 tablespoon brown sugar
1 tablespoon olive oil
2 large red bell peppers
1 tablespoon balsamic vinegar
½ teaspoon dried thyme
¼ teaspoon freshly ground pepper

Wasabi Marinade

Wasabi, also known as Japanese horserad-ish, can be purchased in raw form or as a powder or paste. It adds a hot, pungent flavor to fish and works especially well with salmon. To make a marinade for salmon or other fish, mix 1 teaspoon wasabi powder (or paste) with 2 tablespoons low-sodium soy sauce, ½ teaspoon grated fresh ginger, and 1 teaspoon sesame oil. Coat fish with the marinade and grill.

1. Place salmon in a shallow dish. In a medium bowl, mix together soy sauce, brown sugar, and olive oil and pour over salmon, covering both sides with marinade. Set aside.

2. Prepare roasted red peppers following procedure in sidebar for Roasted Red Pepper and Plum Sauce recipe in Chapter 12. Once peppers are roasted and peeled, cut into strips and sprinkle with balsamic vinegar, thyme, and pepper. Set aside.

3. Heat grill. Remove salmon from the marinade; grill over medium heat approximately 8 minutes on one side. Turn and grill on other side until salmon is cooked and tender, about 4–5 minutes longer. Remove from heat.

4. Top each salmon steak with roasted red peppers.

A-Taste-of-Italy Baked Fish

PER SERVING: Calories: 128 | Protein: 22g | Carbohydrates: 7g | Fat: 1g | Saturated Fat: 0g | Cholesterol: 50mg
Sodium: 312mg | Fiber: 1g | PCF Ratio: 68-23-9 | Exchange Approx.: 2½ Very-Lean Meats, 1½ Vegetables

INGREDIENTS | SERVES 4

1 pound cod fillets
1 (14½-ounce) can stewed tomatoes
¼ teaspoon dried minced onion
½ teaspoon dried minced garlic
¼ teaspoon dried basil
¼ teaspoon dried parsley
⅛ teaspoon dried oregano
⅛ teaspoon sugar
1 tablespoon grated Parmesan cheese

1. Preheat oven to 375°F. Rinse cod with cold water and pat dry with paper towels.

2. In medium baking pan or casserole dish treated with nonstick cooking spray, combine all ingredients except fish and mix together.

3. Arrange fish fillets over mixture, folding thin tail ends under; spoon mixture over fillets. For fillets about 1" thick, bake uncovered 20–25 minutes, or until fish is opaque and flaky.

Grilled Haddock with Peach-Mango Salsa

PER SERVING, INCLUDING ½ CUP PEACH-MANGO SALSA: Calories: 204 | Protein: 22g | Carbohydrates: 11g | Fat: 8g
Saturated Fat: 1g | Cholesterol: 65mg | Sodium: 467mg | Fiber: 2g | PCF Ratio: 43-22-35 | Exchange Approx.: 3 Very-Lean Meats, 1 Fat, ½ Fruit

INGREDIENTS | SERVES 4

2 tablespoons olive oil
2 tablespoons lime juice
¼ teaspoon salt
¼ teaspoon ground pepper
1 pound haddock fillets
Fresh Peach-Mango Salsa (see recipe in Chapter 12)

1. In a shallow dish, mix olive oil, lime juice, salt, and pepper. Add haddock and turn and coat fish with marinade.

2. Heat gas grill or broiler. Spray large piece of aluminum foil with nonstick cooking spray. Place fillets on foil; cook 7–8 minutes on each side, or until fish is tender when pierced with a fork.

3. Top each piece of fish with ½ cup Fresh Peach-Mango Salsa.

Spicy "Fried" Fish Fillet

PER SERVING: Calories: 230 | Protein: 24g | Carbohydrates: 9g | Fat: 10g | Saturated Fat: 2g | Cholesterol: 116mg
Sodium: 412mg | Fiber: 1g | PCF Ratio: 44-17-39 | Exchange Approx.: 3 Very-Lean Meats, 2 Fats, ½ Starch

INGREDIENTS | SERVES 4

⅓ cup cornmeal

½ teaspoon salt

1 teaspoon chipotle seasoning

1 egg

2 tablespoons 1% milk

16 ounces flounder, cut into 4 pieces

2 tablespoons olive oil

1. In a shallow dish, combine cornmeal, salt, and chipotle seasoning.

2. In a separate dish, beat egg and milk together.

3. Dip fish in egg mixture, and then coat each fillet with cornmeal mixture.

4. Heat olive oil in nonstick skillet; brown fillets until golden and crispy, about 6–7 minutes each side.

Crab Cakes with Sesame Crust

PER SERVING: Calories: 108 | Protein: 9g | Carbohydrates: 3g | Fat: 6g | Saturated Fat: 1g | Cholesterol: 45mg
Sodium: 171mg | Fiber: 1g | PCF Ratio: 34-11-55 | Exchange Approx.: 1 Very-Lean Meat, 1½ Fats

INGREDIENTS | SERVES 5

1 pound lump crabmeat

1 egg

1 tablespoon minced fresh ginger

1 small scallion, finely chopped

1 tablespoon dry sherry

1 tablespoon freshly squeezed lemon juice

6 tablespoons real mayonnaise

Sea salt and freshly ground white pepper, to taste (optional)

Old Bay Seasoning (see recipe in Chapter 15), to taste (optional)

¼ cup lightly toasted sesame seeds

1. Preheat oven to 375°F. In large bowl, mix together crab, egg, ginger, scallion, sherry, lemon juice, mayonnaise, and seasonings, if using.

2. Form the mixture into 10 equal cakes. Spread sesame seeds over sheet pan and dip both sides of cakes to coat them.

3. Arrange cakes on baking sheet treated with nonstick cooking spray. Typical baking time is 8–10 minutes, depending on thickness of cakes.

Baked Bread Crumb–Crusted Fish with Lemon

PER SERVING, WITHOUT SALT: Calories: 137 | Protein: 24g | Carbohydrates: 5g | Fat: 3g | Saturated Fat: 1g | Cholesterol: 36mg
Sodium: 73mg | Fiber: 2g | PCF Ratio: 68-14-18 | Exchange Approx.: 2 Very-Lean Meats, ½ Starch, ½ Free Condiment

INGREDIENTS | SERVES 6

2 large lemons

¼ cup bread crumbs

1½ pounds halibut fillets

Kosher or sea salt and freshly ground
white or black pepper, to taste (optional)

Lemon Infusion

Mildly flavored fish such as catfish, cod, halibut, orange roughy, rockfish, and snapper benefit from the distinctive flavor of lemon. Adding slices of lemon to top of fish allows the flavor to infuse into fish.

1. Preheat oven to 375°F. Wash 1 lemon; cut into thin slices. Grate 1 tablespoon of zest from the second lemon, then juice it. Combine grated zest and bread crumbs in small bowl; stir to mix. Set aside.

2. Put lemon juice in shallow dish; arrange a single layer of lemon slices in bottom of baking dish treated with nonstick cooking spray. Dip fish pieces in lemon juice; set on lemon slices in baking dish.

3. Sprinkle bread-crumb mixture evenly over fish pieces along with salt and pepper, if using; bake until crumbs are lightly browned and fish is just opaque, 10–15 minutes. (Baking time will depend on thickness of fish.) Serve immediately, using remaining lemon slices as garnish.

Baked Red Snapper Almondine

**PER SERVING, WITHOUT SALT: Calories: 178 | Protein: 24g | Carbohydrates: 3g | Fat: 7g | Saturated Fat: 2g | Cholesterol: 47mg
Sodium: 73mg | Fiber: 1g | PCF Ratio: 56-7-37 | Exchange Approx.: 3 Lean Meats**

INGREDIENTS | SERVES 4

1 pound red snapper fillets

Kosher or sea salt and freshly ground white or black pepper, to taste (optional)

4 teaspoons all-purpose flour

2 teaspoons olive oil

2 tablespoons ground raw almonds

2 teaspoons unsalted butter

1 tablespoon lemon juice

1. Preheat oven to 375°F. Rinse red snapper fillets and dry between layers of paper towels. Season with salt and pepper on both sides, if using; sprinkle with flour on both sides.

2. In an ovenproof nonstick skillet, sauté fillets in olive oil until nicely browned on both sides, about 5 minutes per side.

3. Combine ground almonds and butter in microwave-safe dish. Microwave on high 30 seconds, or until butter is melted; stir to combine.

4. Pour almond-butter mixture and lemon juice over fillets; bake for 3–5 minutes, or until almonds are nicely browned.

Asian-Style Fish Cakes

PER SERVING: Calories: 66 | Protein: 11g | Carbohydrates: 1g | Fat: 2g | Saturated Fat: 1g | Cholesterol: 41mg | Sodium: 112mg | Fiber: 0mg | PCF Ratio: 69-8-23 | Exchange Approx.: 1 Lean Meat, 1 Free Condiment

INGREDIENTS | SERVES 8

1 pound catfish fillets

2 green onions, minced

1 banana pepper, cored, seeded, and chopped

2 cloves garlic, minced

1 tablespoon grated or minced fresh ginger

1 tablespoon Bragg's Liquid Aminos

1 tablespoon lemon juice

1 teaspoon lemon zest

Old Bay Seasoning (see recipe in Chapter 15) (optional)

Tip

For crunchy fish cakes, coat each side in rice flour and then lightly spritz the tops of the patties with olive or peanut oil before baking as directed.

1. Preheat oven to 375°F. Cut fish into 1" pieces. Combine with green onions, banana pepper, garlic, ginger, Bragg's Liquid Aminos, lemon juice, and lemon zest in food processor; process until chopped and mixed. (You do not want to purée this mixture; it should be a rough chop.) Add Old Bay Seasoning, if using; stir to mix.

2. Form fish mixture into patties of about 2 tablespoons each; you should have 16 patties total. Place patties on baking sheet treated with nonstick cooking spray; bake 12–15 minutes, or until crisp. (Alternatively, you can fry these in a nonstick frying pan about 4 minutes on each side.)

Barley-Spinach-Fish Bake

PER SERVING: Calories: 239 | Protein: 26g | Carbohydrates: 15g | Fat: 8g | Saturated Fat: 1g | Cholesterol: 67mg
Sodium: 418mg | Fiber: 3g | PCF Ratio: 44-26-30 | Exchange Approx.: 3 Lean Meats, ½ Starch, 1 Vegetable, 1½ Fats

INGREDIENTS | SERVES 4

½ tablespoon olive oil

¼ cup chopped scallions

1 clove minced garlic

¼ teaspoon rosemary

¼ teaspoon marjoram

¼ teaspoon salt

1 cup pearl barley, cooked

5 ounces (½ box) frozen chopped spinach, thawed and drained

¼ cup chopped sun-dried tomatoes

4 (12-inch) squares of aluminum foil

4 (4-ounce) fish fillets

3 tablespoons white wine

Salt and freshly ground pepper, to taste

Cooking Barley

Pearl barley takes longer to cook than quick-cooking barley, so you will want to prepare it in advance. To prepare: Bring ½ cup pearl barley and 1 cup water to a boil. Reduce heat, cover, and simmer for 35–45 minutes, or until all water is absorbed. Pearl barley makes a good side dish with the addition of spices or vegetables.

1. Preheat oven to 400°F (or outdoor grill can be used).

2. Heat oil in medium nonstick skillet; add scallions and sauté 2 minutes. Add garlic, rosemary, marjoram, and salt; continue to cook another 3 minutes, until scallions are tender. Add cooked barley, spinach, and sun-dried tomatoes; mix well.

3. Place aluminum foil squares on work surface; place a fish fillet in center of each square. Divide barley mixture equally; place on top of each fillet. Sprinkle with white wine, salt, and pepper.

4. Fold aluminum foil loosely to enclose filling. Place packets on baking sheet (or directly on grill if using outdoor grill); bake 15 minutes, or until fish is tender and flakes easily.

Baked Snapper with Orange-Rice Dressing

**PER SERVING, WITHOUT SALT: Calories: 257 | Protein: 26g | Carbohydrates: 25g | Fat: 5g | Saturated Fat: 2g
Cholesterol: 47mg Sodium: 83mg | Fiber: 1g | PCF Ratio: 41-40-19 | Exchange Approx.: 2 Lean Meats, ½ Fruit, ½ Fat, 1 Starch**

INGREDIENTS | SERVES 4

¼ cup chopped celery

½ cup chopped onion

1 tablespoon lemon juice

½ cup orange juice

1 teaspoon orange zest

1⅓ cups cooked rice

1 pound red snapper fillets

Kosher or sea salt and freshly ground white or black pepper, to taste (optional)

2 teaspoons unsalted butter

2 tablespoons ground raw almonds

1. Preheat oven to 350°F.

2. In a microwave-safe bowl, mix celery and onion with juices and orange zest; microwave on high for 2 minutes, or until mixture comes to a boil. Add rice; stir to moisten, adding water 1 tablespoon at a time if necessary to thoroughly coat rice. Cover and let stand 5 minutes.

3. Rinse fillets and pat dry between paper towels. Prepare baking dish with nonstick cooking spray. Spread rice mixture in dish; arrange fillets on top. Season fillets with salt and pepper, if using.

4. Combine butter and almonds in a microwave-safe bowl; microwave on high for 30 seconds, or until butter is melted. Stir; spoon over top of fillets.

5. Cover and bake for 10 minutes. Remove cover and bake another 5–10 minutes, or until fish flakes easily when tested with a fork and almonds are lightly browned.

Crunchy "Fried" Catfish Fillets

PER SERVING, WITHOUT SALT: Calories: 244 | Protein: 21g | Carbohydrates: 18g | Fat: 9g | Saturated Fat: 2g |
Cholesterol: 53mg | Sodium: 248mg | Fiber: 1g | PCF Ratio: 35-30-35 | Exchange Approx.: 3 Lean Meats, 1 Starch

INGREDIENTS | SERVES 4

4 (4-ounce) catfish fillets

1 egg white (from a large egg), room temperature

¼ cup bread crumbs

¼ cup enriched white cornmeal

1 teaspoon lemon zest

½ teaspoon dried basil

¼ cup all-purpose flour

⅛ teaspoon kosher or sea salt (optional)

¼ teaspoon lemon pepper

Zesty Crunch

Using lemon or lime zest is a great way to add citrus flavor to a crunchy bread-crumb topping for fish.

1. Preheat oven to 450°F; treat shallow baking pan with nonstick cooking spray. Rinse catfish and dry between layers of paper towels.

2. In a shallow dish, beat egg white until frothy. In another dish, combine bread crumbs, cornmeal, lemon zest, and basil. In third dish, combine flour, salt (if using), and lemon pepper.

3. Dip fish into flour mixture to coat 1 side of each fillet. Shake off any excess flour mixture, then dip flour-covered side of fillet into egg white. Next, coat covered side of fillet with bread-crumb mixture.

4. Arrange prepared fillets side by side, coated-sides up, on prepared baking pan. Tuck in any thin edges. Bake for 6–12 minutes, or until fish flakes easily with a fork.

Jon's Fish Tacos

PER SERVING: Calories: 383 | Protein: 29g | Carbohydrates: 40g | Fat: 12g | Saturated Fat: 2g | Cholesterol: 60mg
Sodium: 400mg | Fiber: 4g | PCF Ratio: 30-42-28 | Exchange Approx.: 3½ Very-Lean Meats, 2 Starches, 1 Vegetable, 1 Fat

INGREDIENTS | SERVES 4

¼ cup light mayonnaise

½ cup plain, nonfat yogurt

¼ cup chopped onion

2 tablespoons minced jalapeño pepper

2 teaspoons minced cilantro

2 cups shredded cabbage

¼ cup lime juice

1 clove garlic, minced

1 tablespoon canola oil

1 pound tilapia fillets

4 (6") whole-wheat tortillas

Aluminum foil

Nonstick cooking spray

1 cup chopped tomato

Freshly ground pepper, to taste (optional)

1. In medium bowl, whisk together mayonnaise, yogurt, onion, jalapeño, and cilantro. Stir in shredded cabbage; chill.

2. In separate bowl, combine lime juice, garlic, and canola oil to make a marinade for fish. Pour over fish; cover and refrigerate at least 1 hour.

3. Place fish on aluminum-lined grill (spray aluminum with nonstick cooking spray); cook 6–7 minutes on each side, until fish is tender and beginning to flake.

4. While fish is cooking, loosely wrap whole-wheat tortillas in large piece of aluminum foil to heat.

5. To assemble tacos, cut fish into strips; divide into 4 portions. Place strips in center of each heated tortilla. Top with coleslaw mixture and chopped tomatoes. Add freshly ground pepper, if desired.

Sweet Onion–Baked Yellowtail Snapper

PER SERVING, WITHOUT SALT: Calories: 189 | Protein: 25g | Carbohydrates: 13g | Fat: 4g | Saturated Fat: 1g | Cholesterol: 42mg | Sodium: 77mg | Fiber: 1g | PCF Ratio: 53-28-19 | Exchange Approx.: 1 Lean Meat, 2 Very-Lean Meats, 1 Vegetable, ½ Starch

INGREDIENTS | SERVES 4

2 cups sliced Vidalia onions

1 tablespoon balsamic vinegar

2 teaspoons brown sugar

4 teaspoons olive oil

1 pound skinless yellowtail snapper fillets

Sea salt and freshly ground white or black pepper, to taste (optional)

1. In covered microwave-safe dish, microwave onion on high 5 minutes, or until transparent. Carefully remove cover; stir in vinegar and brown sugar. Cover; allow to sit several minutes so onion absorbs flavors.

2. Heat a nonstick frying pan on medium-high heat and add olive oil. Transfer steamed onion mixture to pan and sauté until browned but not crisp. (Be careful, as onions will burn easily because of brown sugar; if onion browns too quickly, lower heat and add a few tablespoons of water.) Cook until all liquid has evaporated from pan, stirring often. Onions should have a shiny and dark caramelized color. (This can be prepared 2–3 days in advance; store tightly covered in refrigerator.)

3. Preheat oven to 375°F. Rinse snapper in cold water and dry between paper towels. Arrange on baking sheet treated with nonstick cooking spray.

4. Spoon caramelized onions over tops of fillets, pressing to form a light crust over top of fish. Bake for 12–15 minutes, or until fish flakes easily with a fork. Serve immediately with onion sauce divided on 4 plates and fish placed on top. Season with salt and pepper, if desired.

Pasta and Smoked Trout with Lemon Pesto

PER SERVING: Calories: 209 | Protein: 10g | Carbohydrates: 23g | Fat: 8g | Saturated Fat: 1g | Cholesterol: 4mg
Sodium: 151mg | Fiber: 1g | PCF Ratio: 20-45-36 | Exchange Approx.: 1 Fat, 1½ Lean Meats, 1 Carbohydrate/Starch

INGREDIENTS | SERVES 4

2 cloves garlic

2 cups tightly packed fresh basil leaves

⅛ cup pine nuts, toasted

2 teaspoons fresh lemon juice

2 teaspoons water

4 teaspoons extra-virgin olive oil

4 tablespoons grated Parmesan cheese, divided

1⅓ cups uncooked linguini or other pasta (to yield 2 cups cooked pasta)

2 ounces whole boneless smoked trout

Freshly ground black pepper, to taste

1. Put garlic in food processor and pulse until finely chopped. Add basil, pine nuts, lemon juice, and water and process until just puréed. (Note: You can substitute fresh parsley for basil; supplement flavor by adding some dried basil, too, if you do.) Add olive oil and 3 tablespoons of Parmesan cheese; pulse until pesto is smooth, occasionally scraping down side of bowl, if necessary. Set aside.

2. Cook pasta according to package directions. While it is cooking, flake trout. When pasta is cooked, pulse pesto to ensure it has remained blended, then toss pesto and trout with pasta in a large bowl. Sprinkle remaining Parmesan and some pepper on top of each serving. (Although this recipe uses heart-healthy extra-virgin olive oil, it is a little higher in fat but still low in calories. Consult your dietitian if you have any question whether you should include this recipe in your meal plans.)

Baked Fillet of Sole with Shrimp Sauce and Artichokes

PER SERVING: Calories: 332 | Protein: 42g | Carbohydrates: 33g | Fat: 4g | Saturated Fat: 1g | Cholesterol: 108mg
Sodium: 623mg | Fiber: 8g | PCF Ratio: 50-39-11 | Exchange Approx.: 1 Starch, 3½ Vegetables, 4½ Lean Meats

INGREDIENTS | SERVES 2

5 medium shrimp, cooked

1 shallot, chopped

¼ cup low-fat mayonnaise

¼ teaspoon dried dill

2 tablespoons orange juice

1 (9-ounce) package frozen artichoke hearts

2 (6-ounce) sole fillets

Nonstick cooking spray, as needed

Salt and pepper, to taste

4 tablespoons fine bread crumbs

1. Preheat oven to 375°F. In a blender, pulse the shrimp, shallot, mayonnaise, dill, and orange juice. Set the sauce aside.

2. Cook the frozen artichokes according to package directions. Place sole on a baking sheet prepared with nonstick cooking spray. Sprinkle the fillets with salt and pepper. Arrange the artichokes around the sole. Spoon sauce over all. Sprinkle with bread crumbs.

3. Bake for 15 minutes, or until the sole is hot and bubbling and the artichokes are crisply browned on top.

Artichokes

Artichokes are thistle-like plants, and the part we eat is actually the immature flower head. There are many varieties, but the type commonly available in the United States (usually in markets November through May) are globe artichokes. The soft heart or center of the artichoke can be eaten raw or cooked sprinkled with olive oil, salt, and pepper.

Asian Sesame-Crusted Scallops

PER SERVING: Calories: 386 | Protein: 27g | Carbohydrates: 15g | Fat: 25g | Saturated Fat: 4g | Cholesterol: 143mg
Sodium: 703mg | Fiber: 3g | PCF Ratio: 27-15-58 | Exchange Approx.: 1 Vegetable, 3½ Lean Meats, 4 Fats

INGREDIENTS | SERVES 2

2 cups shredded napa cabbage

1 large ripe tomato, sliced

1 tablespoon soy sauce

1 tablespoon sesame oil

Juice of ½ lime

1" fresh gingerroot, peeled and minced

½ pound diver scallops, each weighing 1+ ounces (3–4 per person)

1 egg, beaten

¼ cup sesame seeds

1 tablespoon peanut oil

Salt and pepper, to taste

1. Make beds on 2 serving plates with the cabbage and the tomatoes.

2. In a small bowl, mix together the soy sauce, sesame oil, lime juice, and minced ginger to create sauce. Set aside.

3. Rinse the scallops and pat them dry on paper towels. Dip scallops in beaten egg. Spread sesame seeds on waxed paper, and roll scallops in them to cover.

4. Heat the peanut oil in a nonstick frying pan. Sear the scallops over medium heat until browned on both sides and heated through. Do not overcook, or they will get tough. Arrange the scallops over the greens and tomatoes; add salt and pepper. Drizzle with the prepared sauce.

Stir-Fried Ginger Scallops with Vegetables

PER SERVING: Calories: 145 | Protein: 22g | Carbohydrates: 8g | Fat: 3g | Saturated Fat: 1g | Cholesterol: 37mg
Sodium: 373mg | Fiber: 2g | PCF Ratio: 61-23-16 | Exchange Approx.: 3 Very-Lean Meats, ½ Vegetable

INGREDIENTS | SERVES 4

1 pound scallops

1 teaspoon peanut or sesame oil

1 tablespoon chopped fresh ginger

2 cloves garlic, minced

4 scallions, thinly sliced (optional)

1 teaspoon rice wine vinegar

2 teaspoons Bragg's Liquid Aminos

½ cup low-fat, reduced-sodium chicken broth

2 cups broccoli florets

1 teaspoon cornstarch

¼ teaspoon toasted sesame oil

1. Rinse scallops and pat dry between layers of paper towels. If necessary, slice scallops so they're uniform in size. Set aside.

2. Add peanut oil to heated nonstick deep skillet or wok; sauté ginger, garlic, and scallions if using, 1–2 minutes, being careful ginger doesn't burn. Add vinegar, Liquid Aminos, and broth; bring to a boil. Remove from heat.

3. Place broccoli in large, covered, microwave-safe dish; pour chicken-broth mixture over top. Microwave on high for 3–5 minutes, depending on preference. (Keep in mind that vegetables will continue to steam for a minute or so if cover remains on dish.)

4. Heat skillet or wok over medium-high temperature. Add scallops; sauté 1 minute on each side. (Do scallops in batches if necessary; be careful not to overcook.) Remove scallops from pan when done; set aside. Drain (but do not discard) liquid from broccoli; return liquid to bowl and transfer broccoli to heated skillet or wok. Stir-fry vegetables to bring up to serving temperature.

5. Meanwhile, in small cup or bowl, add enough water to cornstarch to make a slurry or roux. Whisk slurry into reserved broccoli liquid; microwave on high 1 minute. Add toasted sesame oil; whisk again. Pour thickened broth mixture over broccoli; toss to mix. Add scallops back to broccoli mixture; stir-fry over medium heat to return scallops to serving temperature. Serve over rice or pasta; adjust Exchange Approximations accordingly.

Sesame Shrimp and Asparagus

PER SERVING: Calories: 257 | Protein: 28g | Carbohydrates: 23g | Fat: 6g | Saturated Fat: 1g | Cholesterol: 172mg
Sodium: 173mg | Fiber: 3g | PCF Ratio: 44-35-21 | Exchange Approx.: 3 Very-Lean Meats, ½ Vegetable, 1 Starch

INGREDIENTS | SERVES 4

2 teaspoons canola oil

2 cloves garlic, chopped

1 tablespoon grated fresh ginger

1 pound medium shrimp

2 tablespoons dry white wine

½ pound asparagus, cut diagonally into 1" pieces

2 cups cooked whole-grain pasta

½ teaspoon sesame seeds

¼ cup thinly sliced scallions

1 teaspoon sesame oil

1. Heat oil in wok or large nonstick skillet. Stir-fry garlic, ginger, and shrimp over high heat until shrimp begins to turn pink, about 2 minutes.

2. Add white wine and asparagus; stir fry an additional 3–5 minutes.

3. Add pasta, sesame seeds, scallions, and sesame oil; toss lightly and serve.

Garlic Shrimp with Bok Choy

PER SERVING: Calories: 291 | Protein: 29g | Carbohydrates: 25g | Fat: 10g | Saturated Fat: 1g | Cholesterol: 172mg
Sodium: 730mg | Fiber: 5g | PCF Ratio: 39-33-28 | Exchange Approx.: 5 Vegetables, 3 Lean Meats, 1 Fat

INGREDIENTS | SERVES 2

1 tablespoon sesame oil

3 cloves garlic, chopped

1 tablespoon grated fresh ginger

1 pound bok choy

1 cup broccoli florets

1 pound shrimp, peeled and deveined

2 tablespoons low-sodium soy sauce

1. Heat oil in a pan or wok over medium-high heat. Add garlic and ginger, stir, and cook for 30 seconds.

2. Turn heat up to high. Add bok choy and broccoli and stir-fry for 2–3 minutes. Add shrimp and continue stirring.

3. Add soy sauce and cook until shrimp are pink and completely done.

Bok Choy

Bok choy is a Chinese cabbage that is staggeringly simple to prepare and is rich in many important nutrients including vitamin A, vitamin C, and folate.

Creamy Shrimp Pie with Rice Crust

PER SERVING: Calories: 273 | Protein: 26g | Carbohydrates: 27g | Fat: 6g | Saturated Fat: 2g | Cholesterol: 180mg Sodium: 172mg | Fiber: 2g | PCF Ratio: 39-40-21 | Exchange Approx.: 2 Very-Lean Meats, 2 Starches, 1 Fat

INGREDIENTS | SERVES 4

1⅓ cups cooked white rice

2 teaspoons dried parsley

2 tablespoons grated onion

1 teaspoon olive oil

1 tablespoon butter

1 clove garlic, crushed

1 pound shrimp, peeled and deveined

1 recipe Condensed Cream of Mushroom Soup (see recipe in Chapter 8)

1 teaspoon lemon juice

1 cup sliced mushrooms, steamed

Fat-Free Flavor

To add the flavor of sautéed mushrooms or onions without the added fat of butter or oil, roast or grill them first. Simply spread them on a baking sheet treated with non-stick cooking spray. Roasting for 5 minutes in a 350°F oven will be sufficient if the vegetables are sliced, and will not add additional cooking time to the recipe.

1. Preheat oven to 350°F.

2. In a large bowl, combine rice, parsley, and onion; mix well. Use olive oil to coat 10" pie plate and press rice mixture evenly around sides and bottom. This works best if the rice is moist; if necessary, add 1 teaspoon of water.

3. Melt butter in deep, nonstick skillet over medium heat. Add the garlic and sauté. Add shrimp; cook, stirring frequently, until pink, about 5 minutes.

4. Add soup and lemon juice to skillet; stir until smooth and thoroughly heated, about 5 minutes. (If the soup seems too thick, add some water, 1 teaspoon at a time.) Stir mushrooms into soup mixture; pour over rice "crust." Bake for 30 minutes, or until lightly browned on top. Serve hot.

Scallops and Shrimp with White-Bean Sauce

PER SERVING: Calories: 231 | Protein: 27g | Carbohydrates: 18g | Fat: 4g | Saturated Fat: 1g | Cholesterol: 105mg
Sodium: 217mg | Fiber: 7g | PCF Ratio: 49-34-17 | Exchange Approx.: 3 Very-Lean Meats, ½ Fat, 1 Starch, ½ Vegetable

INGREDIENTS | SERVES 4

½ cup finely chopped onion, steamed

2 cloves garlic, minced

2 teaspoons olive oil, divided

¼ cup dry white wine

¼ cup tightly packed fresh parsley leaves

¼ cup tightly packed fresh basil leaves

1⅓ cups canned cannellini (white) beans, drained and rinsed, divided

¼ cup low-fat, reduced-sodium chicken broth

8 ounces shrimp, shelled and deveined

8 ounces scallops

1. In nonstick saucepan, sauté onion and garlic in 1 teaspoon of oil over low heat, for about 5 minutes until onion is soft. Add wine; simmer until wine is reduced by ½. Add parsley, basil, ⅓ cup of beans, and chicken broth; simmer, stirring constantly for 1 minute.

2. Transfer bean mixture to blender or food processor and purée. Pour purée back into saucepan; add remaining beans and simmer for 2 minutes.

3. In nonstick skillet, heat remaining 1 teaspoon of oil over medium-high heat until it is hot but not smoking. Sauté shrimp for 2 minutes on each side, or until cooked through. Using slotted spoon, transfer shrimp to plate; cover to keep warm. Add scallops to skillet; sauté 1 minute on each side, or until cooked through. To serve, divide bean sauce between 4 shallow bowls and arrange shellfish over top.

Lemon-Garlic Shrimp and Vegetables

PER SERVING: Calories: 183 | Protein: 26g | Carbohydrates: 10g | Fat: 5g | Saturated Fat: 1g | Cholesterol: 172mg
Sodium: 744mg | Fiber: 3g | PCF Ratio: 56-22-22 | Exchange Approx.: 2 Vegetables, 3½ Lean Meats

INGREDIENTS | SERVES 2

2 tablespoons low-sodium soy sauce

1 teaspoon lemon zest

1½ tablespoons lemon juice

½ teaspoon agave nectar

½ cup water

Black pepper, to taste

Nonstick cooking spray, as needed

1 stalk celery, sliced

1 cup shredded red cabbage

½ red bell pepper, thinly sliced

3 cloves garlic, chopped

½ cup bean sprouts

1 teaspoon sesame oil

½ pound raw shrimp, peeled and deveined

1. In a small bowl, mix soy sauce, lemon zest, lemon juice, agave nectar, water, and pepper. Set aside.

2. Spray a large frying pan with nonstick cooking spray. Place pan over medium heat.

3. Add celery and cabbage to the pan and sauté for 1 minute. Add bell pepper, garlic, and bean sprouts, and sauté until all vegetables are crisp-tender. Transfer vegetables to a plate and cover.

4. Add oil to the pan, and once oil is hot, place shrimp in the hot pan and cook until opaque. Return vegetables to the pan with the cooked shrimp.

5. Pour soy-sauce mixture over the shrimp and vegetables and cook for 3–4 minutes, until sauce has reduced.

Fresh Tomato and Clam Sauce with Whole-Grain Linguini

PER SERVING: Calories: 361 | Protein: 13g | Carbohydrates: 60g | Fat: 8g | Saturated Fat: 1g | Cholesterol: 7mg
Sodium: 356mg | Fiber: 8g | PCF Ratio: 14-66-20 | Exchange Approx.: 2½ Starches, 1½ Very-Lean Meats, 3 Vegetables, 1½ Fats

INGREDIENTS | SERVES 4

3 dozen littleneck clams

2 tablespoons olive oil

5 cloves garlic, chopped

½ cup chopped red bell pepper

4 cups peeled and chopped fresh tomatoes

3 tablespoons chopped fresh parsley

1 tablespoon chopped fresh basil

¼ teaspoon salt

¼ teaspoon red pepper flakes

½ teaspoon oregano

½ cup dry white wine

8 ounces uncooked whole-grain linguini

Tip

This recipe works well with canned clams if you are unable to get fresh. Canned clams are quite high in sodium, which will need to be taken into consideration. If using canned clams, you will need 1 (8-ounce) can of minced clams and 1 (10-ounce) can of whole clams. Reserve the clam juice and add to the sauce.

1. Before preparing this dish (preferably several hours or more), place clams in bowl of cold water with handful of cornmeal added; keep refrigerated. (This will help purge clams of any sand or other debris.) When ready to cook, rinse and scrub clams.

2. Heat olive oil, garlic, and red pepper in a deep skillet. Add chopped tomatoes, parsley, basil, salt, red pepper flakes, and oregano, bring to quick boil, then reduce heat and simmer for 15–20 minutes.

3. Stir in white wine; add clams on top of tomato sauce. Cover and steam until clams open. (Discard any clams that do not open; they are not suitable for eating.)

4. Meanwhile, boil water and cook pasta to al dente.

5. Serve tomato sauce and clams over pasta.

CHAPTER 8

Casseroles, Soups, and Stews

Condensed Cream of Chicken Soup

PER RECIPE: Calories: 158 | Protein: 4g | Carbohydrates: 35g | Fat: 1g | Saturated Fat: 0g | Cholesterol: 1mg
Sodium: 162mg | Fiber: 2g | PCF Ratio: 9-88-3 | Exchange Approx.: Will depend on serving size and preparation method

INGREDIENTS | MAKES EQUIVALENT OF 1 (10.75-OUNCE) CAN

1 cup water

¾ teaspoon Minor's Low-Sodium Chicken Base

¼ cup Ener-G potato flour

Place all ingredients in blender and process until well blended.

Chicken Broth Variation

You can make Condensed Cream of Chicken Soup with regular chicken broth instead of Minor's Base. For the equivalent of 1 (10.75-ounce) can of condensed chicken soup, blend 1 cup reduced-fat canned chicken broth with ¼ cup Ener-G potato flour. Will last, refrigerated, 3 days. Nutritional Analysis: Calories: 181.20; Protein: 61g; Carbohydrates: 314g; Fat: 1.50g; Saturated Fat: 0.42g; Cholesterol: 0.00mg; Sodium: 7820mg; Fiber: 36g; PCF Ratio: 17-76-7; Exchange Approx.: will depend on serving size and preparation method.

Condensed Cream of Celery Soup

PER RECIPE: Calories: 85 | Protein: 2g | Carbohydrates: 20g | Fat: 0g | Saturated Fat: 0g | Cholesterol: 0mg
Sodium: 79mg | Fiber: 2g | PCF Ratio: 9-89-2 | Exchange Approx.: Will depend on serving size and preparation method

INGREDIENTS | **MAKES EQUIVALENT OF 1
(10.75-OUNCE) CAN**

½ cup chopped celery

½ cup water

⅛ cup Ener-G potato flour

1. In a microwave-safe, covered container, microwave celery 2 minutes, or until tender. Do not drain any resulting liquid. If necessary, add enough water to bring celery and liquid to 1 cup total.

2. Place all ingredients in blender; process. Use immediately, or store in a covered container in refrigerator for use within 3 days. Thickness of concentrate will depend on how much moisture remains in celery; add 1–2 tablespoons of water, if necessary, to achieve a paste.

Condensed Cream of Potato Soup

PER RECIPE: Calories: 103 | Protein: 2g | Carbohydrates: 24g | Fat: 0g | Saturated Fat: 0g | Cholesterol: 0mg | Sodium: 9mg
Fiber: 2g | PCF Ratio: 8-91-1 | Exchange Approx.: Will depend on serving size and preparation method

INGREDIENTS | **MAKES EQUIVALENT OF 1
(10.75-OUNCE) CAN**

½ cup peeled, diced potatoes

½ cup water

1 tablespoon Ener-G potato flour

Tip

The nutrition information for this recipe assumes you'll use the entire tablespoon of Ener-G potato flour; however, the amount needed will depend on the amount of starch in the potatoes you use. For example, new potatoes will require more Ener-G potato flour than larger Idaho potatoes.

1. Place potatoes and water in covered microwave-safe bowl; microwave on high for 4–5 minutes, until potatoes are fork-tender.

2. Pour potatoes and water in blender, being careful of steam. Remove vent from blender lid; process until smooth. Add Ener-G 1 teaspoon at a time while blender is running.

Condensed Cheese Soup

PER RECIPE: Calories: 315 | Protein: 20g | Carbohydrates: 18g | Fat: 18g | Saturated Fat: 11g | Cholesterol: 56mg | Sodium: 384mg | Fiber: 1g | PCF Ratio: 26-23-51 | Exchange Approx.: Will depend on serving size and preparation method

INGREDIENTS | MAKES EQUIVALENT OF 1 (10.75-OUNCE) CAN

½ cup water

⅛ cup Ener-G potato flour

¼ cup nonfat cottage cheese

2 ounces American, Cheddar, or Colby cheese, shredded (to yield ½ cup)

1. Place water, potato flour, and cottage cheese in a blender and process until well blended.

2. Stir in shredded cheese. Cheese will melt as casserole is baked, prepared in microwave, or cooked on stovetop according to recipe instructions.

Be Aware of Your Exchanges

When using any soup preparation method, you'll need to add the appropriate Exchange Approximations for each serving amount (usually ¼ of the total) of whatever condensed soup you make. For example, broth-based soups like chicken and cream of mushroom or celery would be a Free Exchange; cream of potato soup would add 1 Carbohydrate/Starch.

Condensed Cream of Mushroom Soup

PER RECIPE: Calories: 92 | Protein: 3g | Carbohydrates: 21g | Fat: 1g | Saturated Fat: 0g | Cholesterol: 0mg | Sodium: 13mg
Fiber: 3g | PCF Ratio: 12-84-4 | Exchange Approx.: Will depend on serving size and preparation method

INGREDIENTS | MAKES EQUIVALENT OF 1 (10.75-OUNCE) CAN

¾ cup finely chopped fresh mushrooms
Optional ingredients:
    1 teaspoon chopped onion
    1 tablespoon chopped celery
½ cup water
⅛ cup Ener-G potato flour

Potato Flour Substitute?

Instant mashed potatoes can replace potato flour; however, the amount needed will vary according to the brand of potatoes. Also, you'll need to consider other factors such as added fats and hydrogenated oils.

1. In a microwave-safe, covered container, microwave mushrooms (and onion and celery, if using) for 2 minutes, or until tender. (About ¾ cup chopped mushrooms will yield ½ cup steamed ones.) Reserve any resulting liquid; add enough water to equal 1 cup.

2. Place all ingredients in a blender and process. The thickness of soup concentrate will vary according to how much moisture remains in mushrooms. If necessary, add 1–2 tablespoons of water to achieve a paste. (Low-sodium canned mushrooms work in this recipe, but the nutritional analysis assumes fresh mushrooms are used. Adjust sodium content accordingly.)

Condensed Tomato Soup

PER SERVING: Calories: 136 | Protein: 4g | Carbohydrates: 31g | Fat: 1g | Saturated Fat: 0g | Cholesterol: 0mg
Sodium: 352mg | Fiber: 4g | PCF Ratio: 11-83-6 | Exchange Approx.: Will depend on serving size and preparation method

INGREDIENTS | MAKES EQUIVALENT OF 1 (10.75-OUNCE) CAN

1 cup peeled and chopped tomatoes, with juice

¼ teaspoon baking soda

⅛ cup Ener-G potato flour

Direct Preparation

If you'll be making the soup immediately after you prepare the condensed-soup recipe, you can simply add your choice of the additional 1 cup of liquid (such as skim milk, soy milk, or water) to the blender and use that method to mix the milk and soup concentrate together. Pour the combined mixture into your pan or microwave-safe dish.

1. Place tomato in microwave-safe bowl and microwave on high for 2–3 minutes, until tomato is cooked. Add additional tomato juices if necessary to bring mixture back up to 1 cup.

2. Add baking soda; stir vigorously until bubbling stops.

3. Pour cooked tomato mixture into blender; add potato flour, 1 tablespoon at a time, processing until well blended.

Soup Preparation Method

PER SERVING, SKIM MILK: Additional Calories: 21 | **Protein:** 2g | **Carbohydrates:** 3g | **Fat:** 0g | **Saturated Fat:** 0g
Cholesterol: 1mg | **Sodium:** 32mg | **Fiber:** 0g | **PCF Ratio:** 39-56-5 | **Exchange Approx.:** 1 Low-Fat Milk for entire pot of soup; divide accordingly per serving

INGREDIENTS | SERVES 4

Any previous condensed soup recipe

1 cup skim milk (or soy milk or water)

1. To use any of the homemade condensed soup recipes as soup, combine 1 recipe of the soup of choice and 1 cup of skim milk (or soy milk or water) in a saucepan. Stir using a spoon or whisk to blend. Cook over medium heat for 10 minutes until mixture begins to simmer.

2. Season according to taste.

Main Dish Pork and Beans

PER SERVING: Calories: 153 | **Protein:** 11g | **Carbohydrates:** 24g | **Fat:** 2g | **Saturated Fat:** 1g | **Cholesterol:** 18mg
Sodium: 146mg | **Fiber:** 5g | **PCF Ratio:** 29-61-10 | **Exchange Approx.:** 2 Lean Meats, ½ Fruit/Misc. Carbohydrate

INGREDIENTS | SERVES 4

1⅓ cups cooked pinto beans

2 tablespoons ketchup

¼ teaspoon Dijon mustard

¼ teaspoon dry mustard

1 teaspoon cider vinegar

4 tablespoons diced red onion

1 tablespoon 100% pure maple syrup

1 teaspoon brown sugar

4 ounces slow-cooked shredded pork

2 tablespoons apple juice or cider

1. Preheat oven to 350°F. In a casserole dish treated with nonstick cooking spray, combine beans, ketchup, Dijon mustard, dry mustard, vinegar, onion, syrup, and brown sugar.

2. Layer meat over top of bean mixture. Pour apple juice or cider over pork. Bake for 20–30 minutes, or until mixture is well heated and bubbling. Stir well before serving.

Eggplant and Tomato Stew

PER SERVING: Calories: 135 | Protein: 4g | Carbohydrates: 26g | Fat: 3g | Saturated Fat: 1g | Cholesterol: 0mg
Sodium: 22mg | Fiber: 9g | PCF Ratio: 12-69-19 | Exchange Approx.: ½ Fat, 4 Vegetables

INGREDIENTS | SERVES 4

2 eggplants, trimmed but left whole

2 teaspoons olive oil

1 medium Spanish onion, chopped

1 teaspoon chopped garlic

2 cups chopped, unsalted tomatoes (cooked or canned), with liquid

Optional seasonings, to taste:

    Hot pepper sauce

    Ketchup

    Plain, nonfat yogurt

    Fresh parsley sprigs

1. Preheat oven to 400°F.

2. Roast eggplants on baking sheet until soft, about 45 minutes. Scoop out and remove all "meat" from eggplants.

3. In large sauté pan, heat oil. Add the onions and garlic and sauté for 2–3 minutes or until translucent. Add eggplant meat and all other ingredients, except yogurt and parsley. Remove from heat and transfer to food processor; pulse until it becomes creamy.

4. Serve at room temperature, garnished with a dollop of yogurt and parsley, if desired.

Ham and Artichoke Hearts Scalloped Potatoes

PER SERVING, WITHOUT SALT: Calories: 269 | **Protein:** 21g | **Carbohydrates:** 31g | **Fat:** 8g | **Saturated Fat:** 4g | **Cholesterol:** 28mg **Sodium:** 762mg | **Fiber:** 6g | **PCF Ratio:** 31-44-25 | **Exchange Approx.:** 1½ Lean Meats, ½ High-Fat Meat, 1½ Vegetables, 1 Starch

INGREDIENTS | SERVES 4

2 cups frozen artichoke hearts

1 cup chopped onion

4 small potatoes, thinly sliced

Sea salt and freshly ground black pepper, to taste (optional)

1 tablespoon lemon juice

1 tablespoon dry white wine

1 cup Mock Cream (see recipe in Chapter 12)

½ cup nonfat cottage cheese

1 teaspoon dried parsley

1 teaspoon garlic powder

⅛ cup freshly grated Parmesan cheese

4 ounces lean ham, cubed

2 ounces Cheddar cheese, grated (to yield ½ cup)

Simple Substitutions

Artichoke hearts can be expensive. You can substitute cabbage, broccoli, or cauliflower (or a mixture of all 3) for the artichokes in this recipe.

1. Preheat oven to 300°F. Thaw artichoke hearts and pat dry with a paper towel.

2. In a deep casserole dish treated with nonstick cooking spray, layer artichokes, onion, and potatoes; lightly sprinkle salt and pepper over top (if using).

3. In a food processor or blender, combine lemon juice, wine, Mock Cream, cottage cheese, parsley, garlic powder, and Parmesan cheese and process until smooth. Pour over layered vegetables and top with ham.

4. Cover casserole dish (with a lid or foil) and bake for 35–40 minutes, or until potatoes are cooked through.

5. Remove cover; top with Cheddar cheese. Return to oven another 10 minutes, or until cheese is melted and bubbly. Let rest 10 minutes before cutting.

Hearty Beef Stew

PER SERVING: Calories: 326 | Protein: 26g | Carbohydrates: 32g | Fat: 10g | Saturated Fat: 3g | Cholesterol: 88mg
Sodium: 335mg | Fiber: 4g | PCF Ratio: 32-39-28 | Exchange Approx.: 3 Lean Meats, 1 Starch, 3 Vegetables

INGREDIENTS | SERVES 4

1 tablespoon olive oil

12 ounces beef round, cut into 1" cubes

1 cup chopped onion

2 cups chopped (1" pieces) potatoes

½ cup peeled and chopped (1" pieces) carrots

1 cup green beans

½ cup peeled and chopped (1" pieces) turnip

1 tablespoon parsley

¼ teaspoon Tabasco Sauce

1 cup low-sodium V8 juice

¼ teaspoon salt

1 tablespoon all-purpose flour

¼ cup water

1. Heat olive oil in pressure cooker and brown meat. Add onions, potatoes, carrots, green beans, turnip, parsley, Tabasco, V8, and salt.

2. Close cover securely; place pressure regulator on vent pipe and cook for 10–12 minutes with pressure regulator rocking slowly (or follow manufacturer instructions for your pressure cooker). Cool down pressure cooker at once (nonelectric pressure cookers).

3. If desired, make paste of 1 tablespoon flour and ¼ cup water; stir into stew to thicken. Heat and stir liquid until thickened.

Slow-Cook Method for Beef Stew

If you don't have a pressure cooker, you can make this in a slow cooker. First, heat olive oil in a skillet. Dredge meat in 1–2 tablespoons flour; add to skillet and brown. Transfer to slow cooker; add onions, potatoes, carrots, green beans, turnip, parsley, Tabasco, V8, and salt. Cook on low-medium 4–6 hours.

Easy Oven Beef Burgundy

PER SERVING: Calories: 266 | Protein: 34g | Carbohydrates: 12g | Fat: 6g | Saturated Fat: 2g | Cholesterol: 82mg
Sodium: 388mg | Fiber: 2g | PCF Ratio: 56-20-23 | Exchange Approx.: 4 Lean Meats, 2 Vegetables, 1 Fat

INGREDIENTS | SERVES 4

1 pound beef round, cubed
2 tablespoons all-purpose flour
1 cup sliced carrots
1 cup chopped onions
1 cup sliced celery
1 clove garlic, finely chopped
¼ teaspoon pepper
¼ teaspoon marjoram
¼ teaspoon thyme
½ teaspoon salt
2 tablespoons balsamic vinegar
½ cup dry red wine
½ cup water
1 cup sliced fresh mushrooms

1. Preheat oven to 325°F.

2. Dredge meat cubes in flour; place in 3-quart, covered baking dish or Dutch oven. Add carrots, onions, celery, garlic, pepper, marjoram, thyme, salt, and vinegar and stir to combine.

3. Pour red wine and water over mixture. Cover and bake for 1 hour.

4. Remove from oven and mix in mushrooms.

5. Return to oven for 1 hour, or until beef cubes are tender.

Chicken and Mushroom Rice Casserole

PER SERVING: Calories: 165 | Protein: 9g | Carbohydrates: 30g | Fat: 1g | Saturated Fat: 0g | Cholesterol: 15mg
Sodium: 41mg | Fiber: 3g | PCF Ratio: 23-71-6 | Exchange Approx.: 1 Very-Lean Meat, 1 Starch, 1 Vegetable

INGREDIENTS | SERVES 8

1 recipe Condensed Cream of Chicken Soup (see recipe in this chapter)

1 cup diced chicken breast

1 large onion, chopped

½ cup chopped celery

1 cup uncooked rice (not instant rice)

Freshly ground black pepper, to taste (optional)

1 teaspoon dried Herbes de Provence (see recipe in Chapter 15) (optional)

2 cups boiling water

2½ cups chopped broccoli florets

1 cup sliced fresh mushrooms

1. Preheat oven to 350°F.

2. In 4-quart casserole dish (large enough to prevent boil-overs in oven) treated with nonstick cooking spray, combine condensed soup, chicken breast, onion, celery, rice, and seasonings; mix well. Pour boiling water over top and bake, covered, for 30 minutes.

3. Stir casserole; add broccoli and mushrooms. Replace cover; return to oven to bake additional 20–30 minutes, or until celery is tender and rice has absorbed all liquid.

Traditional Stovetop Tuna-Noodle Casserole

PER SERVING: Calories: 245 | Protein: 20g | Carbohydrates: 33g | Fat: 4g | Saturated Fat: 2g | Cholesterol: 46mg
Sodium: 241mg | Fiber: 4g | PCF Ratio: 32-53-15 | Exchange Approx.: 1½ Starches, 1 Vegetable, 1 Medium-Fat Meat

INGREDIENTS | SERVES 4

1⅓ cups uncooked egg noodles

1 recipe Condensed Cream of Mushroom Soup (see recipe in this chapter)

1 teaspoon steamed chopped onion

1 tablespoon steamed chopped celery

½ cup skim milk

1 ounce American, Cheddar, or Colby cheese, shredded (to yield ¼ cup)

1 cup frozen mixed peas and carrots

1 cup steamed sliced fresh mushrooms

1 (6-ounce) can water-packed tuna, drained

1. Cook egg noodles according to package directions. Drain and return to pan.

2. Add all remaining ingredients to pan; stir to blend. Cook over medium heat, stirring occasionally, until cheese is melted. (The nutritional analysis for this recipe assumes egg noodles were cooked without salt.)

Extra-Rich Stovetop Tuna-Noodle Casserole

Add 1 medium egg (beaten) and 1 tablespoon mayonnaise to give the casserole a taste of rich, homemade egg noodles, while still maintaining a good fat ratio. It's still less than 300 calories per serving, too! Nutritional Analysis: Calories: 275; Protein: 21g; Carbohydrates: 34g; Fat: 7g; Saturated Fat: 2g; Cholesterol: 94mg; Sodium: 281mg; Fiber: 4g; PCF Ratio: 30-48-21; Exchange Approx.: 1½ Breads, 1 Vegetable, 1 Meat, 1 Medium-Fat Meat.

Shrimp Microwave Casserole

PER SERVING: Calories: 196 | Protein: 18g | Carbohydrates: 27g | Fat: 2g | Saturated Fat: 1g | Cholesterol: 131mg
Sodium: 290mg | Fiber: 2g | PCF Ratio: 35-56-9 | Exchange Approx.: 1 Starch, 1 Vegetable, 1 Medium-Fat Meat

INGREDIENTS | SERVES 4

1⅓ cups uncooked egg noodles

1 cup chopped green onion

1 cup chopped green pepper

1 cup sliced mushrooms

1 recipe Condensed Cream of Celery Soup (see recipe in this chapter)

1 teaspoon Homemade Worcestershire Sauce (see recipe in Chapter 12)

4 drops Tabasco Sauce (optional)

¼ cup diced canned pimientos

½ cup pitted, chopped ripe olives

½ cup skimmed milk

½ pound cooked, deveined, shelled shrimp

1. Cook egg noodles according to package directions; drain and keep warm.

2. Place green onion and green pepper in covered microwave-safe dish; microwave on high for 1 minute. Add mushrooms; microwave another minute, or until all vegetables are tender.

3. Add soup, Worcestershire sauce, Tabasco (if using), pimientos, olives, and milk and stir well. Microwave, covered, for 1–2 minutes, until mixture is hot and bubbly.

4. Add cooked shrimp and noodles and stir to mix. Microwave for 30 seconds to 1 minute, or until mixture is hot.

CHAPTER 9
Pasta, Rice, Grains, and Beans

Quick Tomato Sauce

PER SERVING, WITHOUT SALT: Calories: 40 | Protein: 1g | Carbohydrates: 6g | Fat: 2g | Saturated Fat: 0g | Cholesterol: 0mg
Sodium: 10mg | Fiber: 1g | PCF Ratio: 9-49-42 | Exchange Approx.: 1 Vegetable, ½ Fat

INGREDIENTS | SERVES 8

2 pounds very ripe tomatoes

2 tablespoons extra-virgin olive oil

2 cloves garlic, minced

½ teaspoon ground cumin

2 large sprigs fresh thyme or ½ teaspoon dried

1 bay leaf

Kosher or sea salt and freshly ground black pepper, to taste (optional)

3 tablespoons total chopped fresh basil, oregano, tarragon, and parsley or cilantro, or a combination of all the listed herbs, to taste. If using dried herbs, reduce the amount to 1 tablespoon.

1. Peel and seed tomatoes; chop with knife or food processor.

2. Heat large skillet over medium heat and add olive oil. Reduce heat to low, add the garlic and cumin, and sauté.

3. Add tomatoes, thyme, bay leaf, and salt and pepper, if using. If using dried herbs, add now. Simmer, uncovered, over medium heat for 8–10 minutes, stirring often; reduce heat to maintain a simmer, if necessary. Simmer until tomatoes are soft and sauce has thickened, about 30 minutes.

4. Discard bay leaf and thyme sprigs; adjust seasoning to taste.

Fresh Garden Tomato Sauce

PER SERVING: Calories: 154 | Protein: 6g | Carbohydrates: 26g | Fat: 5g | Saturated Fat: 1g | Cholesterol: 0mg
Sodium: 867mg | Fiber: 6g | PCF Ratio: 15-61-25 | Exchange Approx.: 5 Vegetables, 1 Fat

INGREDIENTS | SERVES 12

3 tablespoons olive oil

1 cup chopped celery

1 cup finely chopped onion

1 cup chopped green (or sweet red) pepper

2 cloves garlic, crushed

8 cups peeled and crushed fresh tomatoes

1 (5½-ounce) can tomato paste

1 cup grated zucchini

1 tablespoon chopped fresh oregano

1 tablespoon chopped fresh basil

½ teaspoon red pepper flakes

½ cup dry red wine

1. In large, heavy saucepan or Dutch oven, heat oil. Add celery, onion, and peppers and sauté for 5 minutes. Add crushed garlic; sauté additional 2 minutes.

2. Add crushed tomatoes, tomato paste, zucchini, oregano, basil, and red pepper flakes. Bring to a boil; reduce heat and simmer for 2–3 hours.

3. Add wine during last 30 minutes of cooking.

Basic Tomato Sauce

PER SERVING, WITHOUT SALT: Calories: 37 | Protein: 1g | Carbohydrates: 5g | Fat: 2g | Saturated Fat: 0g | Cholesterol: 0mg
Sodium: 9mg | Fiber: 1g | PCF Ratio: 9-55-36 | Exchange Approx.: 1½ Vegetables

INGREDIENTS | MAKES ABOUT 5 CUPS; SERVING SIZE: ¼ CUP

2 tablespoons olive oil

2 cups coarsely chopped yellow onion

½ cup sliced carrots

2 cloves garlic, minced

4 cups canned Italian plum tomatoes with juice

1 teaspoon dried oregano

1 teaspoon dried basil

¼ teaspoon sugar

Kosher or sea salt and freshly ground black pepper, to taste (optional)

Dash ground anise seed (optional)

1. Heat olive oil in large, deep skillet or saucepan over medium-high heat. Add onions, carrots, and garlic and sauté until onions are transparent. (For a richer-tasting sauce, allow onions to caramelize or reach a light golden brown.)

2. Purée tomatoes in food processor.

3. Add the puréed tomatoes, oregano, basil, and sugar to onion mixture along with salt, pepper, and anise, if using. Simmer, partially covered, for 45 minutes.

4. If you prefer a smoother sauce, process sauce in food processor again.

Culinary Antacids

Stir in 2 teaspoons Smucker's Low-Sugar Grape Jelly to tame hot chili or acidic sauces such as tomato sauce. You won't really notice the flavor of the jelly, and it will do a great job of reducing any tart, bitter, or acidic tastes in your sauce.

Grilled Vegetable Sauce for Spaghetti

PER SERVING (INCLUDING PASTA): Calories: 289 | Protein: 5g | Carbohydrates: 42g | Fat: 12g | Saturated Fat: 2g |
Cholesterol: 0mg | Sodium: 271mg | Fiber: 9g | PCF Ratio: 7-57-36 | Exchange Approx.: 2 Starches, 2 Vegetables, 2 Fats

INGREDIENTS | SERVES 4

2 baby eggplants, stemmed and sliced in ⅓" coins

1 medium zucchini, stem removed and cut lengthwise in ⅓" pieces

1 yellow bell pepper, stemmed, seeded, and cut in quarters

4 medium tomatoes, halved

¼ cup Balsamic Vinaigrette and Marinade (see Chapter 12)

1 pound your favorite pasta

2 tablespoons extra-virgin olive oil

4 cloves garlic, chopped

8 fresh basil leaves, torn

Salt and pepper, to taste

Parmesan cheese, for garnish

1. Set the grill on high. Brush the eggplant, zucchini, bell pepper, and tomatoes with the balsamic vinaigrette. Grill until just done, about 3 minutes per side. Grill tomatoes on a piece of aluminum foil.

2. Cook the pasta according to package directions.

3. In a large frying pan, heat the olive oil and sauté the garlic over medium heat. Coarsely chop the grilled vegetables and add to the sautéed garlic.

4. Stir in the basil, salt, and pepper. Drain the pasta, move to a serving bowl, and stir in the vegetables. Garnish with extra pepper and plenty of Parmesan cheese.

Handling Cooked Pasta

Many chefs undercook pasta slightly and add it to the sauce in the pan. This way, the pasta absorbs flavors from the sauce. Remember that if you put pasta into a hot pan of sauce, it will continue to cook—be careful not to overcook and end up with mush!

White Bean, Tomato, and Zucchini Sauce for Polenta or Pasta

PER SERVING (SAUCE ONLY): Calories: 296 | Protein: 12g | Carbohydrates: 32g | Fat: 14g | Saturated Fat: 2g | Cholesterol: 0mg | Sodium: 104mg | Fiber: 8g | PCF Ratio: 16-43-41 | Exchange Approx.: 2 Starches, 1 Vegetable, 2 Fats

INGREDIENTS | SERVES 4

1 pound pasta, or 1 recipe Basic Polenta with Butter and Cheese (see recipe in this chapter)

¼ cup olive oil

3 cloves garlic, minced

1 medium zucchini, trimmed and diced

½ cup chopped sweet onions

1 tablespoon dried rosemary or 2 tablespoons fresh

2 cups crushed or chopped tomatoes (canned are fine)

1 (15-ounce) can large white beans, drained and rinsed

1 teaspoon dried oregano

6 fresh basil leaves, torn

¼ cup beef broth

Salt and pepper, to taste

Chopped fresh parsley, for garnish

1. Cook the pasta or polenta.

2. In a large frying pan over medium heat, add olive oil and sauté garlic, zucchini, and onions. When softened, add the rest of the ingredients except polenta or pasta and parsley. Cover, reduce heat, and simmer for 15–20 minutes.

3. Spoon sauce over polenta or pasta. Garnish with parsley.

Polenta Possibilities

Polenta can be made into different consistencies depending on the purpose you would like it to serve in your meal. Using less water, you can make polenta the consistency of cornbread and grill it, or you can add more water to make thinner polenta that you treat like pasta and serve with sauce, meat, or cheese.

Tuscan Pasta Fagioli

PER SERVING: Calories: 317 | Protein: 15g | Carbohydrates: 54g | Fat: 6g | Saturated Fat: 1g | Cholesterol: 2mg
Sodium: 248mg | Fiber: 11g | PCF Ratio: 18-65-17 | Exchange Approx.: 3 Starches, ½ Vegetable, 1 Fat

INGREDIENTS | SERVES 6

2 tablespoons olive oil

⅓ cup chopped onion

3 cloves garlic, minced

½ pound tomatoes, peeled and chopped

5 cups low-sodium vegetable stock

¼ teaspoon freshly ground pepper

3 cups canned cannellini beans, rinsed and drained, divided

2½ cups whole-grain pasta shells

2 tablespoons Parmesan cheese

1. Heat olive oil in large pot; gently cook onions and garlic until soft but not browned. Add tomatoes, vegetable stock, and pepper.

2. In a food processor or blender, purée 1½ cups of cannellini beans; add to stock mixture. Cover and simmer for 20–30 minutes.

3. While stock is simmering, cook pasta until al dente; drain.

4. Add remaining beans and pasta to stock; heat through. Serve with Parmesan cheese.

Whole-Grain Noodles with Caraway Cabbage

PER SERVING: Calories: 169 | Protein: 6g | Carbohydrates: 27g | Fat: 5g | Saturated Fat: 1g | Cholesterol: 0mg
Sodium: 250mg | Fiber: 5g | PCF Ratio: 14-60-26 | Exchange Approx.: 1 Starch, 1 Vegetable, 1 Fat

INGREDIENTS | SERVES 6

2 tablespoons olive oil

½ cup chopped onion

2 cups coarsely chopped cabbage

1½ cups trimmed and halved Brussels sprouts

2 teaspoons caraway seed

1½ cups low-sodium chicken broth

¼ teaspoon freshly ground pepper

¼ teaspoon salt

6 ounces uncooked whole-grain noodles

1. Heat olive oil in large saucepan; sauté onions for about 5 minutes until translucent.

2. Add cabbage and Brussels sprouts; cook over medium heat for 3 minutes.

3. Stir in caraway seed, broth, pepper, and salt. Cover and simmer for 5–8 minutes, until vegetables are crisp-tender.

4. Cook noodles in boiling water until tender; drain.

5. Mix noodles and vegetables together in a large bowl and serve.

Fusion Lo Mein

PER SERVING: Calories: 126 | Protein: 5g | Carbohydrates: 26g | Fat: 1g | Saturated Fat: 0g | Cholesterol: 0mg
Sodium: 35mg | Fiber: 4g | PCF Ratio: 14-77-9 | Exchange Approx.: 1 Starch, 1 Vegetable, ½ Fruit

INGREDIENTS | SERVES 6

2 tablespoons rice vinegar

2 tablespoons thawed pineapple-orange juice concentrate

2 teaspoons minced shallots

2 teaspoons lemon juice

1 teaspoon cornstarch

1 teaspoon Worcestershire sauce (see recipe for homemade in Chapter 12)

1 teaspoon honey

2 cloves garlic, minced

1 teaspoon olive oil

¾ cup chopped green onions

1 cup diagonally sliced (¼" thick) carrots

1 cup julienned yellow bell pepper

1 cup julienned red bell pepper

3 cups small broccoli florets

1 cup fresh bean sprouts

1½ cups cooked pasta

1. In food processor or blender, combine vinegar, juice concentrate, shallots, lemon juice, cornstarch, Worcestershire, honey, and garlic and process until smooth.

2. Heat wok or large nonstick skillet over medium-high heat until hot and add olive oil. Add onions and stir-fry for 1 minute.

3. Add carrots, bell peppers, and broccoli and stir-fry for another minute. Cover pan and cook for 2 more minutes.

4. Add vinegar mixture and sprouts. Bring mixture to a boil; cook, uncovered, for 30 seconds, stirring constantly.

5. Add cooked pasta and toss to mix.

Roasted Butternut Squash Pasta

PER SERVING: Calories: 216 | Protein: 5g | Carbohydrates: 40g | Fat: 5g | Saturated Fat: 1g | Cholesterol: 0mg
Sodium: 8mg | Fiber: 2g | PCF Ratio: 9-70-21 | Exchange Approx.: 2 Starches, 1 Fat, ½ Vegetable

INGREDIENTS | SERVES 4

1 butternut squash

4 teaspoons extra-virgin olive oil

1 clove garlic, minced

1 cup chopped red onion

2 teaspoons red wine vinegar

¼ teaspoon dried oregano

2 cups cooked pasta

Freshly ground black pepper, to taste (optional)

Tip

For added flavor, use roasted instead of raw garlic. Roasting garlic causes it to caramelize, adding a natural sweetness.

1. Preheat oven to 400°F. Cut squash in half and scoop out seeds.

2. Using nonstick cooking spray, coat 1 side of 2 pieces of heavy-duty foil large enough to wrap squash halves. Wrap squash in foil; place on a baking sheet. Bake for 1 hour, or until tender.

3. Scoop out baked squash flesh and discard rind; rough-chop the squash.

4. Add olive oil, garlic, and onion to nonstick skillet and sauté for about 5 minutes until onion is transparent. (Alternatively, put oil, garlic, and onion in covered microwave-safe dish; microwave on high for 2–3 minutes.)

5. Remove pan from heat; stir in vinegar and oregano. Add squash; stir to coat in onion mixture. Add pasta and toss to mix. Season with freshly ground black pepper, if desired.

Pasta with Artichokes

PER SERVING: Calories: 308 | Protein: 10g | Carbohydrates: 47g | Fat: 9g | Saturated Fat: 2g | Cholesterol: 2mg
Sodium: 87mg | Fiber: 3g | PCF Ratio: 13-60-27 | Exchange Approx.: 1 Medium-Fat Meat, 2 Vegetables, 1 Starch, 2 Fats

INGREDIENTS | SERVES 4

1 (10-ounce) package frozen artichoke hearts

1¼ cups water

1 tablespoon lemon juice

4 teaspoons olive oil

2 cloves garlic, minced

¼ cup drained and chopped sun-dried tomatoes packed in oil

¼ teaspoon red pepper flakes

2 teaspoons dried parsley

2 cups cooked pasta

¼ cup grated Parmesan cheese

Freshly ground black pepper, to taste (optional)

1. Cook artichokes in water and lemon juice according to package directions. Drain, reserving ¼ cup of liquid. Cool artichokes and then cut them into quarters.

2. Heat olive oil in nonstick skillet over medium heat. Add garlic and sauté for 1 minute. Reduce heat to low. Stir in artichokes and tomatoes and simmer for 1 minute. Stir in reserved artichoke liquid, red pepper flakes, and parsley and simmer for 5 minutes.

3. Pour artichoke sauce over pasta in a large bowl; toss gently to coat. Sprinkle with cheese and top with pepper, if desired.

Tip

You can decrease amount of water to 3 tablespoons and add with artichokes and lemon juice to covered microwave-safe dish. Microwave according to package directions; reserve all liquid. This results in stronger lemon flavor, which compensates for lack of salt in recipe.

Whole-Wheat Couscous Salad

PER SERVING: Calories: 153 | **Protein:** 4g | **Carbohydrates:** 15g | **Fat:** 9g | **Saturated Fat:** 1g | **Cholesterol:** 0mg
Sodium: 85mg | **Fiber:** 2g | **PCF Ratio:** 9-38-52 | **Exchange Approx.:** 1 Starch, 2 Fats

INGREDIENTS | SERVES 8

1 cup low-sodium chicken broth

¼ cup dried currants

½ teaspoon ground cumin

¾ cup whole-wheat couscous

¼ cup olive oil

2 tablespoons lemon juice

1 cup chopped broccoli, steamed to crisp-tender

3 tablespoons pine nuts

1 tablespoon chopped fresh parsley

1. In a medium saucepan, combine chicken broth, currants, and cumin and bring to a boil. Remove from heat; stir in couscous. Cover and let sit until cool. Fluff couscous with fork 2–3 times during the cooling process.

2. In a small bowl, whisk together olive oil and lemon juice.

3. Add steamed broccoli and pine nuts to couscous. Pour oil and lemon juice over couscous; toss lightly. Garnish with chopped parsley.

Aren't Currants Just Small Raisins?

Dried currants may look like miniature raisins, but they are actually quite different. Currants are berries from a shrub, not a vine, and there are red and black varieties. Black currants are rich in phytonutrients and antioxidants. They have twice the potassium of bananas and four times the vitamin C of oranges!

Homemade Macaroni and Cheese

PER SERVING: Calories: 358 | Protein: 22g | Carbohydrates: 39g | Fat: 13g | Saturated Fat: 8g | Cholesterol: 42mg
Sodium: 517mg | Fiber: 7g | PCF Ratio: 25-43-32 | Exchange Approx.: 2 Starches, ½ Vegetables, 2½ Lean Meats, 2 Fats

INGREDIENTS | SERVES 5

2 cups uncooked whole-wheat elbow macaroni or penne

2 cups broccoli florets

Nonstick cooking spray, as needed

1 cup low-fat cottage cheese

1 tablespoon Dijon mustard

¼ teaspoon Tabasco Sauce

Salt and pepper, to taste

4 ounces sharp Cheddar cheese, shredded

4 ounces part-skim mozzarella cheese, shredded

1. Boil noodles in a large pot for 6 minutes. Add broccoli and cook for 2 more minutes or until the noodles are al dente. Drain, and reserve ½ cup of cooking liquid. Return noodles and broccoli to the pot.

2. Preheat oven to 400°F. Grease medium soufflé dish using nonstick cooking spray and set aside.

3. In a medium bowl, mix reserved cooking liquid, cottage cheese, mustard, and Tabasco until smooth.

4. Stir cottage-cheese mixture into noodles and broccoli, and season with salt and pepper. Mix in Cheddar and mozzarella cheeses.

5. Transfer to the prepared soufflé dish. Bake for 20 minutes or until cheese is melted and top is golden brown.

Wild Rice with Walnuts and Apples

PER SERVING: Calories: 319 | Protein: 7g | Carbohydrates: 24g | Fat: 23g | Saturated Fat: 2g | Cholesterol: 0mg
Sodium: 4mg | Fiber: 3g | PCF Ratio: 9-29-62 | Exchange Approx.: 2 Starches, 1 Meat, 4 Fats

INGREDIENTS | SERVES 4

2 shallots, chopped

1 tart apple, peeled, cored, and chopped

¼ cup olive oil

2 cups wild rice, cooked according to package directions

½ cup walnuts, toasted

Salt and pepper, to taste

1. In a skillet over medium heat, sauté the shallots and apple in the olive oil for 5 minutes.

2. Just before serving, mix all ingredients together.

Brown Rice and Vegetable Sauté

PER SERVING: Calories: 154 | Protein: 5g | Carbohydrates: 26g | Fat: 4g | Saturated Fat: 1g | Cholesterol: 0mg Sodium: 352mg | Fiber: 3g | PCF Ratio: 12-64-24 | Exchange Approx.: 1 Starch, 1½ Vegetables, 1 Fat

INGREDIENTS | SERVES 4

½ cup brown rice

1 cup water

1 tablespoon olive oil

½ cup chopped onions

1 cup chopped red bell peppers

1 teaspoon minced garlic

4 ounces sliced mushrooms

1 (12-ounce) package fresh bean sprouts

1 tablespoon reduced-sodium soy sauce

1 teaspoon grated fresh ginger

1. Add rice to water in a medium saucepan and bring to a boil. Reduce heat; cover and simmer for 35–40 minutes, until cooked.

2. In large nonstick skillet or wok, heat olive oil. Add onions, red pepper, and garlic and cook until onion is translucent.

3. Add mushrooms, bean sprouts, and soy sauce; cook on low heat for 3 minutes.

4. Add cooked rice and ginger; mix ingredients. Cook on low additional 2–3 minutes.

Squash and Bulgur Pilaf

PER SERVING: Calories: 151 | Protein: 5g | Carbohydrates: 22g | Fat: 6g | Saturated Fat: 1g | Cholesterol: 0mg Sodium: 190mg | Fiber: 5g | PCF Ratio: 13-54-32 | Exchange Approx.: 1 Starch, ½ Vegetable, 2 Fats

INGREDIENTS | SERVES 6

½ cup chopped onions

1 teaspoon minced garlic

1½ cups chopped (½" pieces) yellow summer squash

1 cup bulgur wheat

1 tablespoon olive oil

2 cups low-sodium chicken broth

½ teaspoon cinnamon

¼ cup dried currants

¼ cup chopped walnuts

1. In large nonstick skillet, sauté onions, garlic, yellow squash, and bulgur wheat in olive oil until onions are tender, about 5 minutes.

2. Stir in chicken broth and cinnamon; heat to boiling. Reduce heat and simmer, covered, for 10 minutes.

3. Stir in currants; continue to simmer additional 15 minutes. Add walnuts just before serving.

Herbed Quinoa with Sun-Dried Tomatoes

PER SERVING: Calories: 119 | Protein: 5g | Carbohydrates: 21g | Fat: 2g | Saturated Fat: 0g | Cholesterol: 0mg
Sodium: 193mg | Fiber: 2g | PCF Ratio: 17-71-12 | Exchange Approx.: 1 Starch, ½ Very-Lean Meat, 2 Fats

INGREDIENTS | SERVES 6

½ tablespoon olive oil

¼ cup chopped onion

1 clove garlic, minced

1 cup quinoa

2 cups low-sodium chicken broth

½ cup sliced fresh mushrooms

6 sun-dried tomatoes, cut into ¼" pieces

1 teaspoon Italian-blend seasoning

1. In medium saucepan over medium heat, heat olive oil and sauté onions and garlic.

2. Rinse quinoa in very fine mesh strainer before cooking. Add quinoa and broth to saucepan; bring to a boil for 2 minutes. Add mushrooms, sun-dried tomatoes, and Italian seasoning.

3. Reduce heat and cover. Cook 15 minutes, or until all water is absorbed.

Cooking Time for Quinoa

Quinoa takes no longer to cook than rice or pasta, usually about 15 minutes. You can tell quinoa is cooked when grains have turned from white to transparent and spiral-like germ has separated from seed.

Quinoa with Roasted Vegetables

PER SERVING: Calories: 120 | Protein: 4g | Carbohydrates: 9g | Fat: 4g | Saturated Fat: 0g | Cholesterol: 0mg
Sodium: 151mg | Fiber: 4g | PCF Ratio: 12-62-26 | Exchange Approx.: 1 Starch, 1 Vegetable, 2 Fats

INGREDIENTS | SERVES 4

⅔ cup sliced green pepper

½ cup sliced red pepper (mildly hot variety)

3 cups cubed (1" cubes) eggplant

2 cloves garlic, finely chopped

1 tablespoon olive oil

½ teaspoon Texas Seasoning (see recipe in Chapter 15)

¼ teaspoon ground cumin

½ cup quinoa

1 cup water

¼ teaspoon salt

Another Idea

Cook quinoa as outlined in step 3 and combine with 3 cups of Oven-Roasted Ratatouille recipe found in Chapter 10. Nutritional analysis for 1 cup serving: Calories: 162; Protein: 7g; Carbohydrates: 26g; Fat: 3g; Saturated Fat: 0g; Cholesterol: 1mg; Sodium: 202mg; Fiber: 4g; PCF Ratio: 13-69-18; Exchange Approx.: 1 Starch, 2 Vegetables, ½ Fat.

1. Preheat oven to 375°F. Combine peppers, eggplant, garlic, olive oil, Texas Seasoning, and cumin in 2-quart baking dish. Cover and roast for 20 minutes.

2. Remove cover; continue to roast in oven for about 30 minutes until vegetables are browned and cooked soft. Remove from oven; replace cover.

3. Rinse quinoa in very fine mesh strainer before cooking. Bring water and salt to a boil; add quinoa and bring to a boil for 5 minutes. Cover; remove from heat and let stand for 15 minutes.

4. Once quinoa is cooked and all water is absorbed, add roasted vegetables and serve.

Kasha-Stuffed Red Peppers

PER SERVING: Calories: 383 | Protein: 22g | Carbohydrates: 54g | Fat: 12g | Saturated Fat: 5g | Cholesterol: 40mg
Sodium: 387mg | Fiber: 11g | PCF Ratio: 22-53-25 | Exchange Approx.: 2 Starches, 4 Vegetables, 1½ Lean Meats, 2 Fats

INGREDIENTS | SERVES 4

2 pounds red peppers (4 large)

1 cup kasha

1 egg white, lightly beaten

Nonstick cooking spray

2 cups low-sodium beef broth

4 ounces lean ground beef

1 cup finely chopped onion

5 ounces (½ package) frozen chopped spinach, thawed and drained

½ cup crumbled feta cheese

½ cup canned diced tomatoes

1 teaspoon oregano

⅛ teaspoon red pepper flakes

1½ cups water

Save the Tomato Juice

Most canned tomatoes are packed in juice or puréed tomato. When you open a can, save juices and add to recipes when liquids are called for. In this recipe, tomato juice from a can could substitute for some water used to cook peppers in.

1. Remove tops of red peppers and remove seeds. Set aside. Preheat oven to 375°F.

2. In a small bowl, mix kasha and egg white together.

3. In large nonstick saucepan prepared with nonstick cooking spray, add kasha and cook over high heat for 2–3 minutes, stirring constantly, until kasha kernels are separated.

4. Add beef broth slowly. Reduce heat; cover and cook for 7–10 minutes, until kasha kernels are tender. Transfer to a large bowl.

5. Brown beef in small nonstick skillet. Add onions and cook for 2–3 minutes, until slightly softened.

   Add beef mixture and chopped spinach to cooked kasha; mix well. Stir in feta cheese, diced tomato, oregano, and red pepper flakes. Divide mixture equally; stuff each red pepper. Place peppers upright in 9" × 9" baking dish.

6. Pour water around peppers. Cover with foil and bake in oven for 60–75 minutes, or until peppers are cooked.

Basic Polenta with Butter and Cheese

PER SERVING: Calories: 165 | Protein: 4g | Carbohydrates: 27g | Fat: 4g | Saturated Fat: 2g | Cholesterol: 10mg
Sodium: 663mg | Fiber: 3g | PCF Ratio: 10-66-24 | Exchange Approx.: 1½ Starches, 1 Fat

INGREDIENTS | SERVES 4

3½ cups water

1 teaspoon salt

1 cup coarsely ground yellow cornmeal

1 tablespoon butter or heart-healthy margarine

2 tablespoons grated Parmesan or Fontina cheese

Pepper, to taste

Parsley, for garnish

1. Bring the water to a boil. Add salt. Add the cornmeal in a thin stream, stirring constantly. Reduce heat to low; continue to stir for 20 minutes or until the polenta comes away from the pot.

2. Stir in the butter, cheese, and pepper. Garnish with parsley.

As Versatile as Pasta

In some parts of Italy, polenta is used more than pasta! It is simply cornmeal cooked in boiling water until soft and fluffy like mashed potatoes. When polenta is cooled, it stiffens up, making it useful for frying or grilling. This classic can be used instead of pasta or potatoes. Serve as a base for stews, veggies, or pasta sauces.

Polenta with Broccoli Raab

PER SERVING: Calories: 102 (Add 165 calories for polenta) | Protein: 3g | Carbohydrates: 9g | Fat: 7g | Saturated Fat: 1g Cholesterol: 0mg | Sodium: 38mg | Fiber: 3g | PCF Ratio: 12-30-58 | Exchange Approx.: 1½ Vegetables, 1½ Fats

INGREDIENTS | SERVES 4

1 pound broccoli raab
1 quart boiling, salted water
Cold water, as needed
2 tablespoons olive oil
2 cloves garlic, minced
Juice of ½ lemon
Red pepper flakes, to taste
1 recipe Basic Polenta with Butter and Cheese (see recipe in this chapter)

1. Rinse the broccoli raab and cut in 1½" pieces, trimming off very bottoms of stems.

2. Drop the broccoli raab into the boiling water and cook for 5 minutes. Shock in cold water. Drain thoroughly.

3. In a skillet over medium heat, heat the olive oil and add garlic; sauté for 2–3 minutes. Add the lemon juice, pepper flakes, and drained broccoli raab. Cook and stir until well coated.

4. Serve over hot polenta.

Asian Noodles with Tofu and Edamame

PER SERVING: Calories: 374 | Protein: 21g | Carbohydrates: 49g | Fat: 11g | Saturated Fat: 2g | Cholesterol: 0mg Sodium: 773mg | Fiber: 5g | PCF Ratio: 22-51-27 | Exchange Approx.: 2½ Vegetables, 2 Starches, 1 Meat, 1 Fat

INGREDIENTS | SERVES 2

1½ quarts water
4 ounces soba noodles
1 carrot, sliced
½ cup shelled edamame
½ cup snow peas
½ package firm tofu, cubed
½ cup bean sprouts
1 green onion, chopped
1 tablespoon low-sodium soy sauce
1 teaspoon sesame seeds
Black pepper, to taste

1. Bring water to a boil and cook soba noodles until done.

2. Drain noodles, rinse with cold water, and set aside.

3. In a second pot, steam carrot, edamame, snow peas, and tofu for 3 minutes. Drain excess water.

4. Mix together noodles with vegetables and tofu. Add bean sprouts, green onion, and soy sauce. Sprinkle with sesame seeds and pepper as desired.

Red and White Bean Salad

PER SERVING: Calories: 86 | Protein: 8g | Carbohydrates: 27g | Fat: 6g | Saturated Fat: 1g | Cholesterol: 0mg | Sodium: 7mg | Fiber: 7g | PCF Ratio: 17-55-27 | Exchange Approx.: 1½ Starches, 1 Vegetable, ½ Very-Lean Meat, 2 Fats

INGREDIENTS | SERVES 8

2 cups cooked navy beans

2 cups cooked red beans

¼ cup lemon juice

3 tablespoons olive oil

¼ teaspoon freshly ground pepper

1 cup chopped arugula

1 cup thinly sliced red onion

8 ounces cherry tomatoes, cut in half

1. Combine beans together in a medium bowl.

2. In a separate bowl, whisk together lemon juice, olive oil, and pepper; toss with arugula. Pour mixture over beans.

3. Add onions and toss lightly to mix. Let mixture refrigerate for at least 3 hours.

4. Just before serving, toss in cherry tomatoes and mix lightly.

About Arugula

Arugula has several other names such as rocket, rugula, roquette, and rucola. It is sometimes found in baby greens or mesclun mixes. It has a nutty and peppery flavor, which can add interest to a salad or sandwich. Give arugula a try!

CHAPTER 10

Vegetable Sides

Vegetable Broth

PER SERVING: Calories: 10 | Protein: 0g | Carbohydrates: 2g | Fat: 0g | Saturated Fat: 0g | Cholesterol: 0mg
Sodium: 8mg | Fiber: 1g | PCF Ratio: 11-85-4 | Exchange Approx.: 1 Free Vegetable

INGREDIENTS | MAKES ABOUT 2½ QUARTS; SERVING SIZE: ¾ CUP

4 carrots, peeled and chopped

2 stalks celery with leaves, chopped

1 green bell pepper, seeded and chopped

2 medium zucchini, chopped

1 small onion, chopped

1 cup chopped fresh spinach

2 cups chopped leeks

½ cup chopped scallions

1 cup chopped green beans

1 cup chopped parsnips

2 bay leaves

2 cloves garlic, crushed

Sea salt and freshly ground black pepper, to taste (optional)

3 quarts water

1. Place all ingredients in large pot and bring to a boil. Reduce heat, cover pot, and simmer for 30 minutes, or until vegetables are tender. Discard bay leaf.

2. Use slotted spoon to transfer vegetables to different pot; mix with some of broth for Free Exchange vegetable soup. Freeze mixture in single-serving containers to keep on hand for a quick, heat-in-the-microwave snack.

3. Strain remaining vegetables from broth; purée in blender or food processor and return to broth to add dietary fiber and body. Cool and freeze until needed.

Perpetual Broth

The easiest way to create vegetable broth is to keep a container in the freezer for saving liquid from cooked vegetables. Vegetable broth makes a great addition to sauces, soups, and many other recipes. Substitute it for meat broth in most recipes or use instead of water for cooking pasta, rice, and other grains.

Oven-Baked Red Potatoes

PER SERVING: Calories: 120 | Protein: 2g | Carbohydrates: 26g | Fat: 1g | Saturated Fat: 0g | Cholesterol: 0g
Sodium: 587mg | Fiber: 2g | PCF Ratio: 7-84-9 | Exchange Approx.: 1 Starch

INGREDIENTS | SERVES 4

1 pound small red potatoes, halved
¼ cup fresh lemon juice
1 teaspoon olive oil
1 teaspoon sea salt
¼ teaspoon freshly ground pepper

Remember the Roasting "Rack"

Use caution when roasting potatoes with meat: Potatoes will act like a sponge, soaking up fat. Your best option is to use lean cuts of meat and elevate them and vegetables above fat by putting them on a roasting rack in the pan or making a "bridge" with the celery to elevate the meat. Discard celery when done.

1. Preheat oven to 350°F. Arrange potatoes in 13" × 9" ovenproof casserole dish.

2. In a small bowl, combine remaining ingredients and pour over potatoes. Bake for 30–40 minutes, or until potatoes are tender, turning 3–4 times to baste.

Sweet-Potato Crisps

PER SERVING, WITHOUT SALT: Calories: 89 | Protein: 1g | Carbohydrates: 16g | Fat: 2g | Saturated Fat: 1g Cholesterol: 0mg | Sodium: 7mg | Fiber: 9g | PCF Ratio: 6-70-24 | Exchange Approx.: 1 Starch, ½ Fat

INGREDIENTS | SERVES 2

1 small sweet potato
1 teaspoon olive oil
Sea salt and freshly ground black pepper, to taste (optional)

1. Preheat oven to 400°F.

2. Scrub sweet potato and pierce flesh several times with fork. Place on microwave-safe plate; microwave 5 minutes on high. Remove from microwave; wrap in aluminum foil. Set aside 5 minutes.

3. Remove foil; peel and cut into strips. Spread on baking sheet treated with nonstick cooking spray; spritz strips with olive oil. Bake for 10–15 minutes, or until crisp. There's a risk that sweet-potato strips will caramelize and burn; check often while cooking to ensure this doesn't occur. Lower oven temperature, if necessary.

4. Season with salt and pepper, if desired.

Sweet Potatoes with Onions and Apple

PER SERVING: Calories: 127 | Protein: 2g | Carbohydrates: 28g | Fat: 1g | Saturated Fat: 0g | Cholesterol: 1mg
Sodium: 144mg | Fiber: 4g | PCF Ratio: 6-85-9 | Exchange Approx.: 1 Starch, ½ Vegetable

INGREDIENTS | SERVES 6

1 pound sweet potatoes (about 2 large)
½ teaspoon canola oil
1 cup thinly sliced onion
1 apple, peeled and chopped
½ cup low-sodium chicken broth

1. Wash and dry sweet potatoes; pierce skins several times with fork. Microwave on high for 5–8 minutes, or until tender.

2. While sweet potatoes are cooling, heat oil in large nonstick skillet over medium-high heat. Add onions and sauté until golden brown, about 10 minutes.

3. Add apple and chicken broth to the skillet. Cook until onions are tender and have caramelized.

4. Scoop cooked sweet potato from skins into microwave-safe dish; mash lightly. Cover and microwave on high for 1–2 minutes, or until potatoes are heated. Top with sautéed onions and serve.

Fluffy Buttermilk Mashed Potatoes

PER SERVING, WITHOUT SALT: Calories: 97 | Protein: 2g | Carbohydrates: 18g | Fat: 2g | Saturated Fat: 1g | Cholesterol: 6mg Sodium: 20mg | Fiber: 2g | PCF Ratio: 9-72-19 | Exchange Approx.: 1 Starch, ½ Fat

INGREDIENTS | SERVES 4

¾ pound potatoes, peeled and boiled

¼ cup warm buttermilk

2 teaspoons unsalted butter

Sea salt and freshly ground black pepper, to taste (optional)

1. Place potatoes in large bowl and partially mash.

2. Add warm buttermilk and mix well, mashing potatoes completely.

3. Stir in butter and salt and pepper, if using. If you like your mashed potatoes creamy, add some of the potato water.

Roasted-Garlic Mashed Potatoes

PER SERVING, WITHOUT SALT: Calories: 126 | Protein: 4g | Carbohydrates: 23g | Fat: 2g | Saturated Fat: 1g | Cholesterol: 6mg Sodium: 31mg | Fiber: 3g | PCF Ratio: 13-70-17 | Exchange Approx.: 1 Starch, 1 Vegetable, ½ Fat

INGREDIENTS | SERVES 4

4 cloves dry-roasted garlic (see recipe for Garlic and Feta Cheese Dip in Chapter 3)

1 small onion, chopped

¾ pound potatoes, peeled and cooked

2 cups cauliflower florets, steamed and drained

¼ cup buttermilk

⅛ cup nonfat cottage cheese

2 teaspoons unsalted butter

Sea salt and freshly ground black pepper, to taste (optional)

In a large bowl, combine all ingredients; whip until fluffy. If potatoes or cauliflower are overly moist, add buttermilk gradually until whipped mixture reaches desired consistency. Combining steamed cauliflower with the potatoes allows you to increase the portion size without significantly changing the flavor of the mashed potatoes.

Gravy Substitute

Instead of using gravy, sprinkle crumbled bleu cheese or grated Parmesan over mashed potatoes. Just remember that cheese is a Meat Exchange and adjust approximations accordingly.

Healthy Onion Rings

**PER SERVING, WITHOUT SALT: Calories: 111 | Protein: 4g | Carbohydrates: 22g | Fat: 1g | Saturated Fat: 0g | Cholesterol: 1mg
Sodium: 255mg | Fiber: 1g | PCF Ratio: 16-80-4 | Exchange Approx.: 1 Vegetable, 1 Starch**

INGREDIENTS | SERVES 4

1 cup yellow onion slices (¼" thick)

½ cup flour

½ cup plain, nonfat yogurt

½ cup bread crumbs

Sea salt and freshly ground black pepper, to taste (optional)

1. Preheat oven to 350°F. Dredge onion slices in flour; shake off any excess. Dip onions in yogurt; dredge through bread crumbs.

2. Prepare baking sheet with nonstick cooking spray. Arrange onion rings on pan; bake for 15–20 minutes. Place under broiler additional 2 minutes to brown. Season with salt and pepper, if desired.

French Tarragon Green Beans

**PER SERVING: Calories: 59 | Protein: 0g | Carbohydrates: 5g | Fat: 3g | Saturated Fat: 1g | Cholesterol: 11mg
Sodium: 105mg | Fiber: 1g | PCF Ratio: 3-32-65 | Exchange Approx.: 1 Vegetable, 1 Fat**

INGREDIENTS | SERVES 4

1½ tablespoons butter

¼ cup chopped red onion

½ pound fresh green beans

1 tablespoon finely chopped fresh tarragon

1. Melt butter in nonstick frying pan. Add onions and sauté until translucent.

2. Add green beans. Cover and steam for 2–3 minutes.

3. Add tarragon and combine well. Steam an additional 2–3 minutes.

Roasted Green Beans with Pine Nuts

Calories: 120 | Protein: 6g | Carbohydrates: 12g | Fat: 6g | Saturated Fat: 1g | Cholesterol: 7mg | Sodium: 363mg
Fiber: 5g | PCF Ratio: 19-38-43 | Exchange Approx.: 2 Vegetables, ½ Lean Meat, 1 Fat

INGREDIENTS | SERVES 6

Water, as needed to fill pot

2 pounds green beans, trimmed

Nonstick cooking spray, as needed

2 ounces prosciutto or bacon, thinly sliced

2 teaspoons olive oil

4 cloves garlic, minced

2 teaspoons minced fresh sage

¼ teaspoon salt, divided

Freshly ground pepper, to taste, divided

¼ cup toasted pine nuts

1 teaspoon lemon zest

Toasting Nuts and Seeds

Place nuts or seeds in a dry skillet over medium-low heat and cook for 3–5 minutes. Nuts will have a nutty scent and will be slightly browned.

1. Boil water in a large pot. Add green beans to pot and simmer until tender-crisp, about 4 minutes. Drain green beans and set aside.

2. Spray a large frying pan with nonstick cooking spray and place over medium heat. Add prosciutto and cook, stirring, until crisp. Transfer prosciutto to a paper towel to blot excess oil.

3. Add 2 teaspoons oil to the large pan and return to medium heat. Add green beans, garlic, sage, half of the salt, and pepper to the pan. Cook until the green beans are slightly brown.

4. Add the pine nuts, lemon zest, and prosciutto; season with remaining salt and additional pepper.

Sesame Snap Peas

PER SERVING: Calories: 49 | Protein: 0g | Carbohydrates: 3g | Fat: 4g | Saturated Fat: 0g | Cholesterol: 0mg
Sodium: 149mg | Fiber: 0g | PCF Ratio: 2-27-72 | Exchange Approx.: 1 Vegetable, ½ Fat

INGREDIENTS | SERVES 4

½ tablespoon canola oil
10 ounces fresh snap peas
¼ cup thinly sliced scallions
1 tablespoon grated fresh ginger
2 teaspoons sesame oil
1 tablespoon sesame seeds

1. Heat canola oil in large nonstick skillet or wok.

2. Add snap peas, scallions, and ginger and stir-fry until peas are crisp-tender.

3. Stir in sesame oil and sesame seeds; toss lightly and serve.

Roasted Broccoli with Lemon and Romano Cheese

PER SERVING: Calories: 176 | Protein: 7g | Carbohydrates: 7g | Fat: 14g | Saturated Fat: 4g | Cholesterol: 15mg
Sodium: 200mg | Fiber: 2g | PCF Ratio: 15-15-70 | Exchange Approx.: 1 Vegetable, 1 Meat, 1½ Fats

INGREDIENTS | SERVES 4

4 cups raw broccoli florets
3 tablespoons olive oil
Salt and pepper, to taste
¾ cup grated Romano cheese
Juice of 1 lemon

1. Heat oven to 400°F.

2. Place broccoli in a large glass baking dish, drizzle with oil, and season with salt and pepper as desired. Place broccoli in the oven and roast for 12 minutes.

3. Remove broccoli from the oven and cover the top evenly with cheese and lemon juice. Return the broccoli to the oven and cook until cheese is melted, about 10 minutes.

Amish-Style Turnips

PER SERVING: Calories: 80 | Protein: 2g | Carbohydrates: 12g | Fat: 3g | Saturated Fat: 2g | Cholesterol: 40mg
Sodium: 49mg | Fiber: 2g | PCF Ratio: 10-56-34 | Exchange Approx.: 1 Vegetable, ½ Starch, ½ Fat

INGREDIENTS | SERVES 6

3 cups peeled and cubed (1" cubes) turnips

½ cup water

1 slice whole-wheat bread

1 tablespoon melted butter

2 tablespoons Splenda Brown Sugar Blend

½ cup low-fat milk

1 egg

1. Preheat oven to 375°F.

2. Place turnips in covered, microwave-safe dish with water; microwave on high for 10–15 minutes, until tender. Mash turnips and set aside.

3. Place bread in food processor. Using pulse setting, process until fine bread crumbs form.

4. In medium bowl, mix together bread crumbs, melted butter, Splenda, milk, and egg. Add cooked turnip; mix well.

5. Turn mixture into greased casserole dish. Bake uncovered for 30–35 minutes.

Oven-Roasted Ratatouille

PER SERVING: Calories: 87 | Protein: 2g | Carbohydrates: 11g | Fat: 5g | Saturated Fat: 1g | Cholesterol: 0mg
Sodium: 452mg | Fiber: 3g | PCF Ratio: 9-46-46 | Exchange Approx.: 2 Vegetables, 1 Fat

INGREDIENTS | SERVES 12

5 cups peeled and cubed (½" cubes) eggplant

3 cups chopped (½" pieces) yellow squash

½ pound green beans

½ cup chopped celery

1 cup chopped red onion

4 cloves garlic, chopped

1 (28-ounce) can diced tomatoes

1 tablespoon chopped fresh parsley

¼ teaspoon salt

½ teaspoon rosemary

½ teaspoon thyme

¼ cup olive oil

2 tablespoons balsamic vinegar

1. Preheat oven to 375°F. In large Dutch oven or 9" × 13" baking dish, combine all ingredients except balsamic vinegar.

2. Roast uncovered in oven. Stir after 30 minutes, then continue roasting another 30 minutes, or until vegetables are softened and lightly browned on top.

3. Remove from oven. Stir in balsamic vinegar and serve.

Layered Veggie Casserole

PER SERVING: Calories: 84 | Protein: 5g | Carbohydrates: 16g | Fat: 1g | Saturated Fat: 1g | Cholesterol: 3mg
Sodium: 101mg | Fiber: 4g | PCF Ratio: 20-67-13 | Exchange Approx.: 1 Vegetable, 1 Starch

INGREDIENTS | SERVES 4

1 (10-ounce) package frozen mixed vegetables

½ cup diced onion

½ cup diced green pepper

1 cup unsalted tomato juice

⅛ teaspoon celery seed

⅛ teaspoon dried basil

⅛ teaspoon dried oregano

⅛ teaspoon dried parsley

¼ teaspoon garlic powder

3 tablespoons grated Parmesan cheese, divided

Season First

When readying vegetables for steaming, add fresh or dried herbs, spices, sliced or diced onions, minced garlic, grated ginger, or any other seasoning you'd normally use. Seasonings will cook into vegetables during steaming.

1. Preheat oven to 350°F. In large casserole dish treated with nonstick cooking spray, layer vegetables, onion, and pepper. Mix tomato juice, seasonings, and 2 tablespoons of Parmesan; pour over vegetables. Cover and bake for 1 hour.

2. Uncover; sprinkle with remaining Parmesan. Continue to bake for 10 minutes, or until liquid thickens and mixture bubbles.

Crustless Zucchini and Artichoke Quiche

PER SERVING: Calories: 224 | Protein: 24g | Carbohydrates: 9g | Fat: 10g | Saturated Fat: 4g | Cholesterol: 134mg
Sodium: 798mg | Fiber: 3g | PCF Ratio: 43-16-41 | Exchange Approx.: 1 Vegetable, 1½ Lean Meats, 1½ Fats

INGREDIENTS | SERVES 4

Nonstick cooking spray

1 tablespoon olive oil

¼ cup chopped onions

¾ cup grated zucchini

1 cup chopped (½" pieces) canned artichoke hearts

1½ cups grated light Cheddar cheese

2 eggs

½ cup egg whites

½ cup fat-free cottage cheese

¼ teaspoon cayenne pepper

¼ teaspoon salt

⅛ teaspoon freshly ground pepper

1. Preheat oven to 375°F. Spray 9" pie plate with nonstick cooking spray. In large nonstick skillet, heat olive oil; add onion and sauté until translucent.

2. Add zucchini and artichoke hearts and cook for an additional 3 minutes.

3. Sprinkle grated cheese in bottom of pie plate. Add cooked vegetables on top of cheese.

4. In small bowl, whisk eggs, egg whites, cottage cheese, cayenne, salt, and pepper together and pour over vegetables.

5. Bake for 35–40 minutes, or until set and inserted toothpick comes out clean.

Vegetable Frittata

PER SERVING: Calories: 171 | Protein: 12g | Carbohydrates: 11g | Fat: 9g | Saturated Fat: 4g | Cholesterol: 195mg
Sodium: 252mg | Fiber: 2g | PCF Ratio: 28-24-48 | Exchange Approx.: 1 Vegetable, 1 Lean Meat, 2½ Fats

INGREDIENTS | SERVES 4

1½ tablespoons olive oil

4 ounces red pepper, chopped

3 large eggs

4 ounces egg substitute (or egg whites)

4 ounces asparagus, cut diagonally in 1" pieces

¾ cup cooked and cubed potatoes

⅓ cup crumbled feta cheese

1 teaspoon oregano

1. Preheat oven to 350°F. Using ovenproof nonstick skillet, heat olive oil over medium heat. Add red peppers and cook until softened.

2. In medium bowl, beat together eggs and egg substitute. Add asparagus, potatoes, feta, and oregano.

3. Pour eggs into skillet; gently stir until eggs on bottom of pan begin to set. Gently pull cooked eggs from side of skillet, allowing uncooked egg on top to come in contact with heated skillet. Repeat, working all around skillet, until most of eggs on top have begun to set.

4. Transfer skillet to oven; bake until top is set and dry to the touch, about 3–5 minutes. Loosen frittata around edges of skillet and invert onto serving plate.

Winter Vegetable Casserole

PER SERVING: Calories: 218 | Protein: 5g | Carbohydrates: 36g | Fat: 7g | Saturated Fat: 1g | Cholesterol: 18mg
Sodium: 392mg | Fiber: 5g | PCF Ratio: 9-64-27 | Exchange Approx.: 1½ Starches, 1½ Vegetables, 1 Fat

INGREDIENTS | SERVES 6

Nonstick cooking spray
1½ potatoes
1½ sweet potatoes
1 cup peeled and sliced parsnips
1 cup sliced turnips
3 tablespoons butter
3 tablespoons all-purpose flour
½ teaspoon salt
¼ teaspoon white pepper
1½ cups low-fat milk
½ cup chopped onions

1. Preheat oven to 350°F. Spray 2-quart casserole dish with nonstick cooking spray.

2. Clean, peel, and slice potatoes and sweet potatoes and place in a large bowl. Add the chopped parsnips and turnips and combine.

3. In a small saucepan, melt butter; add flour, salt, and pepper to make a roux. Gradually stir in milk, cooking over low heat; stir well with wire whisk.

4. Bring to a boil, stirring constantly, until roux has thickened into a sauce, about 10 minutes. Remove from heat.

5. Arrange ½ of sliced vegetables in casserole dish; top with ½ of chopped onion and white sauce; repeat to make second layer. Cover and cook for 45 minutes. Uncover and continue to cook until all vegetables are tender, about 60–70 minutes.

6. Let casserole stand 10 minutes before serving.

Winter Root Vegetable Soufflé

PER SERVING: Calories: 224 | Protein: 11g | Carbohydrates: 31g | Fat: 7g | Saturated Fat: 2g | Cholesterol: 248mg
Sodium: 939mg | Fiber: 6g | PCF Ratio: 19-54-27 | Exchange Approx.: 5 Vegetables, 1 Meat, 2 Fats

INGREDIENTS | SERVES 4

½ large Vidalia onion, cut into big chunks
2 carrots, peeled and chopped
2 parsnips, peeled and chopped
2 baby turnips, peeled and chopped
1 teaspoon salt
4 eggs, separated
1 teaspoon dried sage
2 tablespoons chopped fresh parsley
1 tablespoon flour
½ teaspoon Tabasco Sauce, or to taste
½ cup 2% milk
Nonstick cooking spray, as needed

Soufflé Tip

It's okay to have a soufflé flop, especially in the case of cheese and vegetable soufflés. A dessert soufflé should never fall. If, as directed, you start the soufflé with the oven at 400°F and then reduce the temperature, you are more likely to produce a high soufflé!

1. Preheat oven to 400°F. Place the onion, carrots, parsnips, turnips, and salt in a pot of cold water and cover. Bring to a boil; reduce heat and simmer until the veggies are very tender when pierced with a fork.

2. Drain the vegetables and cool slightly. Place in a blender and purée. With the blender running on medium speed, add the egg yolks, one at a time. Then add the sage, parsley, flour, Tabasco, and milk. Pour into a bowl.

3. Prepare a 2-quart soufflé dish with nonstick cooking spray. Beat the egg whites until stiff. Fold the egg whites into the purée. Pour into the soufflé dish.

4. Bake the soufflé for 20 minutes. Reduce heat to 350°F and bake for 20 minutes more. Don't worry if your soufflé flops just before serving; it will still be light and delicious.

Broccoli Raab with Pine Nuts

PER SERVING: Calories: 110 | Protein: 5g | Carbohydrates: 6g | Fat: 8g | Saturated Fat: 1g | Cholesterol: 0mg
Sodium: 229mg | Fiber: 4g | PCF Ratio: 18-20-62 | Exchange Approx.: 1 Vegetable, 1 Fat

INGREDIENTS | SERVES 4

¾ pound broccoli raab, cooked

1 tablespoon olive oil

4 cloves garlic, chopped

¼ cup chopped sun-dried tomatoes

2 tablespoons pine nuts

¼ teaspoon salt

¼ teaspoon red pepper flakes

Preventing Bitter Broccoli Raab

Broccoli raab and other leafy greens (mustard or collard greens) can have a bitter taste once cooked. Rather than add extra salt to offset bitterness, this recipe calls for blanching 2 minutes, which helps reduce bitterness. Blanching should be done as quickly as possible by starting with water at full rolling boil, then removing after 2 minutes of boiling. If allowed to cook too long, the boiling process will reduce the amount of water-soluble nutrients found in the vegetables.

1. Prepare and blanch broccoli before beginning recipe: Rinse well and trim stems. Loosely chop leafy parts and remaining stems, then blanch in 2 quarts boiling water for 2 minutes. Drain well.

2. Heat olive oil in a large skillet. Add garlic and sauté for 1–2 minutes. Add cooked broccoli raab. Toss garlic and broccoli raab together well, so that oil and garlic are mixed evenly.

3. Add remaining ingredients; cook for an additional 2–3 minutes, until broccoli raab is tender.

Greens in Garlic with Pasta

PER SERVING, WITHOUT SALT: Calories: 176 | Protein: 8g | Carbohydrates: 26g | Fat: 5g | Saturated Fat: 1g | Cholesterol: 0mg
Sodium: 17mg | Fiber: 3g | PCF Ratio: 17-58-25 | Exchange Approx.: 1 Free Vegetable, 1 Fat, 1 Starch, ½ Lean Meat

INGREDIENTS | SERVES 4

2 teaspoons olive oil

4 cloves garlic, crushed

6 cups tightly packed loose-leaf greens (baby mustard, turnip, chard)

2 cups cooked pasta

2 teaspoons extra-virgin olive oil

¼ cup freshly grated Parmesan cheese

Salt and freshly ground black pepper, to taste (optional)

Sweet or Salty?

In most cases, when you add a pinch (less than ⅛ teaspoon) of sugar to a recipe, you can reduce the amount of salt without noticing a difference. Sugar acts as a flavor enhancer and magnifies the effect of the salt.

1. Place sauté pan over medium heat. When hot, add olive oil and garlic. Cook, stirring frequently, until golden brown, about 3–5 minutes, being careful not to burn garlic, as that makes it bitter.

2. Add greens and sauté until coated in garlic oil. Remove from heat.

3. In large serving bowl, add cooked greens, pasta, extra-virgin olive oil, and Parmesan cheese; toss to mix. Serve immediately, and season as desired.

Spaghetti Squash and Vegetable Mix

PER SERVING: Calories: 127 | Protein: 4g | Carbohydrates: 16g | Fat: 6g | Saturated Fat: 3g | Cholesterol: 5mg
Sodium: 169mg | Fiber: 2g | PCF Ratio: 12-47-41 | Exchange Approx.: 1 Starch, 1 Fat

INGREDIENTS | SERVES 6

2 pounds spaghetti squash

Nonstick cooking spray

1 cup peas, fresh or frozen

2 tablespoons butter

8 ounces cherry tomatoes, cut in half

1 ounce grated Romano cheese

¼ teaspoon freshly ground pepper

Pasta Alternative

Spaghetti squash is a wonderful alternative to pasta because it is packed with vitamins, minerals, and fiber. While it has a consistency similar to spaghetti, it is much lower in carbohydrates: 1 cup of cooked spaghetti squash has 15 grams of carbohydrate, while 1 cup of cooked spaghetti has approximately 45 grams!

1. Preheat oven to 400°F. Cut spaghetti squash in half and scoop out seeds. Prepare 9" × 13" baking dish with nonstick cooking spray and place squash halves face down. Bake for 45 minutes, or until squash is soft-cooked.

2. When squash is cool enough to handle, use a fork to scoop out cooked squash from the outer shell. Scoop into a medium microwave-safe bowl.

3. In separate small saucepan, lightly steam peas for 2–3 minutes. Add to squash, along with butter; mix well.

4. Place covered bowl in microwave; cook on high for 2–3 minutes.

5. Add cherry tomato halves and top with Romano cheese and pepper before serving.

Brussels-Sprouts Hash with Caramelized Shallots

**PER SERVING: Calories: 118 | Protein: 3g | Carbohydrates: 8g | Fat: 9g | Saturated Fat: 1g | Cholesterol: 0mg
Sodium: 20mg | Fiber: 3g | PCF Ratio: 9-26-65 | Exchange Approx.: 1½ Vegetables, 2 Fats**

INGREDIENTS | SERVES 6

1 pound Brussels sprouts
2 shallots, thinly sliced
¼ cup olive oil
Salt and pepper, to taste
3 tablespoons balsamic vinegar

1. Preheat oven to 400°F.

2. Trim stems off Brussels sprouts and slice in half lengthwise. Place Brussels sprouts and shallots in a shallow baking dish. Coat Brussels sprouts with olive oil; season with salt and pepper as desired.

3. Bake for 20 minutes. Remove dish from the oven, and drizzle vinegar evenly over Brussels sprouts. Return dish to the oven to bake for 3–4 minutes.

Mashed Cauliflower

PER SERVING: Calories: 68 | Protein: 2g | Carbohydrates: 5g | Fat: 5g | Saturated Fat: 1g | Cholesterol: 0mg
Sodium: 19mg | Fiber: 3g | PCF Ratio: 12-27-61 | Exchange Approx.: 1 Vegetable, 1 Fat

INGREDIENTS | SERVES 6

1 head cauliflower
2 tablespoons olive oil
1 tablespoon chopped fresh chives
Salt and pepper, to taste

1. Place cauliflower in a large pot of boiling water, and cook for 10 minutes. Drain well, reserving ¼ cup cooking liquid.

2. Place cauliflower in blender or food processor with oil and ¼ cup cooking liquid and purée until smooth. Add chives and season with salt and pepper as desired.

CHAPTER 11

Salads

Arugula and Fennel Salad with Pomegranate

PER SERVING: Calories: 201 | Protein: 2g | Carbohydrates: 20g | Fat: 14g | Saturated Fat: 2g | Cholesterol: 0mg
Sodium: 18mg | Fiber: 3g | PCF Ratio: 4-37-59 | Exchange Approx.: 1 Fruit, ½ Vegetable, 3 Fats

INGREDIENTS | SERVES 4

2 large navel oranges
1 pomegranate
4 cups arugula
1 cup thinly sliced fennel
4 tablespoons olive oil
Salt and pepper, to taste

1. Cut the tops and bottoms off of the oranges and then cut the remaining peel away. Slice each orange into 10–12 small pieces.

2. Remove seeds from the pomegranate.

3. Place orange pieces, pomegranate seeds, arugula, and fennel slices into a large bowl.

4. Coat the salad with olive oil and season with salt and pepper as desired.

Fennel Facts

Fennel, a crunchy and slightly sweet vegetable, is a popular Mediterranean ingredient. Fennel has a white or greenish-white bulb and long stalks with feathery green leaves stemming from the top. Fennel is closely related to cilantro, dill, carrots, and parsley.

Avocado and Peach Salad

PER SERVING, WITHOUT SALT: Calories: 160 | Protein: 2g | Carbohydrates: 15g | Fat: 11g | Saturated Fat: 2g | Cholesterol: 0mg Sodium: 11mg | Fiber: 4g | PCF Ratio: 6-35-59 | Exchange Approx.: 3 Fats, 1 Free Vegetable, ½ Fruit

INGREDIENTS | SERVES 4

⅛ cup water

⅛ cup frozen orange juice concentrate, thawed

1 clove garlic, crushed

1 teaspoon rice wine vinegar

1 tablespoon extra-virgin olive oil

½ teaspoon vanilla extract

1½ cups tightly packed baby arugula

2 tablespoons fresh tarragon leaves

1 avocado, peeled and diced

1 peach, peeled and diced

½ cup thinly sliced Vidalia onion

Kosher or sea salt and freshly ground black pepper, to taste (optional)

1. In a small bowl, whisk together water, orange juice concentrate, garlic, vinegar, oil, and vanilla until well mixed.

2. Prepare salad by arranging layers of arugula and tarragon, then avocado, peach, and onions, then drizzle with prepared vinaigrette. Season with salt and pepper, if desired, and serve.

Experiment Sensibly

When it comes to new herbs and spices, err on the side of caution. Not sure whether or not you like a seasoning? Mix all other ingredients together and test a bite of salad with pinch of herb or spice before adding it to the entire recipe.

Avocado and Shrimp Salad

**PER SERVING: Calories: 219 | Protein: 10g | Carbohydrates: 14g | Fat: 13g | Saturated Fat: 2g | Cholesterol: 55mg
Sodium: 64mg | Fiber: 5g | PCF Ratio: 18-25-57 | Exchange Approx.: 1 Fruit, 1 Vegetable, 1 Lean Meat, 2 Fats**

INGREDIENTS | SERVES 4

24 raw shrimp

2 tablespoons olive oil

4 green onions, sliced and divided

2 cloves garlic, finely minced

2 tablespoons dry white wine

Salt and pepper, to taste

1 red grapefruit

8 ounces butter lettuce, washed and torn into bite-size pieces

1 ripe avocado, sliced

1. Peel and devein the shrimp.

2. In a pan set over medium-high heat, add the olive oil. Add shrimp and half of the green onions to hot pan. Cook, stirring frequently until shrimp are half-cooked. Add minced garlic and white wine to the pan; cook for an additional minute, then add salt and pepper.

3. Cut grapefruit in half and set one half to the side. Add in juice of half grapefruit to the pan; cook for 2–3 minutes. Cut the peel off the remaining grapefruit half and slice fruit into bite-size pieces.

4. Place lettuce, avocado slices, and remaining green onions on salad plates for serving. Transfer cooked shrimp to plates.

5. Drizzle sauce from pan over top and garnish with grapefruit slices.

Cucumbers with Minted Yogurt

PER SERVING: Calories: 31 | Protein: 2g | Carbohydrates: 4g | Fat: 1g | Saturated Fat: 0g | Cholesterol: 2mg
Sodium: 52mg | Fiber: 1g | PCF Ratio: 27-56-17 | Exchange Approx.: 1 Vegetable

INGREDIENTS | SERVES 8

1 cup plain, nonfat yogurt
1 clove garlic, finely chopped
¼ teaspoon ground cumin
1 teaspoon lemon zest
½ cup fresh mint
1 tablespoon lemon juice
¼ teaspoon salt
4 cups seeded and chopped cucumbers

1. In a blender or food processor, combine all ingredients except cucumbers and blend until smooth.

2. Add yogurt mixture to cucumbers and mix. Chill before serving.

Minted Lentil and Tomato Salad

PER SERVING: Calories: 136 | Protein: 4g | Carbohydrates: 11g | Fat: 9g | Saturated Fat: 1g | Cholesterol: 0mg
Sodium: 211mg | Fiber: 4g | PCF Ratio: 10-31-59 | Exchange Approx.: ½ Starch, 1 Vegetable, ½ Lean Meat, 2 Fats

INGREDIENTS | SERVES 6

1 cup dry lentils
2 cups water
½ cup chopped onion
2 teaspoons minced garlic
¼ cup chopped celery
½ cup chopped green pepper
½ cup finely chopped parsley
2 tablespoons finely chopped fresh mint, or 2 teaspoons dried
¼ cup lemon juice
¼ cup olive oil
½ teaspoon salt
1 cup diced fresh tomato

1. Place lentils and water in medium saucepan; bring to a quick boil. Reduce heat to low; cover and cook 15–20 minutes, or until tender. Drain and transfer to medium bowl.

2. Add onion, garlic, celery, green pepper, parsley, and mint to the bowl and mix well.

3. In a separate small bowl, whisk together lemon juice, olive oil, and salt. Pour into lentils; mix well. Cover and refrigerate several hours.

4. Before serving, mix in diced tomatoes.

Tomato and Cucumber Salad with Mint

PER SERVING: Calories: 68 | Protein: 1g | Carbohydrates: 7g | Fat: 5g | Saturated Fat: 1g | Cholesterol: 0mg
Sodium: 202mg | Fiber: 1g | PCF Ratio: 5-32-63 | Exchange Approx.: 1 Vegetable, 1 Fat

INGREDIENTS | SERVES 6

2 cucumbers
⅓ cup red wine vinegar
1 teaspoon sugar
½ teaspoon salt
2 cups chopped tomatoes
⅔ cup chopped red onion
¼ cup chopped fresh mint
2 tablespoons olive oil

1. Cut cucumbers in ½" pieces; place in a medium bowl.
2. Add vinegar, sugar, and salt to the bowl and stir. Let stand at room temperature for 15 minutes.
3. Add tomatoes, red onion, mint, and olive oil. Toss lightly to blend.

Orange-Avocado Slaw

PER SERVING, WITHOUT SALT: Calories: 60 | Protein: 2g | Carbohydrates: 5g | Fat: 5g | Saturated Fat: 1g | Cholesterol: 0mg
Sodium: 14mg | Fiber: 2g | PCF Ratio: 11-27-62 | Exchange Approx.: 1 Fat, ½ Free Vegetable

INGREDIENTS | SERVES 10

¼ cup orange juice
½ teaspoon curry powder
⅛ teaspoon ground cumin
¼ teaspoon sugar
1 teaspoon white wine vinegar
1 tablespoon olive oil
1 avocado, peeled and chopped
5 cups broccoli slaw mix
Sea salt and freshly ground black pepper, to taste (optional)

1. In a small bowl, whisk together orange juice, curry powder, cumin, sugar, and vinegar. Add oil in stream, whisking until emulsified.
2. In large bowl, toss avocado with slaw mix. Drizzle with vinaigrette. Chill until ready to serve, at least 2 hours. Season with salt and pepper, if desired.

Broccoli-Cauliflower Slaw

PER SERVING: Calories: 117 | Protein: 6g | Carbohydrates: 13g | Fat: 5g | Saturated Fat: 1g | Cholesterol: 0mg
Sodium: 46mg | Fiber: 1g | PCF Ratio: 19-42-39 | Exchange Approx.: 1 Misc. Carbohydrate, 1 Fat

INGREDIENTS | SERVES 8

4 cups raw broccoli florets

4 cups raw cauliflower florets

½ cup real mayonnaise

1 cup 1% fat cottage cheese

3 tablespoons tarragon vinegar

1 tablespoon balsamic vinegar

⅛ cup packed brown sugar

3 tablespoons chopped red onion

Tip

Substituting cottage cheese for some of the mayonnaise called for in a recipe cuts fat and calories considerably. Cut them even more by using nonfat cottage cheese and nonfat mayonnaise.

1. Put broccoli and cauliflower in food processor; pulse until consistency of shredded cabbage is reached. Pour into a bowl.

2. Place remaining ingredients in food processor and process until smooth. Pour resulting dressing over broccoli-cauliflower mixture; stir. Chill until ready to serve.

Old-Town Coleslaw

PER SERVING: Calories: 42 | Protein: 1g | Carbohydrates: 10g | Fat: 1g | Saturated Fat: 0g | Cholesterol: 2mg
Sodium: 280mg | Fiber: 2g | PCF Ratio: 10-80-10 | Exchange Approx.: 2 Vegetables

INGREDIENTS | SERVES 4

¼ cup cider vinegar

1 teaspoon sugar

¼ cup low-fat mayonnaise

¼ teaspoon celery salt

Freshly ground black pepper, to taste

¼ teaspoon celery seeds

3 cups shredded cabbage

½ cup shredded red onion

In a large bowl, mix the cider vinegar, sugar, mayonnaise, celery salt, black pepper, and celery seeds. Add the cabbage and onions. Chill for 1 hour and serve.

Coleslaw History

Food historians believe that the modern coleslaw recipe has actually been around for at least 200 years. Today, coleslaw is served with barbecue, burgers, chicken, and other cooked foods. Shredded carrots and a mix of red and green cabbage can be used to make coleslaw colorful and fun.

Marinated Roasted Peppers and Eggplant

PER SERVING: Calories: 179 | Protein: 2g | Carbohydrates: 14g | Fat: 14g | Saturated Fat: 2g | Cholesterol: 0mg
Sodium: 5mg | Fiber: 6g | PCF Ratio: 5-29-66 | Exchange Approx.: 3 Vegetables, 3 Fats

INGREDIENTS | SERVES 4

1 pound sweet red peppers

1 large eggplant, sliced into ¼" thick rounds

4 tablespoons olive oil, divided

1 tablespoon balsamic vinegar

1 tablespoon finely chopped onion

1 teaspoon oregano

Freshly ground pepper, to taste

1. To roast red peppers, follow procedure in sidebar for Roasted Red Pepper and Plum Sauce recipe in Chapter 12. Set aside.

2. Brush eggplant slices with 2 tablespoons olive oil; place on grill. Grill for about 5 minutes on each side until softened. Remove from grill and place in a container. Add roasted peppers to container.

3. In a small bowl, prepare the marinade by whisking together balsamic vinegar, remaining 2 tablespoons olive oil, onion, oregano, and pepper. Pour over the vegetables. Cover and refrigerate for 3–4 hours before serving.

Spinach Salad with Pomegranate

PER SERVING: Calories: 107 | Protein: 4g | Carbohydrates: 8g | Fat: 8g | Saturated Fat: 1g | Cholesterol: 0mg
Sodium: 259mg | Fiber: 3g | PCF Ratio: 13-26-61 | Exchange Approx.: 1 Vegetable, 2 Fats

INGREDIENTS | SERVES 6

1 pound fresh spinach

½ cup very thinly sliced red onion

8 ounces fresh tomatoes, cut into ½" wedges

⅓ cup chopped walnuts

½ teaspoon salt

¼ cup lemon juice

1½ tablespoons olive oil

¼ cup pomegranate seeds

1. Wash spinach thoroughly and drain well; loosely chop and place in a large bowl.

2. Add onions, tomato, and walnuts; toss lightly.

3. In small bowl, whisk together salt, lemon juice, and olive oil. Drizzle over salad; toss lightly.

4. Garnish salad with pomegranate seeds.

Tabbouleh

PER SERVING: Calories: 144 | Protein: 3g | Carbohydrates: 15g | Fat: 9g | Saturated Fat: 1g | Cholesterol: 0mg
Sodium: 212mg | Fiber: 4g | PCF Ratio: 7-38-55 | Exchange Approx.: ½ Starch, 1 Vegetable, 2 Fats

INGREDIENTS | SERVES 6

1 cup boiling water

½ cup bulgur wheat

1 cup packed finely chopped fresh parsley

⅓ cup finely chopped fresh mint

½ cup finely chopped red onion

1 cup chopped cucumber

¼ cup lemon juice

¼ cup olive oil

½ teaspoon salt

Freshly ground pepper, to taste

1 cup chopped fresh tomato

2 cups leaf lettuce (optional)

1. In small bowl, pour boiling water over bulgur wheat; let stand 20 minutes.

2. When bulgur is softened, drain and squeeze out any excess water using a colander lined with cheesecloth.

3. In a medium bowl, combine parsley, mint, onion, cucumber, and bulgur. Add lemon juice, olive oil, salt, and pepper; mix well.

4. Cover and refrigerate at least 3 hours.

5. Just before serving, add chopped tomatoes; toss lightly. Serve as is or on bed of leaf lettuce.

Tomatoes Stuffed with Quinoa Salad

PER SERVING: Calories: 180 | Protein: 5g | Carbohydrates: 24g | Fat: 9g | Saturated Fat: 2g | Cholesterol: 4mg
Sodium: 78mg | Fiber: 4g | PCF Ratio: 11-49-40 | Exchange Approx.: ½ Starch, 2½ Vegetables, 2½ Fats

INGREDIENTS | SERVES 6

½ cup quinoa

1 cup water

6 large (3 pounds) tomatoes

1½ cups peeled and finely diced cucumber

⅓ cup chopped fresh parsley

¼ cup chopped fresh mint

½ cup finely chopped red onion

3 tablespoons crumbled feta cheese

2 tablespoons lemon juice

3 tablespoons olive oil

1. Rinse quinoa in fine mesh strainer before cooking. To cook: Place quinoa and water in small saucepan; bring to a boil. Reduce heat; cover and cook until all water is absorbed, about 15 minutes. Cool.

2. Prepare tomatoes: Remove caps and hollow out, leaving shell about ½" thick.

3. In a medium mixing bowl, combine cooked quinoa, cucumber, parsley, mint, red onion, and feta cheese.

4. In a small bowl, mix lemon juice and olive oil together. Pour over quinoa and vegetables.

5. Stuff tomatoes with mixture and serve.

Wilted Lettuce with a Healthier Difference

PER SERVING: Calories: 71 | Protein: 2g | Carbohydrates: 7g | Fat: 5g | Saturated Fat: 1g | Cholesterol: 0mg | Sodium: 9mg | Fiber: 2g | PCF Ratio: 8-34-57 | Exchange Approx.: 2 Free Vegetables, 1 Fat

INGREDIENTS | SERVES 1

½ teaspoon olive oil

¼ cup chopped red onion

1½ cups tightly packed loose-leaf lettuce

¼ teaspoon lemon juice or your choice of vinegar

½ teaspoon extra-virgin olive oil, walnut oil, or almond oil

Optional seasonings:

    Pinch dried herbs of your choice, such as thyme or parsley

    Pinch sugar

    Pinch toasted sesame seeds or grated Parmesan cheese

1. In heated nonstick skillet treated with nonstick cooking spray, add olive oil and red onion. Sauté until onion is almost transparent. Add lettuce and sauté until lettuce is warmed and wilted.

2. In salad bowl, whisk lemon juice with extra-virgin olive oil. Add pinch of herbs and sugar, if using; whisk into oil mixture. Add wilted greens; toss with dressing. Top salad with pinch of toasted sesame seeds or Parmesan cheese, if desired. Serve immediately.

Taco Salad

PER SERVING: Calories: 426 | Protein: 23g | Carbohydrates: 58g | Fat: 13g | Saturated Fat: 7g | Cholesterol: 30mg Sodium: 380mg | Fiber: 13g | PCF Ratio: 21-53-26 | Exchange Approx.: 1 Lean Meat, 1 High-Fat Meat, 3 Starches, 2 Vegetables

INGREDIENTS | SERVES 8

8 cups tightly packed salad greens

1 recipe Vegetable and Bean Chili (see recipe in Chapter 4)

8 ounces Cheddar cheese, shredded (to yield 2 cups)

8 ounces nonfat corn chips

Nonstarchy free-exchange vegetables of your choice, such as chopped celery, onion, or banana or jalapeño peppers (optional)

Divide salad greens between 8 large bowls. Top with chili, Cheddar cheese, corn chips, and vegetables or peppers, if using.

Green Bean and Mushroom Salad

PER SERVING: Calories: 131 | Protein: 2g | Carbohydrates: 9g | Fat: 10g | Saturated Fat: 1g | Cholesterol: 0mg
Sodium: 4mg | Fiber: 3g | PCF Ratio: 7-26-67 | Exchange Approx.: 2 Fats, 2 Vegetables

INGREDIENTS | SERVES 4

2 cups fresh small green beans, ends trimmed

1½ cups sliced fresh mushrooms

½ cup chopped red onion

3 tablespoons extra-virgin olive, canola, or corn oil

1 tablespoon balsamic or red wine vinegar

1 clove garlic, minced

½ teaspoon sea salt (optional)

¼ teaspoon freshly ground pepper (optional)

1. Cook green beans in large pot of unsalted boiling water for 5 minutes. Drain in colander; immediately plunge into bowl of ice water to stop cooking process and retain bright green color of the beans.

2. Once beans are cool, drain and place in large bowl. If you'll be serving salad immediately, add mushrooms and onion to bowl; toss to mix. (Otherwise, chill beans separately and add to salad immediately before serving.)

3. To make dressing, combine oil and vinegar in small bowl. Whisk together with garlic; pour over salad. Toss lightly; season with salt and pepper, if desired. Serve immediately.

Spinach Salad with Apple-Avocado Dressing

PER SERVING: Calories: 122 | Protein: 2g | Carbohydrates: 8g | Fat: 10g | Saturated Fat: 1g | Cholesterol: 0mg Sodium: 90mg | Fiber: 3g | PCF Ratio: 7-25-68 | Exchange Approx.: 2½ Fats, 1 Free Vegetable

INGREDIENTS | SERVES 4

¼ cup unsweetened apple juice

1 teaspoon (or up to 1 tablespoon) cider vinegar

1 clove garlic, minced

1 teaspoon Bragg's Liquid Aminos or soy sauce

½ teaspoon Worcestershire sauce (see recipe for homemade in Chapter 12)

2 teaspoons olive oil

1 avocado, peeled and chopped

2½ cups tightly packed spinach and other salad greens

½ cup thinly sliced red onion

½ cup sliced radishes

½ cup bean sprouts

1. In blender or food processor, combine juice, vinegar (the amount of which will depend on how you like your dressing), garlic, Liquid Aminos, Worcestershire, oil, and avocado and process until smooth.

2. In large bowl, toss greens, onion, radishes, and bean sprouts. Pour dressing over salad and toss again.

Mandarin Snap Pea Salad

PER SERVING, WITHOUT DRESSING: Calories: 76 | **Protein:** 4g | **Carbohydrates:** 16g | **Fat:** 0g | **Saturated Fat:** 0g | **Cholesterol:** 0mg | **Sodium:** 344mg | **Fiber:** 4g | **PCF Ratio:** 19-78-3 | **Exchange Approx.:** ½ Starch, 1 Vegetable, ½ Lean Meat, ½ Fat

INGREDIENTS | SERVES 8

¾ pound snap peas, cut into ½" pieces

1 cup drained canned mandarin oranges

1½ cups rinsed and drained canned kidney beans

1 cup thinly sliced red onion

½ cup chopped fresh parsley

2 cups chopped cabbage

⅓ cup Poppy Seed Dressing (see sidebar)

1. In a medium bowl, combine all ingredients except dressing.

2. Mix in Poppy Seed Dressing; refrigerate several hours before serving.

Poppy Seed Dressing

Combine ½ cup red wine vinegar, ¼ cup orange juice, 3 tablespoons lemon juice, ½ cup canola oil, 1 teaspoon Splenda Brown Sugar Blend, 1 teaspoon dry mustard, 1 teaspoon salt, and 1 tablespoon poppy seeds; mix well in covered jar. Store in refrigerator. Nutritional analysis 1 ounce serving (1½ tablespoons): 68 Calories; Protein: 0g; Carbohydrates: 9g; Fat: 7g; Saturated Fat: 1g; Cholesterol: 0mg; Sodium: 148mg; PCF Ration: 1-9-90; Exchange Approx.: 1½ Fats.

Zesty Feta and Olive Salad

PER SERVING: Calories: 109 | Protein: 3g | Carbohydrates: 6g | Fat: 8g | Saturated Fat: 3g | Cholesterol: 132mg
Sodium: 326mg | Fiber: 2g | PCF Ratio: 11-22-66 | Exchange Approx.: 1 Vegetable, 2 Fats

INGREDIENTS | SERVES 4

2 ounces crumbled feta

1 small red onion, diced

½ cup chopped celery

½ cup diced cucumber

1 clove garlic, minced

1 teaspoon lemon zest

1 teaspoon orange zest

1 cup halved very small cherry tomatoes

½ cup pitted and sliced mix of green and kalamata olives

1 tablespoon extra-virgin olive oil

2 tablespoons minced fresh Italian parsley

2 teaspoons minced fresh oregano

1 teaspoon minced fresh mint

1 tablespoon minced fresh cilantro (optional)

4–8 large romaine or butter lettuce leaves

Freshly ground black pepper, to taste

1. In a large bowl, mix feta, onion, celery, cucumber, garlic, lemon zest, orange zest, tomatoes, and olives.

2. Add olive oil and fresh herbs; toss again.

3. Arrange lettuce leaves on 4 salad plates; spoon feta salad on top. Top with pepper and serve.

Greek Salad

PER SERVING: Calories: 221 | Protein: 4g | Carbohydrates: 9g | Fat: 20g | Saturated Fat: 5g | Cholesterol: 17mg
Sodium: 414mg | Fiber: 3g | PCF Ratio: 8-16-76 | Exchange Approx.: 1 Vegetable, ½ Meat, 3½ Fats

INGREDIENTS | SERVES 4

4 cups chopped romaine lettuce

1 large tomato, seeded and chopped

1 small cucumber, sliced

1 green bell pepper, cut into rings

½ cup feta cheese

¼ cup red wine vinegar

Juice of 1 lemon

1 tablespoon Italian seasoning

Salt and pepper, to taste

¼ cup extra-virgin olive oil

2 teaspoons capers

16 kalamata olives

1. In a large bowl, mix lettuce, tomato, cucumber, bell pepper, and feta.

2. To make dressing, whisk vinegar, lemon juice, Italian seasoning, salt, and pepper in a small bowl; mix in olive oil.

3. Coat vegetables with dressing.

4. Place salad on plates. Top salad plates with capers and olives.

Feta Is "Betta"

Feta cheese has been made by Greek shepherds for centuries. Originally it was made from goat's or sheep's milk; today feta cheese is made from pasteurized cow's milk. In Greece, feta cheese is served in restaurants and homes as a garnish on various types of fresh salads.

Wheat Berry Salad

PER SERVING: Calories: 358 | Protein: 4g | Carbohydrates: 34g | Fat: 25g | Saturated Fat: 3g | Cholesterol: 0mg
Sodium: 430mg | Fiber: 5g | PCF Ratio: 4-38-58 | Exchange Approx.: 1 Starch, 1 Fruit, 3 Fats

INGREDIENTS | SERVES 6

4 cups water
1 teaspoon kosher salt
1 cup wheat berries
1 cup French Dressing (see Chapter 12)
2 cups peeled and diced jicama
1 green apple, peeled, cored, and diced
½ pound small seedless red grapes
2 cups mixed baby greens
Freshly ground black pepper, to taste

The Homely Legume

Jicama, also known as a Mexican turnip, is a lumpy root vegetable with a unique and versatile taste. Like a potato, it can be fried, baked, boiled, steamed, or mashed; just keep in mind that the peel is inedible. Jicama can also be eaten raw. Try it as a vehicle for guacamole or use its mild flavor and crunchy texture in fruit salad.

1. Bring the water to a boil in a large pot. Add salt and wheat berries.

2. Cook the wheat berries until crisp-tender, following package directions.

3. Place cooked wheat berries in a large serving bowl. While still warm, toss with the French Dressing. Add jicama, apple, and grapes. Chill for 3–4 hours.

4. Place mixture on plates over mixed baby greens. Add pepper to taste.

Rainbow Potato Salad

PER SERVING: Calories: 146 | Protein: 5g | Carbohydrates: 29g | Fat: 2g | Saturated Fat: 0g | Cholesterol: 0mg
Sodium: 615mg | Fiber: 5g | PCF Ratio: 12-77-11 | Exchange Approx.: 1½ Starches

INGREDIENTS | SERVES 6

2 pounds (6 medium) red potatoes

⅓ cup finely chopped carrots

¼ cup finely chopped onion

¼ cup finely chopped green pepper

¼ cup finely chopped yellow or red bell pepper

2 tablespoons red wine vinegar

2 tablespoons lemon juice

¼ teaspoon celery seed

1 teaspoon sugar

½ teaspoon salt

2 tablespoons light mayonnaise

1. Wash and scrub red potatoes. Place whole potatoes in pot and cover with water. Boil over medium heat for about 20 minutes until potatoes are cooked. Drain; set aside to cool.

2. Combine carrots, onion, peppers, vinegar, lemon juice, celery seed, sugar, and salt in small bowl; mix. Cover and refrigerate for 2–3 hours.

3. After vegetables have marinated, add mayonnaise and mix well.

4. Cut potatoes (with skins on) into ½" cubes.

5. In large bowl, combine potatoes and vegetables; mix well.

Potato and Snow Pea Salad

PER SERVING: Calories: 139 | Protein: 5g | Carbohydrates: 28g | Fat: 1g | Saturated Fat: 0g | Cholesterol: 3mg
Sodium: 223mg | Fiber: 3g | PCF Ratio: 13-78-9 | Exchange Approx.: 1 Starch, 1 Vegetable, ½ Fat

INGREDIENTS | SERVES 8

2 pounds (6 medium) red potatoes

3 slices bacon

½ cup chopped onion

¾ pound snow peas, cut into ½" pieces

½ teaspoon salt

¼ cup apple cider vinegar

1. Wash and scrub red potatoes. Place whole potatoes in pot; cover with water. Boil over medium heat for 20 minutes until potatoes are cooked. Drain and chill for approximately 1 hour. Once chilled, cut into ½" cubes.

2. Cut bacon slices into ½" pieces. Place in nonstick frying pan with onions; fry for 3–4 minutes until crisp. There should be a light coating of fat in pan from bacon. If there is excess fat, pour off before going to Step 3.

3. Add snow peas; toss with bacon and onion for 2 minutes. Remove from heat.

4. In a small bowl, dissolve salt into cider vinegar; mix into snow peas.

5. In large bowl, combine potatoes and snow peas; mix well.

Summary Salad

PER SERVING: Calories: 73 | Protein: 2g | Carbohydrates: 7g | Fat: 5g | Saturated Fat: 1g | Cholesterol: 0mg
Sodium: 109mg | Fiber: 2g | PCF Ratio: 9-36-55 | Exchange Approx.: 1½ Vegetables, 1 Fat

INGREDIENTS | SERVES 6

2 cups chopped (½" pieces) snap peas

2 cups chopped (½" pieces) summer squash

½ cup chopped carrots

3 tablespoons minced mushrooms

2 cups chopped cucumbers

¼ cup thinly sliced onion

2 tablespoons canola oil

2 tablespoons balsamic vinegar

¼ teaspoon salt

¼ teaspoon thyme

¼ teaspoon marjoram

Tip

Add the oil and vinegar dressing just before serving. Minimize the exposure of vinegar to certain vegetables such as snap peas or green beans to retain their bright colors.

1. In a large bowl, combine snap peas, squash, carrots, and mushrooms; steam in microwave for 2–3 minutes, until crisp-tender. Cool and refrigerate.

2. When cooled, add cucumbers and onions.

3. In a small bowl, whisk together canola oil, balsamic vinegar, salt, thyme, and marjoram.

4. Pour dressing over vegetables and toss lightly. Serve.

CHAPTER 12

Salad Dressings, Salsas, and Sauces

Creamy Feta Vinaigrette

PER SERVING: Calories: 31 | Protein: 1g | Carbohydrates: 1g | Fat: 2g | Saturated Fat: 1g | Cholesterol: 4mg Sodium: 57mg | Fiber: 0g | PCF Ratio: 17-17-66 | Exchange Approx.: ½ Fat

INGREDIENTS | MAKES ABOUT ⅔ CUP;
SERVING SIZE:
1 TABLESPOON

½ cup plain, low-fat yogurt
1 tablespoon lemon juice
1 tablespoon olive oil
1½ ounces feta cheese
2 teaspoons fresh mint
½ packet Splenda (optional)
Freshly ground pepper, to taste

Process all ingredients in food processor or blender. Chill before serving.

Raspberry Tarragon Vinaigrette

PER SERVING: Calories: 120 | Protein: 0g | Carbohydrates: 9g | Fat: 9g | Saturated Fat: 1g | Cholesterol: 0mg
Sodium: 0mg | Fiber: 0g | PCF Ratio: 0-33-67 | Exchange Approx.: 2 Fats

INGREDIENTS | MAKES ¾ CUP; SERVING
SIZE: 1 TABLESPOON

½ cup olive oil

¼ cup Raspberry Vinegar (see sidebar)

2 teaspoons lemon juice

½ tablespoon finely chopped fresh
tarragon

Salt and pepper, to taste

Combine all the ingredients in a covered jar; shake thoroughly.

Making Raspberry Vinegar

Combine 2 cups raspberries, lightly mashed; 2 tablespoons honey; and 2 cups red wine vinegar in nonstick saucepan. Simmer uncovered for 10 minutes; cool. Place in covered 1-quart jar; store at room temperature for 3 weeks. Strain vinegar from berries; pour strained vinegar into an empty wine bottle. Cork or cap.

Balsamic Vinaigrette and Marinade

PER SERVING: Calories: 124 | Protein: 0g | Carbohydrates: 1g | Fat: 14g | Saturated Fat: 2g | Cholesterol: 0mg
Sodium: 4mg | Fiber: 0g | PCF Ratio: 0-4-95 | Exchange Approx.: 3 Fats

INGREDIENTS | YIELDS 1 CUP; SERVING SIZE: 2 TABLESPOONS

2 cloves garlic, minced

2 shallots, minced

⅓ cup balsamic vinegar

Juice of ½ lemon

Salt and pepper, to taste

½ teaspoon Dijon mustard

½ cup olive oil

Place all the ingredients except the olive oil in a blender. With the blender running on a medium setting, slowly pour the oil into the blender. Blend until very smooth. Cover and store in the refrigerator for up to 7 days.

Bleu Cheese Dressing

PER SERVING: Calories: 24 | Protein: 1g | Carbohydrates: 1g | Fat: 2g | Saturated Fat: 1g | Cholesterol: 3mg
Sodium: 52mg | Fiber: 0g | PCF Ratio: 21-23-57 | Exchange Approx.: ½ Fat

INGREDIENTS | MAKES 6 TABLESPOONS; SERVING SIZE: 1 TABLESPOON

2 tablespoons plain, nonfat yogurt

1 tablespoon cottage cheese

1 tablespoon real mayonnaise

½ teaspoon lemon juice

½ teaspoon honey

1 tablespoon plus 2 teaspoons crumbled bleu cheese

Place yogurt, cottage cheese, mayonnaise, lemon juice, and honey in a blender and process until smooth. Fold in bleu cheese.

Dijon Vinaigrette

PER SERVING: Calories: 74 | Protein: 0g | Carbohydrates: 1g | Fat: 8g | Saturated Fat: 1g | Cholesterol: 0mg
Sodium: 266mg | Fiber: 0g | PCF Ratio: 1-2-97 | Exchange Approx.: 2 Fats

INGREDIENTS | MAKES ABOUT 5 TABLESPOONS; SERVING SIZE: 1 TABLESPOON

1 tablespoon Dijon mustard
½ teaspoon sea salt
½ teaspoon freshly ground black pepper
1 tablespoon red wine vinegar
3 tablespoons virgin olive oil

Put all the ingredients in small bowl. Use wire whisk or fork to mix.

The Vinegar-Oil Balancing Act

The easiest way to tame too much vinegar is to add some olive oil. Because oil adds fat, the better alternative is to start with less vinegar and add it gradually until you arrive at a flavor you prefer.

Tangy Lemon-Garlic Tomato Dressing

PER SERVING: Calories: 7 | **Protein:** 0g | **Carbohydrates:** 1g | **Fat:** 1g | **Saturated Fat:** 0g | **Cholesterol:** 0mg
Sodium: 1mg | **Fiber:** 1g | **PCF Ratio:** 14-44-42 | **Exchange Approx.:** ½ Free

**INGREDIENTS | MAKES ABOUT ¼ CUP;
SERVING SIZE:
1 TABLESPOON**

1 tablespoon ground flaxseed
2 cloves garlic
⅛ cup cider vinegar
⅛ teaspoon freshly ground pepper
1 small tomato, chopped
¼ teaspoon celery seed
1 tablespoon lemon juice
¼ cup water

Place all the ingredients in blender and blend until smooth.

Friendly Fat and Fiber

In addition to providing fiber, ground flax-seed is a rich source of omega-3 and -6 essential fatty acids. Flaxseed oil is low in saturated fat and therefore a heart-healthy choice. Just remember that flaxseed oil must be refrigerated or it will go rancid.

Lemon-Almond Dressing

PER SERVING: Calories: 25 | Protein: 1g | Carbohydrates: 2g | Fat: 2g | Saturated Fat: 0g | Cholesterol: 0mg
Sodium: 0mg | Fiber: 1g | PCF Ratio: 12-27-61 | Exchange Approx.: ½ Fat

**INGREDIENTS | MAKES ABOUT ⅔ CUP;
SERVING SIZE:
1 TABLESPOON**

¼ cup raw almonds

1 tablespoon lemon juice

¼ cup water

1½ teaspoons honey

¼ teaspoon lemon pepper

½ slice (1" diameter) peeled gingerroot

¼ clove garlic

1½ teaspoons chopped fresh chives, or ½ teaspoon dried

1½ teaspoons chopped fresh basil, or ½ teaspoon dried

Put all ingredients in food processor or blender and process until smooth.

Salad: Undressed

Make a quick salad without dressing by mixing chopped celery, onion, and other vegetables such as cucumbers or zucchini. Add low-salt seasoning or toss vegetables with Bragg's Liquid Aminos or low-sodium soy sauce and serve over salad greens.

Italian Dressing

PER SERVING: Calories: 61 | Protein: 0g | Carbohydrates: 0g | Fat: 7g | Saturated Fat: 1g | Cholesterol: 0mg
Sodium: 0mg | Fiber: 0g | PCF Ratio: 0-2-98 | Exchange Approx.: 1½ Fats

INGREDIENTS | MAKES 1 CUP; SERVING SIZE: 2 TABLESPOONS

⅓ cup balsamic vinegar

½ teaspoon dry mustard

1 teaspoon lemon juice

2 cloves garlic, chopped

1 teaspoon dried oregano, or 1 tablespoon fresh

Salt and pepper, to taste

½ cup extra-virgin olive oil

1. Put all the ingredients except the olive oil into a blender and blend until smooth.

2. Slowly add in the oil in a thin stream. Bottle and give it a good shake before serving.

Sweet and Sour Dressing

PER SERVING: Calories: 27 | Protein: 1g | Carbohydrates: 5g | Fat: 1g | Saturated Fat: 0g | Cholesterol: 0mg
Sodium: 613mg | Fiber: 0g | PCF Ratio: 9-72-19 | Exchange Approx.: 1 Free Condiment

INGREDIENTS | MAKES ½ CUP; SERVING SIZE: 1 TABLESPOON

6 tablespoons soy sauce

1 teaspoon Asian sesame seed oil

1 teaspoon minced fresh ginger

1 tablespoon maple syrup or honey

1 tablespoon frozen concentrated orange juice, thawed

1 tablespoon apricot preserves or jam

1 clove garlic, minced

1 teaspoon Tabasco Sauce, or to taste

Whisk all the ingredients together in a small saucepan over low heat until well blended and serve.

French Dressing

PER SERVING: Calories: 162 | Protein: 0g | Carbohydrates: 1g | Fat: 18g | Saturated Fat: 2g
Cholesterol: 0mg | Sodium: 4mg | Fiber: 0g | PCF Ratio: 0-2-98 | Exchange Approx.: 3½ Fats

INGREDIENTS | MAKES 1 CUP; SERVING SIZE: 2 TABLESPOONS

⅓ cup red wine vinegar

½ teaspoon Worcestershire sauce

1 clove garlic, minced

2 tablespoons fresh parsley, chopped

1 teaspoon thyme, dried

1 teaspoon rosemary, dried

Pinch sugar

⅔ cup extra-virgin olive oil

Mix all ingredients except the olive oil in the blender. Slowly add the oil in a thin stream so that the ingredients emulsify.

Homemade Worcestershire Sauce

PER SERVING: Calories: 14 | Protein: 0g | Carbohydrates: 4g | Fat: 0g | Saturated Fat: 0g | Cholesterol: 0mg
Sodium: 15mg | Fiber: 0g | PCF Ratio: 3-97-0 | Exchange Approx.: 1 Free Condiment

INGREDIENTS | MAKES 1 CUP; SERVING SIZE: 1 TABLESPOON

1½ cups cider vinegar

¼ cup plum jam

1 tablespoon blackstrap molasses

1 clove garlic, minced

⅛ teaspoon chili powder

⅛ teaspoon ground cloves

Pinch cayenne pepper

¼ cup chopped onion

½ teaspoon ground allspice

⅛ teaspoon dry mustard

1 teaspoon Bragg's Liquid Aminos

1. Combine all the ingredients in large saucepan and stir until mixture boils.

2. Lower heat and simmer uncovered for 1 hour, stirring occasionally. Store in covered jar in refrigerator. Will keep in refrigerator up to 2 weeks.

Gingered Peach Sauce

PER SERVING: Calories: 54 | Protein: 1g | Carbohydrates: 5g | Fat: 2g | Saturated Fat: 1g | Cholesterol: 0mg
Sodium: 57mg | Fiber: 1g | PCF Ratio: 5-47-48 | Exchange Approx.: ½ Fat, 1 Fruit

INGREDIENTS | MAKES 2 CUPS; SERVING SIZE: ½ CUP

2 teaspoons olive oil

1 tablespoon chopped shallot

2 teaspoons grated fresh ginger

⅓ cup dry white wine

1 small peach, peeled and diced

1 tablespoon frozen unsweetened orange juice concentrate

1 teaspoon Bragg's Liquid Aminos

½ teaspoon cornstarch

1. Heat olive oil in nonstick skillet over medium heat; sauté shallot and ginger. Add wine; simmer until reduced by half. Add peach, orange juice concentrate, and Bragg's Liquid Aminos; return to simmer, stirring occasionally.

2. In separate container, mix cornstarch with a tablespoon of sauce; stir to create a slurry, mixing well to remove any lumps. Add slurry to sauce; simmer for 5–7 minutes until mixture thickens. Transfer to blender or food processor; process until smooth. Will keep in refrigerator up to 2 weeks.

Country Barbecue Sauce

PER SERVING: Calories: 119 | Protein: 3g | Carbohydrates: 21g | Fat: 4g | Saturated Fat: 1g | Cholesterol: 0mg
Sodium: 743mg | Fiber: 4g | PCF Ratio: 9-63-28 | Exchange Approx.: 3 Vegetables, 1 Fat

**INGREDIENTS | MAKES 1 QUART;
SERVING SIZE: 4 OUNCES**

4 cloves garlic, chopped

2 large yellow onions, chopped

2 sweet red peppers, chopped

2 serrano chili peppers, cored, seeded, and minced (optional)

2 tablespoons olive oil

1 teaspoon salt, or to taste

2 teaspoons black pepper

1 teaspoon Tabasco Sauce, or to taste

2 ounces cider vinegar

2 tablespoons Dijon mustard

1 (28-ounce) can tomato purée

2 tablespoons molasses

1 teaspoon liquid smoke

4 whole cloves

1 cinnamon stick

1 teaspoon hot paprika

1 tablespoon sweet paprika

1. In a large soup pot, sauté the garlic, onions, and peppers in olive oil. Stirring constantly, add the rest of the ingredients. Bring to a boil. Reduce heat.

2. Cover the pot and simmer for 2 hours. If you don't like the texture, purée in a blender. Will keep in refrigerator up to 2 weeks.

Sweet, Spicy, or Both

The amount of heat you add to barbecue sauce is a matter of personal taste, as is the amount of sweetness. Some people prefer the flavor of honey over molasses; others use brown sugar. You can also change the flavor of the sauce by adding a chopped lemon, orange juice, or lime juice. Experiment!

Cucumber, Dill, and Sour Cream Sauce

PER SERVING: Calories: 59 | Protein: 2g | Carbohydrates: 6g | Fat: 4g | Saturated Fat: 2g | Cholesterol: 12mg
Sodium: 612mg | Fiber: 1g | PCF Ratio: 10-36-54 | Exchange Approx.: ½ Milk, 1 Fat

INGREDIENTS | SERVES 4

1½ cups peeled and chopped cucumber

½ cup finely chopped red onion

Juice of 1 lemon

1 teaspoon Tabasco Sauce

½ cup low-fat sour cream

1 teaspoon celery salt, or to taste

½ cup finely minced fresh dill

2 tablespoons minced fresh chives

½ teaspoon sweet paprika, or to taste

Mix all the ingredients in a medium bowl. Cover and refrigerate for 1 hour. Serve chilled. Use for dipping vegetables or recipes calling for sour cream garnish.

Pesto Sauce

PER SERVING: Calories: 37 | Protein: 1g | Carbohydrates: 1g | Fat: 4g | Saturated Fat: 1g | Cholesterol: 1mg
Sodium: 14mg | Fiber: 0g | PCF Ratio: 10-6-85 | Exchange Approx.: 1 Fat

INGREDIENTS | MAKES ABOUT 3 CUPS; SERVING SIZE: 1 TABLESPOON

¾ cup pine nuts
4 cups tightly packed fresh basil leaves
½ cup freshly grated Parmesan cheese
3 large garlic cloves, minced
¼ teaspoon salt
1 teaspoon freshly ground black pepper
½ cup extra-virgin olive oil, divided

1. Preheat oven to 350°F. Spread pine nuts on baking sheet. Bake for about 5 minutes and stir. Continue to bake for 10 minutes until nuts are golden brown and highly aromatic, stirring occasionally. Let nuts cool completely, then chop finely.

2. Fill medium heavy saucepan halfway with water. Place over medium heat; bring to a boil. Next to pot, place large bowl filled with water and ice. Using tongs, dip a few basil leaves into boiling water. Blanch for 3 seconds; quickly remove from boiling water and place in ice water. Repeat process until all basil has been blanched, adding ice to water as needed. Drain basil in colander and pat dry with a towel.

3. In blender or food processor, combine pine nuts, blanched basil, cheese, garlic, salt, pepper, and all but 1 tablespoon olive oil; process until smooth and uniform. Pour into airtight container and add remaining olive oil to top to act as protective barrier. Mix oil layer on top into pesto before using. Pesto can be stored in refrigerator for up to 5 days.

4. To freeze pesto, mix in oil on top; place it in a tightly sealed container. To freeze small amounts of pesto, pour into ice cube trays and freeze until solid. Once frozen, you can remove the pesto cubes and place them in sealed freezer bags.

Roasted Red Pepper and Plum Sauce

PER SERVING: Calories: 38 | Protein: 0g | Carbohydrates: 10g | Fat: 1g | Saturated Fat: 0g | Cholesterol: 0mg
Sodium: 76mg | Fiber: 1g | PCF Ratio: 3-95-2 | Exchange Approx.: ½ Misc. Carbohydrate

INGREDIENTS | MAKES 2 CUPS; SERVING SIZE: 1 TABLESPOON

1 large roasted red pepper, pulp only (see sidebar)

½ pound apricots, quartered and pitted

¾ pound plums, quartered and pitted

1⅓ cups apple cider vinegar

⅔ cup water

⅓ cup white sugar

½ cup brown sugar

2 tablespoons corn syrup

2 tablespoons grated fresh ginger

1 teaspoon salt

1 tablespoon toasted mustard seeds

4 scallions, chopped (white parts only)

1 teaspoon minced fresh garlic

½ teaspoon cinnamon

1. Place all ingredients together in large pot and bring to a boil. Reduce heat; simmer, covered, for 30 minutes.

2. Uncover and simmer for another hour.

3. Place in blender or food processor; process to desired consistency. The sauce can be stored in refrigerator for 4–6 weeks.

Roasting Red Peppers

The traditional method of roasting a red pepper is to use a long-handled fork to hold the pepper over the open flame of a gas burner until it's charred. Of course, there are a variety of other methods as well. You can place the pepper on a rack set over an electric burner and turn it occasionally, until the skin is blackened. This should take about 4 to 6 minutes. You can also put the pepper over direct heat on a preheated grill. Use tongs to turn the pepper occasionally. Another method is to broil the pepper on a broiler rack about 2 inches from the heat, turning the pepper every 5 minutes. Total broiling time will be about 15 to 20 minutes, or until the skins are blistered and charred. The key to peeling the peppers is letting them sit in their steam in a closed container until they are cool. Once the peppers are cool, the skin will rub or peel off easily.

Mock White Sauce

PER RECIPE: Calories: 61 | Protein: 2g | Carbohydrates: 6g | Fat: 3g | Saturated Fat: 2g | Cholesterol: 9mg
Sodium: 190mg | Fiber: 0g | PCF Ratio: 20-36-44 | Exchange Approx.: ½ Fat, ½ Skim Milk

INGREDIENTS | MAKES ABOUT 1 CUP; SERVING SIZE: ½ CUP

1 tablespoon unsalted butter
1 tablespoon flour
¼ teaspoon sea salt
Pinch white pepper
1 cup Mock Cream (see recipe in this chapter)

1. In medium heavy nonstick saucepan, melt butter over very low heat. Butter should gently melt; you do not want it to bubble and turn brown. While butter is melting, mix together flour, salt, and white pepper in small bowl.

2. Once butter is melted, add flour mixture; stir constantly. (A heat-safe, flat-bottom spoon safe for nonstick pans works well for this.) Once mixture thickens and starts to bubble, about 2 minutes, slowly pour in some Mock Cream; stir until blended with roux. Add a little more Mock Cream; stir until blended. Add remaining Mock Cream; continue cooking, stirring constantly to make sure sauce doesn't stick to bottom of pan. Once sauce begins to steam and appears it's just about to boil, reduce heat and simmer until sauce thickens, about 3 minutes. This sauce can be used in recipes calling for a white sauce. Once prepared, it can be refrigerated for up to 3 days.

Fat-Free Roux

PER SERVING, ROUX ONLY: Calories: 13 | **Protein:** 0g | **Carbohydrates:** 2g | **Fat:** 0g | **Saturated Fat:** 0g | **Cholesterol:** 0mg
Sodium: 1mg | **Fiber:** 0g | **PCF Ratio:** 1-99-0 | **Exchange Approx.:** 1 Free

INGREDIENTS | MAKES ENOUGH TO THICKEN 1 CUP OF LIQUID; SERVING SIZE: ¼ CUP

1 tablespoon cornstarch
2 tablespoons wine (Use red wine for a defatted beef broth gravy. Use white wine for chicken or seafood gravy or sauce.)

1. In a small bowl, whisk ingredients together until well blended, making sure there are no lumps.
2. To use as thickener for 1 cup of broth, heat broth until it reaches a boil. Slowly whisk roux into broth; return to a boil. Reduce heat; simmer, stirring constantly, until mixture thickens enough to coat back of spoon. (A gravy or sauce made in this manner will thicken more as it cools. It's important to bring a cornstarch slurry to a boil; this helps it thicken and removes the starchy taste.)

Mock Cream

PER RECIPE: Calories: 147 | **Protein:** 14g | **Carbohydrates:** 21g | **Fat:** 1g | **Saturated Fat:** 1g | **Cholesterol:** 8mg
Sodium: 221mg | **Fiber:** 0g | **PCF Ratio:** 39-57-3 | **Exchange Approx.:** 1½ Skim Milks

INGREDIENTS | MAKES 1¼ CUPS; SERVING SIZE: 2 TABLESPOONS

1 cup skim milk
¼ cup nonfat dry milk

Process all the ingredients in a blender until mixed. Use as a substitute for heavy cream. Once prepared, refrigerate in airtight container for up to 3 days.

Comparative Analysis

Using 1¼ cups heavy cream would give you the following breakdown: Calories: 5,102; Protein: 6g; Carbohydrates: 17g; Fat: 527g; Saturated Fat: 340g; Cholesterol: 2,079mg; Sodium: 516mg; Fiber: 0g; PCF Ratio: 2-3-95; Exchange Approx.: 11 Fats.

Horseradish Mustard

PER SERVING: Calories: 10 | Protein: 0g | Carbohydrates: 1g | Fat: 1g | Saturated Fat: 0g | Cholesterol: 0mg
Sodium: 68mg | Fiber: 0g | PCF Ratio: 12-25-63 | Exchange Approx.: 1 Free Condiment

INGREDIENTS | MAKES ¾ CUP; SERVING SIZE: 1 TEASPOON

¼ cup dry mustard
2½ tablespoons prepared horseradish
1 teaspoon sea salt
¼ cup white wine vinegar
1 tablespoon olive oil
Cayenne pepper, to taste (optional)

Combine all the ingredients in food processor or blender and process until smooth. Pour into decorative jar; store in refrigerator. Will keep in refrigerator for up to 2 weeks.

Caribbean Kiwi Salsa

PER SERVING: Calories: 79 | Protein: 2g | Carbohydrates: 19g | Fat: 0g | Saturated Fat: 0g | Cholesterol: 0mg
Sodium: 28mg | Fiber: 3g | PCF Ratio: 9-87-5 | Exchange Approx.: 1 Fruit, ½ Vegetable

INGREDIENTS | SERVES 6

1 cup peeled and chopped kiwi
1 cup chopped pineapple
1 cup peeled and chopped mango
⅓ cup chopped red onion
1 cup chopped red bell pepper
⅓ cup cooked black beans
3 tablespoons chopped fresh cilantro
2 tablespoons lime juice
½ teaspoon chili powder
Dash cayenne pepper

1. Mix all the ingredients together in a medium bowl.
2. Chill at least 2 hours before serving.

Zesty Black Bean Salsa

PER SERVING: Calories: 91 | Protein: 4g | Carbohydrates: 13g | Fat: 3g | Saturated Fat: 0g | Cholesterol: 0mg
Sodium: 125mg | Fiber: 4g | PCF Ratio: 15-55-30 | Exchange Approx.: ½ Starch, 1 Vegetable, ½ Fat

INGREDIENTS | SERVES 10

1 cup chopped red onion
¼ cup chopped cilantro
¼ cup chopped parsley
3 tablespoons chopped jalapeño pepper
1½ cups cooked black beans
4 cups chopped tomato
3 tablespoons lime juice
2 tablespoons olive oil

1. Place onion, cilantro, parsley, and jalapeño in food processor and chop finely.

2. In a medium bowl, combine onion mixture, black beans, and tomatoes.

3. In a small bowl, whisk together lime juice and olive oil. Pour over black-bean mixture and mix well.

4. Chill well before serving.

Fresh Peach-Mango Salsa

PER SERVING: Calories: 45 | Protein: 1g | Carbohydrates: 10g | Fat: 1g | Saturated Fat: 0g | Cholesterol: 0mg
Sodium: 104mg | Fiber: 2g | PCF Ratio: 9-82-9 | Exchange Approx.: ½ Fruit

INGREDIENTS | SERVES 6

1 cup peeled and diced mango, peeled and cut into ¼" pieces
1 peach, peeled and diced
1 cup finely chopped red onion
1 cup peeled and diced cucumber
1 tablespoon balsamic vinegar
1 tablespoon lime juice
1 teaspoon chili powder
½ teaspoon ground cumin
1 tablespoon chopped fresh cilantro
1 tablespoon chopped parsley
¼ teaspoon salt

1. Mix all the ingredients together in a medium bowl.

2. Chill for at least 4 hours before serving.

Pineapple-Chili Salsa

PER SERVING: Calories: 29 | Protein: 1g | Carbohydrates: 7g | Fat: 0g | Saturated Fat: 0g | Cholesterol: 0mg
Sodium: 2mg | Fiber: 1g | PCF Ratio: 8-87-5 | Exchange Approx.: ½ Fruit

INGREDIENTS | SERVES 4

½ cup unsweetened diced pineapple

½ cup roughly chopped papaya, peach, or mango

1 small poblano chili pepper, chopped

¼ cup chopped red bell pepper

¼ cup chopped yellow bell pepper

1 tablespoon fresh key lime or lime juice

¼ cup chopped red onion

Combine all the ingredients in bowl and toss to mix.

Green Salsa

PER SERVING: Calories: 41 | Protein: 1g | Carbohydrates: 2g | Fat: 3g | Saturated Fat: 2g | Cholesterol: 6mg
Fiber: 1g | PCF Ratio: 8-23-70 | Exchange Approx.: ½ Fat

INGREDIENTS | MAKES 1 CUP; SERVING SIZE: 2 TABLESPOONS

1 cup blanched fresh or thawed frozen corn kernels

1 small banana pepper, seeded and chopped

¼ cup diced red radishes

⅛ cup thinly sliced green onion

1 avocado, diced

1 tablespoon lime juice

½ teaspoon white wine vinegar

1 teaspoon extra-virgin olive oil

¼ teaspoon dried oregano

Dash of ground cumin

Dash of Tabasco sauce

Freshly ground black pepper (optional)

Place all the ingredients in the blender or food processor and pulse until coarsely chopped. Rest in refrigerator for 2 hours. Serve chilled.

Avocado-Corn Salsa

PER SERVING: Calories: 133 | Protein: 2g | Carbohydrates: 14g | Fat: 9g | Saturated Fat: 1g | Cholesterol: 0mg
Sodium: 10mg | Fiber: 4g | PCF Ratio: 7-37-56 | Exchange Approx.: ½ Starch/Vegetable, 2 Fats

INGREDIENTS | SERVES 4

1 cup blanched fresh or thawed frozen corn kernels

1 small banana pepper, seeded and chopped

¼ cup diced red radishes

⅛ cup thinly sliced green onion

1 avocado, diced, divided

1 tablespoon lime juice

½ teaspoon white wine vinegar

1 teaspoon extra-virgin olive oil

¼ teaspoon dried oregano

Dash ground cumin

Dash Tabasco Sauce

Freshly ground black pepper (optional)

1. In a medium bowl, combine corn, banana pepper, radish, and green onion.

2. In another bowl, combine ½ of diced avocado and lime juice; stir to thoroughly coat.

3. In blender, combine the other ½ of avocado, vinegar, oil, oregano, cumin, and Tabasco; process until smooth. Pour over corn mixture and stir.

4. Add avocado mixture. Add black pepper if desired. Serve immediately.

Cranberry Orange Relish

PER SERVING: Calories: 62 | Protein: 0g | Carbohydrates: 16g | Fat: 0g | Saturated Fat: 0g | Cholesterol: 0mg
Sodium: 3mg | Fiber: 2g | PCF Ratio: 3-96-1 | Exchange Approx.: 1 Fruit

INGREDIENTS | SERVES 12; SERVING SIZE: ½ CUP

16 ounces fresh cranberries

1½ cups orange sections

2 teaspoons orange zest

¼ cup brown sugar

⅓ cup Splenda Granulated

1 teaspoon cinnamon

1. Chop cranberries and orange sections in food processor using pulse setting until coarsely chopped. Transfer to a medium saucepan.

2. Bring cranberry mixture, orange zest, brown sugar, and Splenda to boil over medium heat. Cook for 2 minutes.

3. Remove from heat; stir in cinnamon. Chill before serving.

Roasted Corn Salsa

PER SERVING: Calories: 104 | Protein: 4g | Carbohydrates: 24g | Fat: 1g | Saturated Fat: 0g | Cholesterol: 0mg
Sodium: 77mg | Fiber: 3g | PCF Ratio: 12-80-8 | Exchange Approx.: 1 Starch, ½ Vegetable

INGREDIENTS | SERVES 6

2 ears corn

1½ cups skinned and chopped fresh tomatoes

½ cup chopped red onion

3 tablespoons finely chopped jalapeño pepper

1 tablespoon rice wine vinegar

¼ cup chopped roasted red pepper

1½ tablespoons chopped cilantro

1 teaspoon finely chopped garlic

1 tablespoon lime juice

½ teaspoon ground cumin

2 teaspoons red wine vinegar

1. Husk corn and place on grill. Cook for about 10–12 minutes until lightly browned and tender. Set aside to cool.

2. Combine all other ingredients in a medium bowl.

3. When corn has cooled, cut kernels off cobb and add to bowl. Mix and serve immediately.

Pepper and Corn Relish

PER SERVING: Calories: 39 | Protein: 2g | Carbohydrates: 9g | Fat: 1g | Saturated Fat: 0g | Cholesterol: 0mg
Sodium: 7mg | Fiber: 2g | PCF Ratio: 14-78-8 | Exchange Approx.: ½ Starch

INGREDIENTS | MAKES 2 CUPS; SERVING SIZE: ½ CUP

4 banana or jalapeño peppers, seeded and chopped

⅓ cup frozen corn, thawed

⅓ cup chopped red onion

⅛ teaspoon ground coriander

2 teaspoons lime juice

Freshly ground black pepper, to taste

In a large bowl, toss all the ingredients. Relish can be served immediately, or chilled and served the next day.

Tip

For a colorful, mild relish, use a combination of 2 tablespoons chopped green bell pepper and an equal amount of chopped red pepper in place of the jalapeño peppers.

Caramelized Onions

PER SERVING: Calories: 68 | Protein: 1g | Carbohydrates: 9g | Fat: 3g | Saturated Fat: 0g | Cholesterol: 0mg
Sodium: 3mg | Fiber: 1g | PCF Ratio: 5-52-43 | Exchange Approx.: 2 Vegetables, ½ Fat

INGREDIENTS | MAKES 1 CUP; SERVING SIZE: ¼ CUP

3 large Vidalia or other sweet onions, sliced ⅛" thick

1 tablespoon olive oil

Place the onions in a large sauté pan with olive oil. Over very low heat, sauté for 20 minutes, or until onions are browned but not burned.

Timesaving Tip

This recipe can be made ahead of time and kept on hand in a small glass jar for 3–5 days to use as a condiment and add flavor to many dishes. Caramelized onions are wonderful on everything from sandwiches to salads and as a garnish for roasts and stews.

Honey and Cider Glaze for Baked Chicken

PER SERVING, GLAZE ONLY: Calories: 10 | Protein: 0g | Carbohydrates: 2g | Fat: 0g | Saturated Fat: 0g | Cholesterol: 0mg
Sodium: 55mg | Fiber: 0g | PCF Ratio: 9-90-1 | Exchange Approx.: 1 Free Condiment

INGREDIENTS | SERVES 4

3 tablespoons apple cider or apple juice

½ teaspoon honey

1 teaspoon lemon juice

1 teaspoon Bragg's Liquid Aminos

½ teaspoon lemon zest

1. Preheat oven to 375°F. Combine all ingredients in microwave-safe bowl; microwave on high 30 seconds. Stir until honey is dissolved.

2. To use glaze, arrange 4 boneless, skinless chicken pieces on rack placed in roasting pan or broiling pan. Brush or spoon 1 teaspoon of glaze over top of each piece. Baste halfway through cooking time, and again 5 minutes before chicken is done. Allow chicken to sit 5 minutes before serving.

Spice Tea Chicken Marinade

Steep 4 orange or lemon spice tea bags in 2 cups boiling water for 4 minutes. Dissolve 1 teaspoon honey into the tea, pour it over 4 chicken pieces, and marinate for 30 minutes. Occasionally turn and baste any exposed portions of chicken. Pour the tea into the roasting pan to provide moisture—discard it after cooking.

Breads and Muffins

Hawaiian-Style Bread

PER SERVING (1 SLICE): Calories: 89 | Protein: 2g | Carbohydrates: 17g | Fat: 1g | Saturated Fat: 1g | Cholesterol: 11mg
Sodium: 103mg | Fiber: 1g | PCF Ratio: 11-75-14 | Exchange Approx.: 1 Starch

INGREDIENTS | MAKES 1 LARGE LOAF; 20 THIN SLICES

1 egg

½ cup pineapple juice, or ⅛ cup frozen pineapple juice concentrate and ⅜ cup water

¾ cup water

2 tablespoons butter

1 teaspoon vanilla extract

½ teaspoon ground ginger

1 teaspoon salt

1½ cups unbleached bread flour

2⅛ cups unbleached all-purpose flour

¼ cup sugar

2 tablespoons nonfat milk powder

1 package (2½ teaspoons) active dry yeast

Unless instructions for your bread machine differ, add ingredients in order listed here. Use light-crust setting.

Honey Oat Bran Bread

PER SERVING (1 SLICE): Calories: 86 | Protein: 3g | Carbohydrates: 16g | Fat: 1g | Saturated Fat: 0g | Cholesterol: 8mg
Sodium: 109mg | Fiber: 1g | PCF Ratio: 15-72-13 | Exchange Approx.: 1 Starch

**INGREDIENTS | MAKES 1 LARGE LOAF;
20 THIN SLICES**

1¼ cups skim milk

2 tablespoons nonfat buttermilk powder

1 tablespoon olive or canola oil

1 medium egg

1 cup oat bran

1 teaspoon sea salt

½ cup whole-wheat flour

2½ cups unbleached all-purpose or bread flour

1 tablespoon honey

1 package (2½ teaspoons) active dry yeast

Use light-crust setting on your bread machine. Add ingredients in order recommended by manufacturer. Be careful yeast doesn't come in contact with salt.

Cheddar Cornbread

PER SERVING (1 SLICE): Calories: 102 | Protein: 3g | Carbohydrates: 16g | Fat: 3g | Saturated Fat: 2g | Cholesterol: 8mg
Sodium: 172mg | Fiber: 1g | PCF Ratio: 13-63-24 | Exchange Approx.: 1 Starch, ½ Fat

**INGREDIENTS | MAKES 1 LARGE LOAF;
12 SLICES**

1¼ cups water

1 tablespoon honey

3 tablespoons butter

¼ cup nonfat milk powder

1 package (2½ teaspoons) active dry yeast

2½ cups unbleached all-purpose or bread flour

1 cup yellow cornmeal

1½ teaspoons sea salt

⅔ cup grated Cheddar cheese

1. Use light-crust setting. Add all ingredients except cheese in order suggested by bread machine manual. Process on basic bread cycle according to manufacturer's directions.

2. At the beep (or end of first kneading), add cheese.

7-Grain Bread

**PER SERVING (1 SLICE): Calories: 82 | Protein: 3g | Carbohydrates: 15g | Fat: 1g | Saturated Fat: 0g | Cholesterol: 8mg
Sodium: 108mg | Fiber: 1g | PCF Ratio: 14-73-12 | Exchange Approx.: 1 Starch**

INGREDIENTS | MAKES 1 LARGE LOAF

1¼ cups skim milk

2 tablespoons nonfat milk powder

1 tablespoon olive or canola oil

¾ cup dry 7-grain cereal

½ cup oat bran

1 teaspoon sea salt

2¼ cups unbleached all-purpose or bread flour

½ cup whole-wheat flour

1 tablespoon honey

1 package (2½ teaspoons) dry yeast

Add ingredients to bread machine in order recommended by manufacturer, being careful that yeast doesn't come in contact with salt. Bake on whole-wheat bread setting.

Lactose-Free Bread

When cooking for someone who is lactose intolerant, substitute equal amounts of water or soy milk for any milk called for in bread recipes.

Cottage Cheese Bread

PER SERVING (1 SLICE): Calories: 76 | Protein: 3g | Carbohydrates: 13g | Fat: 1g | Saturated Fat: 1g | Cholesterol: 11mg
Sodium: 114mg | Fiber: 1g | PCF Ratio: 16-68-16 | Exchange Approx.: 1 Starch

INGREDIENTS | MAKES 1 LARGE LOAF;
20 THIN SLICES

¼ cup water

1 cup nonfat cottage cheese

2 tablespoons butter

1 egg

1 tablespoon sugar

¼ teaspoon baking soda

1 teaspoon salt

3 cups unbleached all-purpose or bread flour

1 package (2½ teaspoons) active dry yeast

1. Add ingredients in order recommended by manufacturer, being careful yeast doesn't come in contact with salt. Bake at white bread setting, light crust.

2. Check bread machine at "beep" to make sure dough is pulling away from sides of pan and forming a ball. Add water or flour, if needed. (Note: You do not want dough to be overly dry.)

Why Breads Need Salt

Salt is only used in bread to enhance the flavor. If salt comes directly in contact with yeast before yeast has had a chance to begin to work, it can hinder the action of the yeast. Keep that in mind when adding ingredients to your bread machine.

Basic White Bread

PER SERVING (1 SLICE): Calories: 77 | Protein: 2g | Carbohydrates: 15g | Fat: 1g | Saturated Fat: 0g | Cholesterol: 0mg
Sodium: 175mg | Fiber: 1g | PCF Ratio: 11-79-10 | Exchange Approx.: 1 Starch

INGREDIENTS | MAKES 2 LARGE LOAVES; 20 THIN SLICES

5½–6 cups flour, divided

1 package (2½ teaspoons) active dry yeast

¼ cup warm water

2 tablespoons sugar

1¾ cups warm water

2 tablespoons shortening

1 tablespoon sea salt

1. Place ⅓ of flour in large bowl and set aside. Mix yeast with ¼ cup warm water in another bowl, stirring well. Add sugar and 1¾ cups warm water to yeast. Add mixture to flour; stir well. Set aside 5 minutes to allow yeast to proof.

2. Stir; cut in shortening using a pastry blender or your hands. Stir in salt and as much of remaining flour as possible. Dough has enough flour when it's still somewhat sticky to the touch, yet pulls away from side of bowl as it's stirred. Turn dough onto lightly floured work surface. Knead for 8–10 minutes, until smooth and elastic, adding flour as necessary. Dough will take on an almost glossy appearance once it's been kneaded sufficiently.

3. Transfer dough to bowl treated with nonstick cooking spray. Cover with damp cloth; place in warm, draft-free area. Allow to rise until it doubles in volume, about 1–1½ hours.

4. Punch dough down and let rise a second time, until almost doubled in volume.

5. Treat two 9" x 5" bread pans with nonstick cooking spray. Punch dough down again; divide into 2 loaves. Shape loaves; place in bread pans. Cover and let rise until almost doubled.

6. Preheat oven to 350°F. Bake 20–30 minutes, or until golden brown. Remove from pans and allow to cool on rack.

Fiber-Enriched Cheddar Bread

PER SERVING (1 SLICE): Calories: 141 | **Protein:** 6g | **Carbohydrates:** 25g | **Fat:** 1g | **Saturated Fat:** 0g | **Cholesterol:** 2mg
Sodium: 546mg | **Fiber:** 1g | **PCF Ratio:** 19-73-8 | **Exchange Approx.:** 1½ Starches

INGREDIENTS | MAKES 1 LOAF; 12 SLICES

1½ cups warm water

1 package (2½ teaspoons) active dry yeast

2½ teaspoons salt

½ cup wheat bran

3 cups bread flour

⅔ cups reduced-fat Cheddar cheese, grated

1 tablespoon grated Parmesan cheese

Cornmeal for baking sheet

1. Combine water, yeast, and salt in mixer bowl or food processor. Add remaining ingredients; mix well using dough hook or dough attachment until very soft dough is formed.

2. Transfer dough to large, loosely covered bowl; allow to rise at room temperature for 2 hours. Dough can be used after rising, but is much easier to handle after it has been refrigerated several hours or overnight.

3. When ready to bake, sprinkle a light dusting of flour on top of dough. With floured hands, remove dough from bowl; shape into round loaf.

4. Place dough on a baking sheet liberally covered with cornmeal. Lightly cover and allow dough to rise at room temperature for 45 minutes.

5. Preheat oven to 450°F with pizza stone placed on center rack of oven. Before transferring dough to hot stone, slash dough across top using floured sharp knife. Slide dough onto hot baking stone; place shallow pan of hot water on lower rack of oven to create steam underneath bread.

6. Bake for 40 minutes, or until bread is deeply browned and has a hardened crust. Remove to a cooling rack; allow to cool before slicing.

Golden Raisin Bread

PER SERVING (1 SLICE): Calories: 163 | Protein: 6g | Carbohydrates: 34g | Fat: 1g | Saturated Fat: 0g | Cholesterol: 0mg
Sodium: 497mg | Fiber: 3g | PCF Ratio: 13-82-5 | Exchange Approx.: 1½ Starches; ½ Fruit

INGREDIENTS | MAKES 1 LOAF; 12 SLICES

1½ cups warm water

2½ teaspoons active dry yeast

2½ teaspoons salt

⅓ cup wheat germ

1 cup whole-wheat flour

2 cups bread flour

2 tablespoons honey

1 teaspoon cinnamon

½ cup golden raisins

1 egg white

½ tablespoon water

Tools of the Trade

Nonstick pans with a dark surface absorb too much heat, which causes breads to burn. Chicago Metallic makes muffin, mini-muffin, and other bread pans with lighter-colored Silverstone nonstick coating that are much better suited for baking.

1. Combine water, yeast, and salt in mixer bowl or food processor. Using dough hook or dough attachment for food processor, add in remaining ingredients except egg white and ½ tablespoon water; mix well until very soft dough is formed.

2. Transfer dough to loosely covered large bowl; allow to rise at room temperature for 2 hours. Dough can be used after rising; however, it is much easier to handle after it has been refrigerated several hours or overnight.

3. When ready to bake, lightly grease 9" × 4" × 3" loaf pan. Scoop dough out of bowl with wet hands (this makes it easier to handle); shape into elongated loaf and place in loaf pan. Cover and allow dough to rise for 1 hour.

4. Preheat oven to 375°F. Brush loaf with egg wash of 1 tablespoon egg white and ½ tablespoon water.

5. Bake on middle rack of preheated oven. Place shallow pan of hot water on the lower rack to create steam under bread.

6. Bake for 45–50 minutes, until bread is golden brown. Cool in pan for 10 minutes, then remove to wire rack. Allow bread to cool completely before slicing.

Whole-Wheat Bread

PER SERVING (1 SLICE): Calories: 86 | Protein: 2g | Carbohydrates: 17g | Fat: 1g | Saturated Fat: 0g | Cholesterol: 0mg Sodium: 118mg | Fiber: 1g | PCF Ratio: 10-77-13 | Exchange Approx.: 1 Starch

INGREDIENTS | MAKES 2 LOAVES; 20 THIN SLICES

1 package (2½ teaspoons) active dry yeast

2 cups warm water

3 cups unbleached all-purpose or bread flour

2 tablespoons sugar

½ cup hot water

2 teaspoons salt

½ cup brown sugar

3 tablespoons shortening

3 cups whole-wheat flour

History Lesson

The sponge process of making bread was more popular years ago, when foods were less processed and the quality of yeast was less reliable. The yeast works in a batter and the dough rises only once. The sponge process produces a loaf that is lighter but coarser grained.

1. Add yeast to 2 cups warm water. Stir in all-purpose flour and sugar; beat until smooth, either by hand or with mixer. Set in warm place to proof until it becomes foamy and bubbly, up to 1 hour.

2. Combine ½ cup hot water, salt, brown sugar, and shortening; stir. Allow to cool to lukewarm. (Stirring sugar until it's dissolved should be sufficient to cool water; test to be sure, as adding liquid that's too warm can kill yeast.) Add to bubbly flour mixture. Stir in whole-wheat flour; beat until smooth, but do not knead.

3. Divide dough into 2 lightly greased 8" × 4" × 2-½" loaf pans. Cover; set in warm place until doubled in size. Preheat oven to 350°F; bake for 50 minutes. Let cool before slicing.

Multigrain Cornbread

PER SERVING (1 SLICE): Calories: 124 | Protein: 4g | Carbohydrates: 20g | Fat: 3g | Saturated Fat: 1g | Cholesterol: 16mg
Sodium: 220mg | Fiber: 2g | PCF Ratio: 12-65-23 | Exchange Approx.: 1 Starch, ½ Fat

INGREDIENTS | MAKES 1 (8" × 8") PAN

Nonstick cooking spray
1 egg
2 tablespoons egg whites
3 tablespoons butter, melted
1½ cups low-fat buttermilk
1 teaspoon vanilla extract
1¾ cups cornmeal
¾ cup whole-wheat pastry flour
1 tablespoon ground flaxseed
3 tablespoons Splenda Granulated
1 tablespoon sugar
4 teaspoons baking powder
½ teaspoon baking soda
Pinch salt

1. Preheat oven to 375°F. Spray 8" × 8" square baking pan with nonstick cooking spray.

2. In medium bowl, whisk together egg, egg whites, butter, buttermilk, and vanilla. Set aside.

3. In larger bowl, combine cornmeal, flour, flaxseed, Splenda, sugar, baking powder, baking soda, and salt; mix well.

4. Make well in center of dry ingredients; pour in buttermilk mixture. Mix gently with spoon until all dry ingredients are moistened; do not over-mix.

5. Spoon batter into prepared pan. Bake for 25–30 minutes, or until center springs back when lightly touched. Cool on wire rack before slicing into pieces.

Don't Have Buttermilk?

You can make your own buttermilk substitution with just a few simple ingredients. To replace 1 cup of buttermilk in a recipe, stir 1 tablespoon of white vinegar or fresh lemon juice into 1 cup of fresh milk. Let the milk stand for 5 minutes, or until milk thickens.

Fiber-Enriched Banana Bread

PER SERVING (1 SLICE): Calories: 65 | Protein: 5g | Carbohydrates: 29g | Fat: 4g | Saturated Fat: 1g | Cholesterol: 22mg
Sodium: 348mg | Fiber: 4g | PCF Ratio: 12-67-21 | Exchange Approx.: 1 Starch, ½ Fruit, 1 Fat

INGREDIENTS | MAKES 1 LARGE LOAF; 12 SLICES

Nonstick cooking spray
½ cup buttermilk
¼ cup wheat bran
1 cup mashed ripe banana
1 egg
¼ cup egg whites
2 tablespoons canola oil
1 teaspoon vanilla extract
2 tablespoons honey
1¼ cups whole-wheat pastry flour
½ cup all-purpose flour
⅓ cup Splenda Granulated
1 teaspoon baking soda
1½ teaspoons baking powder
½ teaspoon salt

1. Preheat oven to 375°F. Spray 9" × 4" × 3" loaf pan with nonstick cooking spray.

2. In a medium bowl, place buttermilk and wheat bran. Allow wheat bran to soak 10 minutes. Stir in banana, egg, egg whites, oil, vanilla, and honey.

3. In larger bowl, sift together flours, Splenda, baking soda, baking powder, and salt; add dry ingredients to banana mixture. Using a large spoon, stir just until dry ingredients are moistened; do not over-mix.

4. Spoon batter into prepared loaf pan. Bake for 45 minutes, or until top is lightly browned and inserted toothpick comes out clean. Cool in pan for 10 minutes before removing to wire rack.

Whole-Wheat Zucchini Bread

PER SERVING (1 SLICE): Calories: 178 | Protein: 4g | Carbohydrates: 29g | Fat: 6g | Saturated Fat: 1g | Cholesterol: 25mg
Sodium: 243mg | Fiber: 3g | PCF Ratio: 9-63-28 | Exchange Approx.: 1½ Starches, 1 Fat

INGREDIENTS | MAKES 4 MINI LOAVES (5 SLICES PER MINI LOAF; 20 SLICES TOTAL)

Nonstick cooking spray
2 eggs
1 egg white
½ cup honey
2 cups shredded zucchini
⅔ cup unsweetened applesauce
⅓ cup canola oil
2 teaspoons vanilla extract
2 cups whole-wheat pastry flour
1 cup all-purpose flour
¼ cup Splenda Granulated
1 teaspoon salt
2 teaspoons baking powder
1 teaspoon baking soda
2 teaspoons cinnamon
½ teaspoon nutmeg
⅓ cup sunflower seeds, toasted

1. Preheat oven to 350°F. Spray 4 aluminum mini-loaf pans with nonstick cooking spray.

2. In large mixing bowl, beat egg and egg whites until foamy. Mix in honey, zucchini, applesauce, canola oil, and vanilla.

3. In separate mixing bowl, sift together whole-wheat flour, all-purpose flour, Splenda, salt, baking powder, baking soda, cinnamon, and nutmeg.

4. Gradually add dry ingredients to zucchini mixture; mix until all ingredients are combined, but do not over-mix. Stir in sunflower seeds.

5. Divide batter evenly into prepared mini-loaf pans. Bake for 35–40 minutes, or until tops are browned and inserted toothpick comes out clean.

6. Remove pans to wire rack and cool for 10 minutes before removing from pans. Cool completely before slicing.

Variations

For a variation on this recipe, ⅓ cup dried cranberries, currants, raisins, or chopped nuts can be added in place of the sunflower seeds.

Applesauce Buckwheat Muffins

PER MUFFIN, WITH CRISP TOPPING: Calories: 182 | Protein: 5g | Carbohydrates: 27g | Fat: 7g | Saturated Fat: 1g | Cholesterol: 24mg | Sodium: 302mg | Fiber: 3g | PCF Ratio: 11-56-34 | Exchange Approx.: 1 Starch, ½ Fruit, 1 Fat

INGREDIENTS | MAKES 12 MUFFINS; SERVING SIZE: 1 MUFFIN

1 cup buttermilk

½ cup unsweetened applesauce

¼ cup canola oil

1 egg

1 egg white

2 tablespoons maple syrup

1 teaspoon vanilla extract

1¼ cups whole-wheat pastry flour

¾ cup light buckwheat flour

¼ cup Splenda Granulated

1½ teaspoons baking powder

1½ teaspoons baking soda

¼ teaspoon salt

2 teaspoons cinnamon

¼ teaspoon ground allspice

Crisp Topping (optional):

1 tablespoon Splenda Brown Sugar Blend

¼ teaspoon cinnamon

¼ cup oats

2 teaspoons ground flaxseed

1 tablespoon whole-wheat pastry flour

1 tablespoon butter, melted

1. Preheat oven to 375°F. Prepare muffin pan with nonstick cooking spray.

2. In a medium bowl, whisk together buttermilk, applesauce, oil, egg, egg white, maple syrup, and vanilla. In separate bowl, sift together whole-wheat flour, buckwheat flour, Splenda, baking powder, baking soda, salt, and spices. Gradually add dry ingredients to liquid mixture; mix just enough to combine ingredients. Do not over-mix. Spoon batter evenly into prepared muffin pan.

3. In a small bowl, mix together all ingredients for crisp topping. Sprinkle evenly on top of each muffin.

4. Bake for 20–25 minutes, or until center of muffin springs back when lightly touched. Cool in muffin pan for 5 minutes before removing to wire rack.

Pear Walnut Muffins

PER MUFFIN, WITH CRISP TOPPING: Calories: 195 | Protein: 5g | Carbohydrates: 27g | Fat: 8g | Saturated Fat: 1g | Cholesterol: 24mg | Sodium: 289mg | Fiber: 3g | PCF Ratio: 11-54-35 | Exchange Approx.: 1 Starch, ½ Fruit, 1 Fat

INGREDIENTS | MAKES 12 MUFFINS; SERVING SIZE: 1 MUFFIN

1 cup buttermilk

3 tablespoons canola oil

1 egg

1 egg white

⅔ cup peeled and chopped pears

2 tablespoons honey

1¼ cups whole-wheat pastry flour

¾ cup all-purpose flour

3 tablespoons Splenda Granulated

1½ teaspoons baking powder

1½ teaspoons baking soda

¼ teaspoon salt

1 teaspoon cinnamon

¼ teaspoon ginger

⅓ cup chopped walnuts

Crisp Topping (optional):

1 tablespoon Splenda Brown Sugar Blend

Pinch ground ginger

¼ cup oats

2 teaspoons ground flaxseed

1 tablespoon whole-wheat pastry flour

1 tablespoon butter, melted

1. Preheat oven to 375°F. Prepare muffin pan with nonstick cooking spray.

2. In a medium bowl, whisk together buttermilk, oil, egg, egg white, pears, and honey.

3. In a separate bowl, sift together whole-wheat flour, all-purpose flour, Splenda, baking powder, baking soda, salt, spices, and walnuts. Gradually add dry ingredients to liquid mixture; stir just enough to combine ingredients. Do not over-mix. Spoon batter evenly into prepared muffin pan.

4. In a small bowl, mix together all ingredients for crisp topping. Sprinkle evenly on top of each muffin.

5. Bake for 20–25 minutes, or until center of muffin springs back when lightly touched. Cool in muffin pan for 5 minutes before removing to wire rack.

Whole-Wheat Pastry Flour

Whole-wheat pastry flour is a finer grind of soft white wheat. When used in quick-bread and muffin recipes, it delivers more nutrition and fiber than white flour and yields a lighter texture than whole-wheat flour.

Angelic Buttermilk Batter Biscuits

PER SERVING: Calories: 74 | Protein: 2g | Carbohydrates: 12g | Fat: 2g | Saturated Fat: 1g | Cholesterol: 6mg
Sodium: 55mg | Fiber: 1g | PCF Ratio: 11-64-26 | Exchange Approx.: 1 Starch

**INGREDIENTS | MAKES 24 BISCUITS;
SERVING SIZE: 1 BISCUIT**

3 tablespoons nonfat buttermilk powder

2 tablespoons granulated sugar

¾ cup warm water

1 tablespoon active dry yeast

2½ cups unbleached all-purpose flour

½ teaspoon sea salt

½ teaspoon baking powder

¼ cup unsalted butter

¼ cup plain, nonfat yogurt

Why Breads Need Sugar

Bread recipes need sugar or another sweetener, like honey, to "feed" the yeast. This helps the yeast work, which in turn helps the bread rise.

1. Put buttermilk powder, sugar, and warm water in food processor; process until mixed. Sprinkle yeast over top; pulse once or twice to mix. Allow mixture to sit at room temperature for about 5 minutes, or until yeast begins to bubble. Add all remaining ingredients to food processor; pulse until mixed, being careful not to over-mix.

2. Preheat oven to 400°F. Drop 1 heaping teaspoon per biscuit onto baking sheet treated with nonstick cooking spray. Set tray in warm place; allow biscuits to rise for about 15 minutes.

3. Bake biscuits for 12–15 minutes.

Orange Date Bread

PER SERVING (1 SLICE): Calories: 79 | Protein: 2g | Carbohydrates: 16g | Fat: 1g | Saturated Fat: 0g | Cholesterol: 8mg
Sodium: 130mg | Fiber: 1g | PCF Ratio: 9-80-10 | Exchange Approx.: 1 Starch

INGREDIENTS | MAKES 4 MINI LOAVES; 20 SLICES

2 tablespoons thawed frozen orange juice concentrate

2 tablespoons orange zest

¾ cup pitted and chopped dates

½ cup brown sugar

¼ cup granulated sugar

1 cup plain, nonfat yogurt

1 egg

1¼ cups all-purpose flour

¾ cup whole-wheat flour

1 teaspoon baking soda

1 teaspoon baking powder

½ teaspoon salt

1 tablespoon vegetable oil

1 teaspoon vanilla extract

1. Preheat oven to 350°F. Spray 4 mini-loaf pans with nonstick cooking spray.

2. In food processor, process orange juice concentrate, orange zest, dates, sugars, yogurt, and egg until mixed. (This will cut dates into smaller pieces, too.) Add remaining ingredients; pulse until mixed, scraping down side of bowl if necessary.

3. Divide mixture evenly between the pans. Bake for 15–20 minutes, or until a toothpick inserted into center of loaf comes out clean.

4. Cool bread in pans on wire rack for 10 minutes. Remove bread to rack and cool to room temperature.

Are Your Eyes Bigger Than Your Stomach?

Use mini-loaf pans. It's much easier to arrive at the number of servings in the form of a full slice when you use smaller loaf pans. There's a psychological advantage to getting a full rather than half slice.

CHAPTER 14

Desserts

Chocolate Cheesecake Mousse

**PER SERVING: Calories: 83 | Protein: 3g | Carbohydrates: 7g | Fat: 5g | Saturated Fat: 2g | Cholesterol: 9mg
Sodium: 47mg | Fiber: 0g | PCF Ratio: 13-32-55 | Exchange Approx.: ½ Skim Milk, 1 Fat**

INGREDIENTS | SERVES 4

1 tablespoon semisweet chocolate chips

¾ cup Mock Whipped Cream (see recipe in this chapter), divided

1 ounce cream cheese

1½ teaspoons cocoa

1 teaspoon vanilla extract

1. Put chocolate chips and 1 tablespoon of Mock Whipped Cream in microwave-safe bowl and microwave on high for 15 seconds.

2. Add cream cheese and microwave on high for another 15 seconds. Whip mixture until well blended and chocolate chips are melted.

3. Stir in cocoa and vanilla. Fold in remaining Mock Whipped Cream. Chill until ready to serve.

Whipped Lemon Cheesecake Mousse

**PER SERVING: Calories: 81 | Protein: 4g | Carbohydrates: 8g | Fat: 4g | Saturated Fat: 3g | Cholesterol: 14mg
Sodium: 65mg | Fiber: 0g | PCF Ratio: 18-38-44 | Exchange Approx.: 1 Skim Milk**

INGREDIENTS | SERVES 10; SERVING SIZE: ½ CUP

4 ounces cream cheese, room temperature

1 tablespoon lemon juice

1 teaspoon lemon zest

¼ cup powdered sugar

1 recipe Nonfat Whipped Milk Base (see recipe in this chapter)

1. In a small bowl, combine cream cheese, lemon juice, lemon zest, and sugar. Using fork or whisk, beat until well blended.

2. Fold mixture into Whipped Milk Base. Chill for at least 1 hour before serving.

Whipped Mocha Mousse

PER SERVING: Calories: 82 | Protein: 4g | Carbohydrates: 16g | Fat: 1g | Saturated Fat: 0g | Cholesterol: 1mg
Sodium: 37mg | Fiber: 1g | PCF Ratio: 19-77-3 | Exchange Approx.: 1 Skim Milk

INGREDIENTS | SERVES 10; SERVING SIZE: ½ CUP

¼ cup cold water

1 envelope Knox Original Unflavored Gelatine

¾ cup hot water

2 teaspoons instant espresso powder

½ cup sugar

¼ cup unsweetened cocoa

1½ teaspoons vanilla extract

Cinnamon (optional)

1 recipe Nonfat Whipped Milk Base (see recipe in this chapter)

1. Pour cold water into blender and sprinkle gelatine over it; let stand for 1 minute.

2. Add hot water and instant espresso powder; blend at low speed until gelatine is completely dissolved. Add sugar, cocoa, vanilla, and cinnamon if using; process at high speed until blended. Allow mixture to cool to at least room temperature before folding into Whipped Milk Base. Chill until ready to serve.

Mock Whipped Cream

PER SERVING: Calories: 24 | Protein: 1g | Carbohydrates: 2g | Fat: 1g | Saturated Fat: 0g | Cholesterol: 1mg
Sodium: 17mg | Fiber: 0g | PCF Ratio: 21-41-38 | Exchange Approx.: ½ Fat

**INGREDIENTS | MAKES 3½ CUPS;
SERVING SIZE: 2
TABLESPOONS**

1 envelope Knox Unflavored Gelatine
¼ cup cold water
½ cup hot water
2 tablespoons almond oil
3 tablespoons powdered sugar
1 teaspoon vanilla extract
1 cup ice water
1¼ cups nonfat milk powder

Know Your Ingredients

"Gelatine" is the name of the commercial Knox Original Unflavored Gelatine product used to make gelatin. Although any unflavored gelatin will work, the nutritional analyses for all recipes are based on the Knox brand.

1. Allow gelatine to soften in cold water and then pour into blender. Add hot water and blend for 2 minutes, until gelatine is dissolved.

2. While continuing to blend mixture, gradually add almond oil, powdered sugar, and vanilla. Chill in freezer for 15 minutes, or until mixture is cool but hasn't begun to set.

3. Using hand mixer or whisk, add ice water and nonfat milk powder to a chilled bowl; beat until peaks start to form. Add chilled gelatine mixture to whipped milk; continue to whip for 10 minutes until stiffer peaks begin to form. This whipped topping will keep several days in refrigerator. Whip again to reintroduce more air into topping before serving.

Nonfat Whipped Milk Base

PER RECIPE: Calories: 290 | Carbohydrates: 42g | Protein: 28g | Fat: 1g | Saturated Fat: 0g | Cholesterol: 11mg Sodium: 310mg | Fiber: 0g | PCF Ratio: 39-59-2 | Exchange Approx.: 2 Skim Milks, 1 Carbohydrate

INGREDIENTS | MAKES ABOUT 3 CUPS

¼ cup nonfat milk powder

⅛ cup powdered sugar

1 cup chilled skim milk, divided

1½ envelopes Knox Original Unflavored Gelatine

Whipping Methods

Because you don't need to whip the Nonfat Whipped Milk Base until it reaches stiff peaks, you can use a blender or food processor; however, you won't be whipping as much air into the mixture if you do, so the serving sizes will be a bit smaller.

1. In a chilled bowl, combine milk powder and sugar; mix until well blended. Pour ¼ cup milk and gelatine into blender. Let sit for 1–2 minutes to allow gelatine to soften.

2. In microwave-safe container, heat remaining milk on high until it almost reaches boiling point, 30–45 seconds.

3. Add milk to blender with gelatine; blend 2 minutes, or until gelatine is completely dissolved. Chill for 15 minutes, or until mixture is cool but gelatine hasn't yet begun to set.

4. Using hand mixer or whisk, beat until doubled in size. (It won't form stiff peaks like whipped cream; however, you'll notice it will get creamier in color.) Chill until ready to use in desserts. If necessary, whip again immediately prior to folding in other ingredients.

Raspberry Yogurt Delight

PER SERVING: Calories: 121 | Protein: 6g | Carbohydrates: 18g | Fat: 3g | Saturated Fat: 2g | Cholesterol: 12mg
Sodium: 74mg | Fiber: 1g | PCF Ratio: 19-59-22 | Exchange Approx.: 1 Milk, ½ Fat

INGREDIENTS | SERVES 4; SERVING SIZE: ½ CUP

1½ cups plain, nonfat yogurt

3 tablespoons Splenda Granulated, divided

4 tablespoons heavy cream

¼ cup Raspberry Sauce (see recipe in this chapter)

1. Combine yogurt and 2 tablespoons Splenda Granulated in a medium bowl. Chill in refrigerator.

2. In a separate bowl, whip heavy cream until moderately stiff; stir in remaining 1 tablespoon Splenda Granulated.

3. To make dessert: Gently fold cream into yogurt. Spoon mixture into 4 dessert or parfait cups. Swirl 1 tablespoon prepared Raspberry Sauce into each cup and serve.

Raspberry Sauce

PER SERVING: Calories: 38 | Protein: 1g | Carbohydrates: 9g | Fat: 0g | Saturated Fat: 0g | Cholesterol: 0mg
Sodium: 1mg | Fiber: 3g | PCF Ratio: 5-89-6 | Exchange Approx.: ½ Fruit

INGREDIENTS | **MAKES 12 SERVINGS;
SERVING SIZE: ¼ CUP**

4 cups raspberries
2 tablespoons Splenda Granulated
2 tablespoons honey
1 teaspoon cornstarch
½ tablespoon lemon juice

1. Rinse berries and drain. Put in small saucepan and mash.

2. Add Splenda and honey; cook over medium heat until mixture reaches slow boil. Reduce heat and simmer another 10 minutes.

3. Strain berry juice through mesh sieve to remove seeds. Return to saucepan.

4. In separate small bowl, mix cornstarch with lemon juice until dissolved; add to strained berry juice. Bring liquid to a boil, stirring frequently until mixture thickens slightly, about 10 minutes.

5. Cool and store in refrigerator for up to 1 week. Use as dessert topping or mixed in yogurt or pudding.

Creamy Fruit Cup

PER SERVING, without additional applesauce or jelly: | Calories: 128 | Protein: 7g | Carbohydrates: 26g | Fat: 1g | Saturated Fat: 0g | Cholesterol: 0mg | Sodium: 89mg | Fiber: 2g | PCF Ratio: 19-77-3 | Exchange Approx.: ½ Skim Milk, 1½ Fruits

INGREDIENTS | SERVES 1

4 ounces plain, nonfat yogurt

1 tablespoon unsweetened applesauce

1 teaspoon lemon juice

½ cup cubed fresh or frozen cantaloupe, thawed

¼ cup cubed or sliced apple

6 seedless red or green grapes

Lemon zest, to taste (optional)

1. In a small bowl, mix together yogurt, applesauce, and lemon juice. Drizzle over mixed fruit. (If you prefer a sweeter dressing, you can add another tablespoon of applesauce or blend in 2 teaspoons of low-sugar apple jelly without increasing the number of fruit exchanges; adjust calorie count accordingly.)

2. Sprinkle lemon zest over top, if using.

Just Juice?

Fruit and fruit juice provide healthy nutrients, and, in most cases, fiber, too. That's the good news. The downside is they also convert quickly to glucose. For that reason, many people can only consume them as part of a meal, rather than alone as a snack.

Rice Pudding with Sour Cherries

PER SERVING: Calories: 184 | Protein: 6g | Carbohydrates: 27g | Fat: 5g | Saturated Fat: 3g | Cholesterol: 92mg
Sodium: 54mg | Fiber: 1g | PCF Ratio: 14-59-27 | Exchange Approx.: 1 Starch, 1 Fruit, 1 Fat

INGREDIENTS | SERVES 6

Nonstick cooking spray, as needed
2 cups cooked basmati rice
1½ cups 2% milk
2 eggs
1 teaspoon vanilla extract
1 teaspoon salt
¼ cup sugar substitute
¼ teaspoon nutmeg
¼ teaspoon ground mace
1 cup sour pie cherries, drained, not in sugar syrup
1 tablespoon butter, softened

Family Favorite

This recipe is wonderful for kids, giving them long-lasting carbohydrates, fruit, and milk. Its creamy sweetness blended with fall spices makes grownups love it, too!

1. Preheat oven to 325°F. Spray a 2-quart baking dish with nonstick cooking spray. Add the rice.

2. In a medium bowl, whisk together the milk, eggs, vanilla, salt, sugar substitute, nutmeg, and mace. Stir in cherries and butter. Mix into the rice.

3. Bake for 50 minutes. Serve warm or chilled.

Baked Pumpkin Custard

PER SERVING: Calories: 130 | Protein: 7g | Carbohydrates: 23g | Fat: 2g | Saturated Fat: 1g | Cholesterol: 63mg
Sodium: 89mg | Fiber: 2g | PCF Ratio: 20-68-12 | Exchange Approx.: 1 Milk, 1 Vegetable, ½ Fat

INGREDIENTS | SERVES 6; SERVING SIZE: ½ CUP

2 cups solid pack or mashed cooked pumpkin

¼ cup sugar

⅓ cup Splenda Granulated

2 teaspoons cinnamon

½ teaspoon ground ginger

⅛ teaspoon ground cloves

2 eggs, slightly beaten

¼ cup egg whites

12 ounces evaporated skim milk

1. Preheat oven to 350°F.

2. In a medium bowl, mix together pumpkin, sugar, Splenda, cinnamon, ginger, and cloves. Add eggs, egg whites, and evaporated milk; whisk until well blended.

3. Pour into 6 custard cups or a 1½-quart casserole dish. Set cups or casserole in large baking pan. Put pan on rack in oven and pour hot water into pan to within ½" of top of custard.

4. Bake in custard cups for 40–45 minutes, 1½-quart casserole for 60–70 minutes, until a toothpick inserted in center comes out clean. Remove immediately from hot water. Serve warm or chilled.

Pumpkin Pie

If using this recipe for pumpkin pie, pour filling in prepared pie shell and bake in a 350°F oven for 40–45 minutes, or until filling is set. The nutrition information per serving is: Calories: 244; Protein: 8g; Fat: 9g; Saturated fat: 3g; Cholesterol: 63mg; Carbohydrate: 33g; Sodium: 206mg; PCF ratio: 13-33-5; Exchange Approx.: 1 Starch, 1 Milk, 1 Vegetable, 3 Fats.

Fall Fruit with Yogurt Sauce

PER SERVING: Calories: 126 | Protein: 3g | Carbohydrates: 26g | Fat: 3g | Saturated Fat: 1g | Cholesterol: 2mg
Sodium: 48mg | Fiber: 3g | PCF Ratio: 10-72-19 | Exchange Approx.: 1 Fruit, ½ Milk

INGREDIENTS | SERVES 8; SERVING SIZE:
½ CUP

2 cups cubed apples

1½ cups halved red seedless grapes

1½ cup cubed pears

2 teaspoons lemon juice, divided

8 ounces light vanilla yogurt

1 tablespoon honey

¼ cup chopped walnuts

1. In a medium bowl, combine apples, grapes, and pears. Drizzle 1 teaspoon lemon juice over fruit to prevent turning brown.

2. In a small bowl, combine remaining 1 teaspoon lemon juice, yogurt, and honey.

3. Portion ½ cup fruit per serving. Spoon yogurt dressing over fruit and top with chopped walnuts.

Fruit Compote

PER SERVING: Calories: 117 | Protein: 1g | Carbohydrates: 24g | Fat: 2g | Saturated Fat: 1g | Cholesterol: 3mg
Sodium: 29mg | Fiber: 3g | PCF Ratio: 3-80-17 | Exchange Approx.: 1½ Fruits, ½ Fat

INGREDIENTS | SERVES 4; SERVING SIZE:
½ CUP

2 cups chopped apples

2 tablespoons dried cranberries

6 dried apricots, diced

¼ teaspoon cinnamon

2 tablespoons water

1 tablespoon brandy (optional; if not used, add additional 3 tablespoons water)

1 tablespoon finely chopped walnuts

1. In a small saucepan, combine apples, cranberries, apricots, cinnamon, water, and brandy.

2. Cook over medium heat until apples are softened, about 10 minutes. Remove from heat and cover 5 minutes. Stir in walnuts before serving.

Peach Bread Pudding

PER SERVING: Calories: 164 | Protein: 7g | Carbohydrates: 23g | Fat: 5g | Saturated Fat: 3g | Cholesterol: 63mg
Sodium: 175mg | Fiber: 2g | PCF Ratio: 16-55-29 | Exchange Approx.: 1 Starch, ½ Fruit, 1 Fat

INGREDIENTS | SERVES 9; SERVING SIZE: ½ CUP

Nonstick cooking spray
2 cups 1% milk
2 tablespoons butter

2 eggs
⅓ cup egg whites
1 teaspoon vanilla extract
2 teaspoons cinnamon
⅓ cup Splenda Brown Sugar Blend
6 slices whole-wheat bread, cubed
2 cups sliced peaches

1. Preheat oven to 350°F. Spray 9" x 9" baking dish with nonstick cooking spray.

2. Heat milk in a small saucepan over low heat. Melt butter in milk. Cool.

3. In a medium bowl, beat eggs, egg whites, vanilla, cinnamon, and Splenda.

4. Combine milk and egg mixtures.

5. Place cubed bread in an even layer in prepared baking dish. Place sliced peaches on top of bread cubes. Pour egg mixture over bread and peaches. Bake for 40–45 minutes.

Cranberry Pecan Biscotti

PER SERVING: Calories: 98 | Protein: 3g | Carbohydrates: 15g | Fat: 3g | Saturated Fat: 1g | Cholesterol: 20mg
Sodium: 39mg | Fiber: 2g | PCF Ratio: 10-59-3 | Exchange Approx.: 1 Starch, ½ Fat

INGREDIENTS | MAKES 30 BISCOTTI; SERVING SIZE: 1 BISCOTTI

4 tablespoons butter, softened
½ cup sugar
½ cup Splenda Granulated
2 eggs
½ cup egg whites
1 teaspoon vanilla extract
1 teaspoon lemon zest
2½ cups all-purpose flour
⅛ teaspoon salt
½ teaspoon baking powder
½ cup chopped pecans
½ cup dried cranberries

1. Preheat oven to 350°F. In medium bowl, beat butter, sugar, Splenda, eggs, egg whites, vanilla, and lemon zest until smooth.

2. In a separate bowl, sift flour, salt, and baking powder. Add dry ingredients to liquid ingredients; mix well. Add pecans and cranberries. Chill dough for 1–2 hours, which makes it easier to handle.

3. Divide dough in ½; shape each ½ into a slightly flattened 3" × 9" loaf. Place loaves on greased baking sheet; bake for 25 minutes.

4. Remove from oven; when cooled enough to handle, cut into ½" slices. Lay out slices on baking sheet and return to oven for 20 minutes until toasted on bottom.

5. Remove from oven; turn over and bake for 15 minutes until other side is toasted as well. Remove from oven and cool on wire rack.

Key Lime Pie

PER SERVING: Calories: 203 | Protein: 4g | Carbohydrates: 29g | Fat: 8g | Saturated Fat: 4g | Cholesterol: 20mg
Sodium: 331mg | Fiber: 1g | PCF Ratio: 8-57-35 | Exchange Approx.: 1½ Starches, 1½ Fats

INGREDIENTS | SERVES 10; SERVING SIZE: 1 SLICE

1 cup graham-cracker crumbs

1 tablespoon plus ½ cup Splenda Granulated, divided

2 tablespoons butter, melted

½ teaspoon key lime or lime zest (sometimes key limes are hard to find and regular limes will work)

6 ounces low-fat (Neufchâtel) cream cheese

1 package instant sugar-free vanilla pudding mix

½ cup 1% milk

1 cup key lime juice (5–6 limes), divided

1 tablespoon Knox Original Unflavored Gelatine

1. Prepare graham-cracker crust: Preheat oven to 350°F. Combine graham crumbs and 1 tablespoon Splenda. Add melted butter and mix well. Press crumbs into 9" pie plate with help of flat surface such as bottom of glass. Bake for 10 minutes; remove from oven and cool.

2. In mixer or food processor, combine lime zest and ½ cup Splenda. Add cream cheese and process for 30 seconds. Add pudding mix and milk and blend well.

3. Pour ¼ cup lime juice into small microwave-safe bowl; heat in microwave for 1 minute. Add gelatine to heated juice; dissolve completely.

4. Mix dissolved gelatine in rest of lime juice. Turn on mixer or food processor; pour lime juice into mixture slowly. Process until all ingredients are well combined.

5. Pour filling into pie crust; refrigerate for 3–4 hours before serving. If desired, top with Mock Whipped Cream (see recipe in this chapter).

Strawberry Ricotta Pie

PER SERVING: Calories: 238 | Protein: 10g | Carbohydrates: 27g | Fat: 10g | Saturated Fat: 5g | Cholesterol: 86mg
Sodium: 183mg | Fiber: 1g | PCF Ratio: 18-45-37 | Exchange Approx.: 1 Starch, 1 Lean Meat, 2 Fats

INGREDIENTS | SERVES 8; SERVING SIZE: 1 SLICE

2 cups part-skim ricotta cheese

1 cup graham-cracker crumbs

3 tablespoons plus ¼ cup Splenda Granulated, divided

2 tablespoons butter, melted

2 eggs, separated

1 teaspoon lemon extract

2 tablespoons honey

¼ cup egg whites

¼ teaspoon cream of tartar

2 cups sliced strawberries

1 tablespoon cornstarch

1 tablespoon lemon juice

1 teaspoon balsamic vinegar

1. Place ricotta cheese in fine mesh strainer lined with coffee filter; allow excess water to drain from cheese for 2–3 hours.

2. Prepare graham-cracker crust: Preheat oven to 350°F. Combine graham crumbs and 1 tablespoon Splenda. Add melted butter; mix well. Press crumbs into 9" pie plate with help of flat surface such as bottom of glass. Bake for 10 minutes, remove from oven, and cool.

3. Prepare pie filling: In a medium bowl, mix ricotta cheese, ¼ cup Splenda, egg yolks, lemon extract, and honey.

4. In the mixer bowl, beat egg whites (2 separated plus ¼ cup additional egg whites) with cream of tartar until soft peaks begin to form. Gently fold egg whites into ricotta mixture. Turn into pie shell; bake at 350°F for 45 minutes, or until mixture is set and top is golden brown. Remove to wire rack and cool completely.

5. Prepare glaze: In a medium saucepan, combine 2 tablespoons Splenda, strawberries, and cornstarch until dry ingredients have coated strawberries. Add lemon juice and balsamic vinegar and cook over medium heat, stirring constantly. Cook mixture for 5–7 minutes, or until cornstarch liquid is clear and gently bubbling. Cool.

6. Spread cooled strawberry glaze on top of cooled pie. Chill until ready to serve.

Meringue Pie Crust

PER SERVING (⅛ CRUST): Calories: 94 | Protein: 3g | Carbohydrates: 10g | Fat: 5g | Saturated Fat: 0g | Cholesterol: 0mg
Sodium: 28mg | Fiber: 0g | PCF Ratio: 13-42-45 | Exchange Approx.: 2 Fats

INGREDIENTS | MAKES 1 (9") PIE CRUST

Nonstick cooking spray, as needed

4 egg whites

Pinch salt

1 teaspoon vinegar

½ cup sugar substitute, or to taste

½ cup toasted walnuts, hazelnuts, or pecans

1. Prepare a 9" pie pan with nonstick cooking spray.

2. In a medium bowl, beat egg whites by adding salt and then vinegar and sugar substitute. When stiff, fold in nuts.

3. Pile into pie pan. Bake at 175°F for 3–4 hours.

4. Let cool before filling. The meringue should be used the same day it's made and served immediately after it's filled. Once filled or sitting out in a humid room, it will turn soggy.

Fruit and Cream Filling for Meringue Pie Crust

PER SERVING (CRUST NOT INCLUDED): Calories: 85 | Protein: 1g | Carbohydrates: 8g | Fat: 6g | Saturated Fat: 3g | Cholesterol: 20mg | Sodium: 6mg | Fiber: 1g | PCF Ratio: 4-38-58 | Exchange Approx.: ½ Fruit, 1 Fat

INGREDIENTS | SERVES 8

1 Meringue Pie Crust (see recipe in this chapter)

1 banana

1 cup heavy cream

2 teaspoons plus 1 tablespoon sugar substitute, divided

1 teaspoon vanilla extract

1 pint strawberries, washed and hulled; half sliced, half left whole for top of pie

1. Using a cool Meringue Pie Crust, slice the banana over the bottom of the crust.

2. In a medium bowl, whip the cream with 2 teaspoons sugar substitute and vanilla. Spread half the whipped cream over bananas.

3. Cover with the sliced strawberries and sprinkle with remaining sugar substitute.

4. Cover with remaining whipped cream and arrange the rest of the berries on top. Serve immediately.

Pavlova

This is the classic filling for Pavlova cake, a wonderful Australian dessert. The cake is sometimes topped with peeled, sliced kiwi fruit in addition to strawberries, which you could do for this recipe as well.

Summer Fruit Cobbler

PER SERVING: Calories: 152 | Protein: 3g | Carbohydrates: 26g | Fat: 5g | Saturated Fat: 0g | Cholesterol: 0mg
Sodium: 248mg | Fiber: 4g | PCF Ratio: 8-65-27 | Exchange Approx.: ½ Starch, ½ Fruit, 1 Fat

**INGREDIENTS | SERVES 8; SERVING SIZE:
½ CUP**

Nonstick cooking spray

1½ cups raspberries

1½ cups peeled and sliced peaches

1 cup sliced strawberries

¼ cup plus 1 tablespoon sugar, divided

1 tablespoon Splenda Granulated

2 tablespoons plus ¾ cup whole-wheat pastry flour, divided

1 teaspoon cinnamon

1½ teaspoons baking powder

½ teaspoon salt

2½ tablespoons canola oil

2 tablespoons milk

2 tablespoons egg whites

1. Preheat oven to 350°F. Spray 9" × 9" square baking pan with nonstick cooking spray. Put mixed fruit in bottom of baking dish.

2. In a small bowl, mix ¼ cup sugar, Splenda, 2 tablespoons flour, and cinnamon; sprinkle evenly over fruit.

3. In a small bowl, sift together 1 tablespoon sugar, ¾ cup flour, baking powder, and salt. Add oil, milk, and egg whites; stir quickly until just mixed.

4. Drop dough by spoonfuls over fruit. If desired, loosely spread dough over fruit. Bake for 25–30 minutes, until dough is golden brown.

Fun Fruits

Any combination of fresh fruit will work well with this recipe. You will need a total of 4 cups of fruit. Fruit suggestions include blueberries, blackberries, peaches, mangoes, or plums. Keep in mind that calories will vary somewhat with different fruit combinations.

Strawberry Rhubarb Cobbler

PER SERVING: Calories: 138 | Protein: 3g | Carbohydrates: 27g | Fat: 3g | Saturated Fat: 0g | Cholesterol: 7mg
Sodium: 223mg | Fiber: 3g | PCF Ratio: 7-76-17 | Exchange Approx.: ½ Starch, ½ Fruit, ½ Fat

INGREDIENTS | SERVES 9; SERVING SIZE: ½ CUP

Nonstick cooking spray
4 cups chopped rhubarb
2 cups thickly sliced strawberries
¼ teaspoon lemon zest
⅓ cup plus 1 tablespoon sugar, divided
¼ cup Splenda Granulated
2 tablespoons cornstarch
2 tablespoons water
¾ cup whole-wheat pastry flour
¼ teaspoon ground ginger
1½ teaspoons baking powder
½ teaspoon salt
2½ tablespoons canola oil
2 tablespoons milk
2 tablespoons egg whites

1. Preheat oven to 375°F. Spray 8" × 8" baking dish with nonstick cooking spray.

2. In a mixing bowl, combine rhubarb, strawberries, lemon zest, ⅓ cup sugar, and Splenda.

3. In a small bowl, dissolve cornstarch in water. Pour over fruit and stir to coat. Place in prepared baking dish and set aside.

4. In a small bowl, sift together 1 tablespoon sugar, flour, ginger, baking powder, and salt. Add oil, milk, and egg whites; stir quickly until just mixed.

5. Drop dough by spoonfuls over fruit. If desired, loosely spread dough over fruit. Bake for 25–30 minutes, until dough is golden brown.

Baked Pear Crisp

PER SERVING: Calories: 200 | Protein: 2g | Carbohydrates: 42g | Fat: 4g | Saturated Fat: 2g | Cholesterol: 8mg
Sodium: 53mg | Fiber: 3g | PCF Ratio: 3-82-15 | Exchange Approx.: 1 Fruit, 1 Fat, 1 Starch

**INGREDIENTS | SERVES 4; SERVING SIZE:
½ CUP**

2 pears
2 tablespoons frozen unsweetened
pineapple juice concentrate
1 teaspoon vanilla extract
1 teaspoon dark rum
1 tablespoon butter
⅛ cup Ener-G Brown Rice Flour
⅓ cup firmly packed brown sugar
½ cup oat bran flakes

1. Preheat oven to 375°F. Treat 9" × 13" baking dish or large flat casserole dish with nonstick cooking spray. Core and cut up pears; place in baking dish. (Except for any bruised spots, it's okay to leave skins on.)

2. In a small microwave-safe bowl, microwave frozen juice concentrate for 1 minute. Stir in vanilla and rum and pour over pears.

3. Using same bowl, microwave butter 30–40 seconds, until melted; set aside.

4. Toss remaining ingredients in a separate bowl, being careful not to crush cereal. Spread uniformly over pears. Drizzle melted butter over top. Bake for 35 minutes, or until mixture is bubbling and top is just beginning to brown. Serve hot or cold.

Flourless Hazelnut Chocolate Cake

PER SERVING: Calories: 302 | Protein: 9g | Carbohydrates: 27g | Fat: 18g | Saturated Fat: 1g | Cholesterol: 0mg
Sodium: 56mg | Fiber: 4g | PCF Ratio: 12-35-53 | Exchange Approx.: 3½ Fats, 1 Lean Meat

INGREDIENTS | SERVES 12

Nonstick cooking spray, as needed
3½ cups ground roasted hazelnuts
1½ cups Splenda Granulated
2 tablespoons vanilla extract
¾ cup unsweetened cocoa
12 egg whites

1. Preheat oven to 350°F. Coat a 10" springform pan with nonstick cooking spray.

2. In a medium bowl, mix hazelnuts, Splenda, vanilla, and cocoa.

3. In a small bowl, beat egg whites until stiff. Gently fold the egg whites into the cocoa mixture.

4. Pour batter into greased pan. Bake for 40–50 minutes or until toothpick inserted into cake comes out clean.

5. Cool in pan before serving.

Coconut Macaroons

PER SERVING: Calories: 67 | Fat: 6g | Carbohydrates: 3g | Protein: 2g | Saturated Fat: 5g | Cholesterol: 0mg
Sodium: 20mg | Fiber: 1g | PCF Ratio: 10-20-70 | Exchange Approx.: 1 Fat

INGREDIENTS | MAKES APPROXIMATELY 60 SMALL MACAROONS

6 egg whites
Pinch salt
⅓ cup agave nectar
1 teaspoon vanilla extract
¼ teaspoon almond extract
3 cups shredded unsweetened coconut

1. Preheat oven to 350°F. In a medium bowl, using an electric mixer, beat egg whites and salt until stiff.

2. In a second bowl, combine agave nectar, vanilla, and almond extract. Using a folding motion, combine agave mixture and coconut with egg whites.

3. Place tablespoon-size portions of coconut batter onto a baking sheet lined with parchment paper. Using fingers, mold macaroons into a round shape.

4. Bake for 15 minutes, until slightly golden brown.

Almond Cookies

PER SERVING: Calories: 232 | Fat: 19g | Carbohydrates: 13g | Protein: 7g | Saturated Fat: 3g | Cholesterol: 8mg
Sodium: 50mg | Fiber: 4g | PCF Ratio: 12-20-68 | Exchange Approx.: 1 Starch, 1 Lean Meat, 3 Fats

INGREDIENTS | MAKES 36 (1") COOKIES

2 cups almonds
¼ cup pecans
½ teaspoon salt
⅓ cup rolled oats
⅓ cup ground flaxseed
1 teaspoon baking powder
1 teaspoon vanilla extract
1 teaspoon cinnamon
3 tablespoons butter, softened
⅔ cup agave nectar
Nonstick cooking spray, as needed

1. Chop almonds and pecans; set aside 3 tablespoons chopped almonds. Lightly toast the nuts in the oven. Place nuts in a food processor and grind until a butter-like consistency forms.

2. Add all remaining ingredients except the agave nectar and process. Finally, add the agave nectar to the dough and process until incorporated.

3. Spray a baking sheet with nonstick cooking spray or line with parchment paper. Make dough into 1" balls, place on baking sheet, and flatten down. Sprinkle with reserved chopped almonds.

4. Bake at 350°F for 10 minutes, until just slightly browned.

Chocolate-Dipped Fruit

PER SERVING: Calories: 186 | Protein: 2g | Carbohydrates: 31g | Fat: 6g | Saturated Fat: 3g | Cholesterol: 0mg
Sodium: 4mg | Fiber: 5g | PCF Ratio: 4-70-26 | Exchange Approx.: 2 Fruits, 1 Fat

INGREDIENTS | SERVES 3

6 large strawberries
1 pear
1 under ripe banana
3 cups water
⅓ cup dark chocolate chips

1. Wash fruit and peel banana. Slice banana into 1"-thick pieces. Core pear and slice into 6 pieces.

2. Add water to the bottom of a double boiler. Bring water to a simmer and then turn heat down to low. Add chocolate to the top of the double boiler and stir with a wooden spoon until melted.

3. Using fingers or a skewer, dip fruit pieces halfway into the chocolate to coat. Place dipped fruit onto a tray covered with parchment paper.

4. Place the tray in the refrigerator to allow chocolate to harden. Results are best if served the same day.

CHAPTER 15

Salt-Free Spice Mixes

Barbecue Blend

4 tablespoons dried basil

4 tablespoons dried rubbed sage

4 tablespoons dried thyme

4 teaspoons freshly ground black pepper

4 teaspoons dried savory

1 teaspoon dried lemon peel

Cajun Blend

2 tablespoons paprika

1½ tablespoons garlic powder

1 tablespoon onion powder

½ tablespoon black pepper

2 teaspoons cayenne pepper

2 teaspoons dried oregano

2 teaspoons dried thyme

Caribbean Blend

1 tablespoon curry powder

1 tablespoon ground cumin

1 tablespoon ground allspice

1 tablespoon ground ginger

1 teaspoon cayenne pepper

Country Blend

5 teaspoons dried thyme

4 teaspoons dried basil

4 teaspoons dried chervil

4 teaspoons dried tarragon

Fish and Seafood Herbs

5 teaspoons dried basil

5 teaspoons crushed fennel seed

4 teaspoons dried parsley

1 teaspoon dried lemon peel

French Blend

1 tablespoon crushed dried tarragon

1 tablespoon crushed dried chervil

1 tablespoon onion powder

Herbes de Provence

4 teaspoons dried oregano

2 teaspoons dried basil

2 teaspoons dried sweet marjoram

2 teaspoons dried thyme

1 teaspoon dried mint

1 teaspoon dried rosemary

1 teaspoon dried sage

1 teaspoon fennel seed

1 teaspoon dried lavender (optional)

Italian Blend

1 tablespoon crushed dried basil

1 tablespoon crushed dried thyme

1 tablespoon crushed dried oregano

2 tablespoons garlic powder

Middle Eastern Blend

1 tablespoon ground coriander

1 tablespoon ground cumin

1 tablespoon turmeric

1 teaspoon cinnamon

1 teaspoon crushed dried mint

Mediterranean Blend

1 tablespoon dried sun-dried tomatoes

1 tablespoon dried basil

1 teaspoon dried oregano

1 teaspoon dried thyme

1 tablespoon garlic powder

TIP: If you don't have a food processor, you can freeze the sun-dried tomatoes so they will be easier to crush; however, that adds moisture to the herb blend, so it can't be stored.

Old Bay Seasoning

1 tablespoon celery seed

1 tablespoon whole black peppercorns

6 bay leaves

½ teaspoon whole cardamom

½ teaspoon mustard seed

4 whole cloves

1 teaspoon sweet Hungarian paprika

¼ teaspoon ground mace

Pacific Rim

1 tablespoon Chinese five-spice powder

1 tablespoon paprika

1 tablespoon ground ginger

1 teaspoon black pepper

Sonoran Blend

1 tablespoon chili powder

1 tablespoon black pepper

1 tablespoon crushed dried oregano

1 tablespoon crushed dried thyme

1 tablespoon ground coriander

1 tablespoon garlic powder

Stuffing Blend

6 tablespoons dried rubbed sage

3 tablespoons dried sweet marjoram

2 tablespoons dried parsley

4 teaspoons dried celery flakes

Texas Seasoning

3 tablespoons dried cilantro

2 tablespoons dried oregano

4 teaspoons dried thyme

2 tablespoons pure good-quality chili powder

2 tablespoons freshly ground black pepper

2 tablespoons ground cumin

2 small crushed dried chili peppers

1 teaspoon garlic powder

APPENDIX A

Your 10-Week Plan to Kick Pre-Diabetes!

The 10-Week Plan to Kick Pre-Diabetes is designed to help you set modest goals and put what you have learned into practice. Each week has a healthy lifestyle theme along with two suggested goals to help you achieve success.

Week 1: Check Your Portions

Portion control is everything, even when you choose healthy foods! If you eat large portions, you will have trouble controlling your calories. One simple approach to controlling portions is to use the plate method. The concept is designed to help you put together healthy meals in correct portions and distribute carbohydrates evenly in meals. Using the plate method at lunch and dinner, fill half of your plate with vegetables, one-quarter of the plate with starches, and one-quarter of the plate with meat or meat substitute. A serving of milk and fruit are also added to the meal.

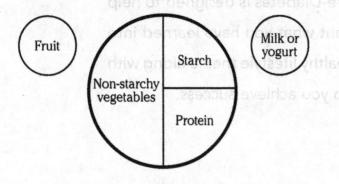

YOUR GOALS FOR WEEK 1

- Give the plate method a try as a means to reduce portion sizes.
- For several days, measure or weigh your food so you can see just how much you are eating.

Week 2: Eat More Vegetables and Fruit Every Day

The recommendation to eat five to nine servings of fruit and vegetables every day sounds like a lot of food, but once you know how to incorporate these foods into your plan it becomes easy. Why that many servings? Because fruit and vegetables are nutrient-dense foods that are high in fiber and low in calories.

YOUR GOALS FOR WEEK 2

- Take two pieces of fruit from home each day to have for a mid-meal snack or with lunch.
- Keep raw vegetables washed, cut up, and ready to eat for quick snacks or salads. If they are there, you will eat them!

Week 3: Get Walking!

Start walking, even if you are only able to manage a few minutes at a time. No matter how long you are able to walk, doing it consistently is most important. Aim for walking most days of the week. Make sure that you have comfortable walking shoes or sneakers.

- Walk for as long as you are comfortably able to. Keep a written record of when and how long you are walking.
- Wear a pedometer so you can track how many steps you take each day. Use the number of steps you take as a motivator to help you increase it each day.

Week 4: Switch to Whole Grains

Begin to switch out the white flour and white grain products in your kitchen for whole-grain foods. Whole grains provide more fiber and nutrients, and have less impact on your blood glucose. Look for products that list whole-grain flour rather than enriched flour as one of the first ingredients.

YOUR GOALS FOR WEEK 4

- Add whole-grain pasta or brown rice to a favorite dish or in combination with vegetables or beans.
- Purchase a new whole-grain food that you haven't used before and try it as a replacement for rice, pasta, or potatoes. Some suggestions: quinoa, kasha, or bulgur.

Week 5: Manage Your Stress

Take stress seriously and find ways to reduce it. Chronic stress can wreak havoc on health and well-being by lowering your immunity and making you more susceptible to many types of illness. You are working on ways to halt pre-diabetes in its tracks; don't let stress derail you!

YOUR GOALS FOR WEEK 5

- Add stretching exercises, meditation, or deep breathing exercises to your daily routine.
- Allow yourself some downtime from the daily grind each day. Make this time for yourself by choosing a relaxing activity that you enjoy.

Week 6: Get Adequate Sleep

Insufficient sleep can have a negative impact on your health. New research has shown that poor-quality sleep on a regular basis can contribute to insulin resistance, metabolic syndrome, and diabetes—just what you are trying to avoid!

YOUR GOALS FOR WEEK 6

- Even if you are very busy or have a demanding schedule, resist the urge to skimp on sleep. Make enough time to get seven to eight hours of sleep each night.

- Develop good sleeping habits by rising and retiring at about the same time each day. Avoid distractions such as the television at times when you should be going to sleep.

Week 7: Don't Forget the Snacks

Having meals and snacks at regular times can go a long way toward controlling your appetite and blood glucose. Snacking during the day is fine, as long as you make good choices that are low in calories and have nutritional value.

GOALS FOR WEEK 7

- When you grocery shop, buy healthy snacks to have on hand at all times.
- Come up with at least two new snack options this week to prevent boredom.
- If necessary, prepare snacks ahead of time, so they are always ready to go (e.g., cut up vegetables, pre-measure nuts into individual containers/baggies, etc.).

Week 8: Ramp Up Your Exercise

You may have started an exercise plan several weeks ago, but it's time to take it up a notch. This is important because exercising the same muscles or at the same intensity all of the time will eventually stall your efforts at weight loss.

GOALS FOR WEEK 8

- Turn your moderate walk into a brisk walk. Step up the pace of your walk and add additional steps by using your pedometer to measure your progress.
- Add a few flexibility or weight-bearing exercises to your routine in addition to the walking.

Week 9: Change Your Food Behaviors

Negative food habits are not always easy to change. Make a conscious effort to correct eating habits that cause you to get off track.

GOALS FOR WEEK 9

- Slow down when you eat. Fast eating or mindless eating can cause you to eat too much food before you realize that you've had enough. Place your fork down between each bite and allow more time to eat your meal or snack.
- Drink plenty of water. Take a water bottle with you wherever you go, set one on your desk at work, or find ways to remind yourself to drink more water. Most people need about 64 ounces of fluid a day; make most of it water!

Week 10: Progress Check—Putting It All Together

Monitor your overall progress by looking at how well you have done with various aspects of your plan.

GOALS FOR WEEK 10

- Make a list of all of the things you have been able to achieve, as well as the goals that still need work.
- Seeing in writing all that you have accomplished is very satisfying and motivates you to keep going. Congratulate and reward yourself for a job well done!

APPENDIX B
Resources

As you learn more about diabetes, you may have more questions or want to find out additional information. The following resources provide a wealth of information regarding diabetes in general, as well as diets, forums, and frequently asked questions.

Online Sources for Diabetes Information

ACADEMY OF NUTRITION AND DIETETICS
www.eatright.org
The Academy of Nutrition and Dietetics is the world's largest organization of food and nutrition professionals. This site provides nutrition information and resources on food, food safety, and weight management, as well as a tool to find a dietitian in your area.

AMERICAN DIABETES ASSOCIATION
www.diabetes.org
This site, maintained by the recognized authority on diabetes, is dedicated to providing up-to-date diabetes information and research findings, and advocating for people with diabetes.

ASK THE DIETITIAN
www.dietitian.com
Joanne Larsen, MS, RD, LD, maintains this site. You can use it to post specific diet-related questions or read the answers to questions from other visitors.

CORNERSTONES4CARE
www.cornerstones4care.com
An interactive website with menu-planning tools, articles, and a free diabetes e-book that you can download.

DLIFE
www.dLife.com
An interactive diabetes website that includes diabetes information, tips for healthy eating, a recipe bank, and a diabetic community.

MEDLINEPLUS
www.nlm.nih.gov/medlineplus/diabetes.html
A service of the U.S. National Library of Medicine and National Institutes of Health, this site has research, references, interactive tutorials, consumer materials, and guidebooks to download or order online.

NATIONAL INSTITUTE OF DIABETES AND DIGESTIVE AND KIDNEY DISEASES (NIDDK)
www.niddk.nih.gov
Site for general diabetes information, where brochures and articles can be downloaded.

Online Sources for Ingredients and Equipment

The quality of the foods you prepare is based on the quality of the ingredients you use; that's elementary. The equipment you use can make a difference, too. Even if you don't have a gourmet grocery or cooking supply store nearby, you don't have to forgo using ingredients or products you've been wanting to try. Chances are you can order them online through one of these sites or find out where products are located near you.

ANCIENT HARVEST QUINOA
www.quinoa.net

BARILLA PLUS PASTA
www.barilla.com

BOB'S RED MILL
www.bobsredmill.com

CABOT CHEESE
www.cabotcheese.coop

CHEFS CATALOG
www.chefscatalog.com

KING ARTHUR FLOUR
www.kingarthurflour.com

MCCORMICK
www.mccormick.com

MEXGROCER.COM
www.mexgrocer.com

MRS. DASH
www.mrsdash.com

Visit these sites to find a location near you:

LOCALHARVEST
www.localharvest.org
Use this website to find farmers' markets, family farms, and other sources of sustainably grown food in your area, where you can buy produce, grass-fed meats, and many other locally grown foods.

TRADER JOE'S
www.traderjoes.com

WHOLE FOODS MARKET
www.wholefoodsmarket.com

For an online food exchange list:

MAYO CLINIC
www.mayoclinic.com/health/diabetes-diet/ DA00077

Standard U.S./Metric Measurement Conversions

VOLUME CONVERSIONS

U.S. Volume Measure	Metric Equivalent
⅛ teaspoon	0.5 milliliter
¼ teaspoon	1 milliliter
½ teaspoon	2 milliliters
1 teaspoon	5 milliliters
½ tablespoon	7 milliliters
1 tablespoon (3 teaspoons)	15 milliliters
2 tablespoons (1 fluid ounce)	30 milliliters
¼ cup (4 tablespoons)	60 milliliters
⅓ cup	90 milliliters
½ cup (4 fluid ounces)	125 milliliters
⅔ cup	160 milliliters
¾ cup (6 fluid ounces)	180 milliliters
1 cup (16 tablespoons)	250 milliliters
1 pint (2 cups)	500 milliliters
1 quart (4 cups)	1 liter (about)

WEIGHT CONVERSIONS

U.S. Weight Measure	Metric Equivalent
½ ounce	15 grams
1 ounce	30 grams
2 ounces	60 grams
3 ounces	85 grams
¼ pound (4 ounces)	115 grams
½ pound (8 ounces)	225 grams
¾ pound (12 ounces)	340 grams
1 pound (16 ounces)	454 grams

OVEN TEMPERATURE CONVERSIONS

Degrees Fahrenheit	Degrees Celsius
200 degrees F	95 degrees C
250 degrees F	120 degrees C
275 degrees F	135 degrees C
300 degrees F	150 degrees C
325 degrees F	160 degrees C
350 degrees F	180 degrees C
375 degrees F	190 degrees C
400 degrees F	205 degrees C
425 degrees F	220 degrees C
450 degrees F	230 degrees C

BAKING PAN SIZES

U.S.	Metric
8 × 1½ inch round baking pan	20 × 4 cm cake tin
9 × 1½ inch round baking pan	23 × 3.5 cm cake tin
11 × 7 × 1½ inch baking pan	28 × 18 × 4 cm baking tin
13 × 9 × 2 inch baking pan	30 × 20 × 5 cm baking tin
2 quart rectangular baking dish	30 × 20 × 3 cm baking tin
15 × 10 × 2 inch baking pan	30 × 25 × 2 cm baking tin (Swiss roll tin)
9 inch pie plate	22 × 4 or 23 × 4 cm pie plate
7 or 8 inch springform pan	18 or 20 cm springform or loose bottom cake tin
9 × 5 × 3 inch loaf pan	23 × 13 × 7 cm or 2 lb narrow loaf or pâté tin
1½ quart casserole	1.5 liter casserole
2 quart casserole	2 liter casserole

Index